New Hard-Boiled Writers
1970s–1990s

New Hard-Boiled Writers 1970s–1990s

LeRoy Lad Panek

Bowling Green State University Popular Press
Bowling Green, OH 43403

By the same author

Watteau's Shepherds: The Detective Novel in Britain, 1914–1940

The Special Branch: The British Spy Novel, 1890–1980

An Introduction to the Detective Story

Probable Cause: Crime Fiction in America

Library of Congress Cataloging-in-Publication Data

Panek, LeRoy.
    New hard-boiled writers, 1970-1990s / LeRoy Lad Panek.
        p.   cm.
    ISBN 0-87972-819-1 (cloth) -- ISBN 0-87972-820-5 (paper)
        1. Detective and mystery stories, American--History and criticism.
    2. American fiction--20th century--History and criticism. I. Title.

    PS374.D4 P34 2000
    813'.087209--dc21

                                                        00-037889

Cover design by Dumm Art

For

Keith, Del, and Ray

CONTENTS

PREFACE

In a commencement address, Meyer Abrams once recounted an anecdote from his youth in which a teacher told the young Abrams that "if you take a drink every day you will end as a drunkard, but if you read a book every day you will end up as a learned person." I'm not so sure that this is the case with detective stories—or I'm not so sure that it is always or even often the case with detective stories. The seductive and addictive qualities of any popular genre, especially those of the detective story, make a virtue of immediate and transitory gratification. There is the reader/writer game of the classical story which authors and critics alike characterize by summoning up the metaphor of the crossword or the jigsaw puzzle. In each case, finishing is the principal object: there's the satisfaction of having completed a task or knowing the Sanskrit word for potter's wheel. But neither one has much to do with becoming a learned person, with asking hard questions about human behavior and the human condition. The same is true with hard-boiled stories. A lot of the narrative technology of the hard-boiled story is designed to race the reader through the plot. Indeed, hard-boiled writers traditionally were not even supposed to pause for analytical or reflective comments on what their fictions mean. They began, after all, in the single most disposable form of literature, the pulp magazine. On top of all of this, the fact that most detective stories are written as part of a series also dissuades readers from considering them as more than fleeting entertainment, as more than diversion, as more than a game.

It has always been my contention that reading detective stories can indeed help to make one a learned person—even though it may take a bit more conscious effort than reading writers with avowedly "serious" purposes—the kind who receive three-column reviews in the *New York Times* or the *Washington Post*. The best writers in every period and every subgenre of detective fiction use their works as a means of confronting readers with some of the same issues one finds in "regular" literature. One of the principal purposes of the following pages, therefore, is to discuss the ways in which ten hard-boiled writers identify and present serious issues, issues that are both contemporary and sometimes universal. With these writers, one of the singular advantages a reader possesses is that each wrote a number of books. It's an advantage because every writer ultimately has only one book to write. But it takes him or her lots

of volumes to get it written. Sometimes a book will succinctly and elo-
quently articulate one part of a writer's vision and flub up another.
Sometimes that part comes across but another gets glossed over. I hope
that looking at all of each of these writers' books together will give readers the most accurate version of the ways in which each of them extends
his or her fiction beyond the superficial delights of the genre.

In addition to this, I will admit to having historical longings. The
kind of fiction these writers have chosen—hard-boiled fiction—extends
back to the 1920s. The kinds of things Hammett and Chandler, particularly Chandler, did shape the ways in which Parker and Estleman and
Paretsky and Emerson and the rest make their fictions. The ways in
which each writer responds to the conventions of the genre have real and
specific impact on the style they choose as well as upon the characters
and worlds they create. Indeed, I believe that the writers I discuss (and a
number of other writers I pass over because of the demands of space and
time) participate in what amounts to a hard-boiled renaissance which
occurred for discernible reasons and which possesses discrete characteristics. I touch on some of them. But like my historical longings, I also
long for independent wealth, universal approbation, fitness without exercise, and a lot of other things I'm not going to get. What follows, then,
while it has some leanings toward history, is not intended to deliver the
real historical goods. Those places in which I touch on literary history
will serve, I hope, as partial material for a genuine history of hard-boiled
fiction that will some day be written.

In the pages that follow I have asked myself a number of questions.
Since writers are distinct individuals, these have not always been the
same questions. Attempting to answer them has made the works of the
individual writers as well as the genre richer for me and, I hope, for the
reader. Inevitably, however, there are questions I have not asked and
questions I cannot answer—or at least that I cannot answer yet—and
questions that have not even occurred to me. I hope that what follows
will encourage others to ask them and to provide the answers I have not.

As always, I have more debts than I can ever repay: to Joan and
Anita for help with enigmatic and intractable computers; to Pam, Becky,
Mary, Gail, and all of the others who showed interest in my work; to the
librarians at Hoover Library at Western Maryland College; to all of the
scholars I mention in the first chapter who helped make the contemporary hard-boiled story what it has become—without any of the royalties;
to the writers I discuss in the following chapters for writing books I wish
I had not read so that I could read them again for the first time; to Pat
and Ray Browne for twenty good years; and especially to Chris. I am
poor in thanks, but I thank you all.

INTRODUCTION

Vietnam, rock and roll, yuppies, firepower, women, urban decay, pornography, child abuse: all of them had something to do with remaking the hard-boiled detective story in the last quarter of the twentieth century. They're also all going to have to wait until later because my focus here begins with the literary background of the relatively recent renaissance in hard-boiled writing.

From the perspective of 1960 it didn't look like the hard-boiled story would last long enough to have a renaissance. *Black Mask* sputtered, fizzled, and then finally died in the early fifties. Raymond Chandler didn't make it to the 1960s and Dashiell Hammett lived only one year into the decade. And the fifties were hardly productive years for either writer, Chandler mourning the death of his wife and Hammett—written out a decade earlier—persecuted by Senator Joseph McCarthy and the House Committee on Un-American Activities. Granted, the fifties had the MacDonalds, John D. and Ross, and Mickey Spillane, but even with them, the hard-boiled story—realistically the hard-boiled novel—gave every indication of dying in the not so distant future. It looked like the future belonged to James Bond. But it didn't. Instead of shuffling off unmourned, in the 1970s the hard-boiled novel came back, gaining as much energy and probably a much wider and more diverse readership than it had during its first real years of life.

One of the reasons for this renaissance resides in the fact that in the seventies and eighties readers who had never seen or even heard of pulp magazines could read the hard-boiled fiction of the 1930s for the first time. All of Hammett's novels had been available since Knopf's omnibus edition in 1965, but both Hammett and Chandler were reprinted in the seventies: Vintage reprinted Hammett's novels in paperback as well as *The Big Knockover* (with an introduction by Lillian Hellman) in 1972 and Random House published *The Continental Op* two years later. Along with reprints of his novels, the seventies saw most of Chandler's short stories reprinted in Ballantine's 1972 issue of *Trouble Is My Business, Pickup on Noon Street, Killer in the Rain,* and *The Simple Art of Murder.* Come the 1980s, readers could even get hold of some of the lesser-known hard-boiled writers: Raoul Whitfield was reprinted in 1985 and so was Fredric Brown; Paul Cain's *Fast One* reappeared in 1987 and so did Gerald Butler's *Kiss the Blood off My Hands*; and the next year

1

Jonathan Latimer's *Solomon's Vineyard* and *The Lady in the Morgue* hit the book racks—or at least the specialty catalogs. Even a couple of Robert Leslie Bellem's soft-porn Dan Turner stories from *Spicy Detective* appeared again in 1986.

Other than Hammett and Chandler's books, though, hard-boiled writers' works appeared only from small presses: Winds of the World Press published Bellem's Dan Turner stories and International Polygonics printed a facsimile of Carroll John Daly's *Murder from the East* in 1978. A few die-hard fans and obscure academics bought these books. A lot more people, however, first came to know about the hard-boiled story through anthologies. The first of these was Ron Goulart's *The Hardboiled Dicks* (1967), and this was followed by Herbert Ruhm's *The Hard-Boiled Detective: Stories from the Black Mask Magazine 1920-1951*, published by Random House (1977); William Kittredge and Steven M. Krauzer's *Great American Detective* (New American Library, 1978); Bill Pronzini's *The Arbor House Treasury of Detective and Mystery Stories from the Great Pulps* (1983); and William Nolan's *The Black Mask Boys* (Morrow, 1985). Pronzini, for example, gave readers long-forgotten stories by Hammett, Carroll John Daly, Horace McCoy, Frederick Nebel, Paul Cain, Cornell Woolrich, Norbert Davis, Fredric Brown, and Robert Leslie Bellem. Nolan, too, reprinted pulp stories by Hammett, Daly, Nebel, McCoy, and Cain, and added to them pieces by Chandler, Raoul Whitfield, and Erle Stanley Gardner. Yep, Gardner, the Perry Mason Gardner, started out in *Black Mask*, too. And those who read these works for the first time in the sixties and seventies found images of their own times, their own selves, and their own country in hard-boiled stories written thirty or forty years earlier.

A lot of these readers were academics. Imagine "Gee Professor Millar, I'd like to do a dissertation on the hard-boiled detective story. What do you think?" Together with William Kinney's dissertation "The Dashiell Hammett Tradition and the Modern Detective Novel" at Michigan in 1964, there were eight doctoral theses written on major hard-boiled writers before 1978. The graduate faculties at Texas (Austin), Connecticut, Michigan State, Bowling Green, Chicago, and Penn all okayed work on Hammett, Chandler, and Ross Macdonald. Then, too, there was Robert B. Parker's "The Violent Hero, Wilderness Heritage and Urban Reality: A Study of the Private Eye Novels of Dashiell Hammett, Raymond Chandler, and Ross Macdonald" at Boston University in 1971. We'll come back to that one. In addition to the dissertations, moreover, academic publishing took an interest in hard-boiled fiction in the sixties and early seventies. First came some groundwork. Matthew Bruccoli published checklists for Chandler (1968) and Ross Macdonald

(1971)—Kent State and Gale, respectively—and Kent State issued E. H. Mundell's *A List of Original Appearances of Dashiell Hammett's Magazine Work* in 1968. There was literary criticism, too. Early works included Durham's *Down These Mean Streets a Man Must Go: Raymond Chandler's Knight,* published by North Carolina in 1963, and Southern Illinois' edition of David Madden's collection of critical essays, *Tough Guy Writers of the Thirties,* in 1968. And then there was biography: by the mid-'80s nine lives of Chandler and Hammett had rolled off the presses, three of them on Hammett (William Nolan's, Dennis Dooley's, and Diane Johnson's) appearing in the same year, 1983. Indeed, in that same year, Francis Ford Coppola released his film *Hammett,* based on Joe Gores' 1975 historical detective story of Hammett returning to his profession as a detective in the San Francisco of 1928.

One can argue, in fact, that both the serious study and the widespread appreciation of all detective literature really began in the 1970s. Otto Penzler, Chris Steinbrunner, Dilys Winn, Bill Pronzini, Allen J. Hubin—to mention only a few of the significant names—published a shelf full of important guides and reference books during the decade.

It would be gratifying, of course, to believe that the emergence of new hard-boiled writers was purely a literary event. But nothing is that simple any more—or at least since the screening of *The Jazz Singer.* After all, a lot of the original hard-boiled writers took themselves to the movies. Who hasn't seen John Huston's 1941 version of *The Maltese Falcon?* Dick Powell, Humphrey Bogart, and Robert Montgomery all played Marlowe in the '40s. In the seventies and eighties, films influenced the new hard-boiled writers in three ways. First, like the reprints, they brought back the works of classic writers. Paul Newman brought Ross Macdonald to the screen, first with *Harper* (1966) and then with *The Drowning Pool* (1975). After *Marlowe,* with James Garner, in 1969, three more Chandler films appeared in the seventies: *The Long Goodbye* (1973), *Farewell, My Lovely* (1975), and *The Big Sleep* (1978). In 1969 there was even a cinematic version of Horace McCoy's 1935 novel *They Shoot Horses, Don't They?* Along with these remakes, Roman Polanski used the form and the atmosphere of the forties to transmit his dark and violent version of the hard-boiled story to the seventies with his *Chinatown* in 1974. Evident especially in Loren Estleman's *Never Street* (1997), the revival of interest in the *noir* films of the forties also had an impact on the new hard-boiled writers. And in the eighties and nineties the mores of the hard-boiled hero became attached to the heroes of action/adventure films. Films with stars like Mel Gibson and Bruce ("Die Hard") Willis focused on the same qualities—determination, responsibility, wit, perseverance, cynicism, violence, etc.—highlighted in hard-boiled novels of the thirties and forties. Private eye Leo Haggerty, in fact, talks about the appropriateness of Gibson's Mad Max character to his own world in Benjamin Schutz's *A Tax in Blood* (1987):

Two white-knuckled, goggle-eyed hours later I stood with Max staring at the sand leaking out of the overturned tanker, stunned but wanting to laugh. Out there alone, in the middle of nowhere, he'd done it all. He'd totaled the vermin. For a truckfull of sand. The homesteaders were long gone, hauling the petrol north. Crafty bastards. Walking out of the theatre I couldn't shake the feeling that what I'd seen was a documentary. (55)

If films confirm, transmit, and, to some extent, update the hard-boiled vision of the world, television tried to do so as well but did not do very much in the way of influencing writers. The early seventies certainly had enough private eye shows, including "Mannix" (starting in 1967), "Cannon" (starting in 1974), "Banacek" (starting in 1972), and "The Rockford Files" (starting in 1974), and "Magnum P.I." ran from 1980 to 1988. Judging from references in contemporary hard-boiled novels, however, other than keeping the character of the private eye in front of a very large public, these shows had negligible impact on hard-boiled fiction. Indeed, most frequently, writers refer to the fact that their heroes are not like the heroes featured in "The Rockford Files" or "Magnum P.I."

Coincidence or not, one of the movements toward the contemporary hard-boiled novel had pretty close ties to the cinema. Historical detective stories have been a fairly conspicuous subgenre of mainstream detective stories at least since Lillian de la Torre's *Dr. Sam. Johnson, Detector* of 1944. Anachronistic or historical or nostalgic hard-boiled novels became an occasional part of the genre in the seventies starting with Andrew Bergman's *The Big Kiss Off of 1944* (1974) and continuing with Stuart Kaminsky's Toby Peters books that began in 1977. They extend into the eighties with writers like Richard Blaine and his Mike Garrett mysteries (beginning with *The Silver Setup*, 1988) set in the forties and Gaylord Dold with his Mitch Roberts books (starting with *Snake Eyes*, 1987) set in the fifties. The originators of the nostalgic hard-boiled novel, Bergman and Kaminsky, both earned film credentials before turning to hard-boiled fiction: Bergman wrote a history of American movies in the 1930s as well as coauthoring the screenplay for *Blazing Saddles*, and Kaminsky is a professor of film history. Along with their appeal based on nostalgia for recent historical trivia—Bergman's Jack LeVine, for example, is surprised by a car with fluid drive in *Hollywood and LeVine* and one of Toby's cars is a Crosley—these writers demonstrated the basic but superficial imitability of hard-boiled writing. The principal exterior features of the genre are easy to spot and are not difficult (and are even fun) to copy. The world they portray, however, is not that of their readers, and this approach to updating the hard-boiled story suggests, after the manner of all historical novels, that the hero's attributes are particular to the time and place of the setting. They suggest that the hard-boiled hero can only exist in bygone times.

Not everyone agreed with this. And the following chapters discuss ten writers who bring together the hard-boiled hero and the complexity and confusion unique to the last quarter of the twentieth century in the United States. In so doing they participated in the renaissance of hard-boiled fiction.

ROBERT B. PARKER

So here you have Robert B. Parker in 1971. He'd finished his dissertation, "The Violent Hero, Wilderness Heritage and Urban Reality: A Study of the Private Eye in the Novels of Dashiell Hammett, Raymond Chandler, and Ross Macdonald," and got a teaching job at Northeastern, pulling down maybe ten grand a year. What he was supposed to do in his spare time was to spin his dissertation into a bunch of articles for learned journals or, even better, wave it under the noses of editors of university presses in hopes of getting it in print. But he didn't do that. Instead Parker spent his time using the patterns he found in American hard-boiled fiction to create his own hard-boiled world with its own hard-boiled hero.

In many ways the publication of Parker's *The Godwulf Manuscript* in 1972 signaled the beginning of the hard-boiled renaissance, and no one can say that Parker was anything but adroit at recognizing and employing many of the elements of the classic story. At the same time, however, as much as he admires and would at least like to write like Raymond Chandler, no one can say that Parker's adaptation of those elements to his own inclinations (as well as to the marketplace) has remained entirely faithful to the essential hero, world, and attitude that he found in Hammett, Chandler, and Macdonald back in graduate school when he, no doubt, lived on Cheez-Whiz instead of brie.

We can see some of this in Parker's first book. *The Godwulf Manuscript* does a pretty good job of capturing some of the fundamental features of the hard-boiled story. First of all, the plot shows a bit of the genre's requisite complexity. Parker brings together the stolen manuscript, the revolutionary student underground, college officials of varying stripes, a loopy religious cult, the mob, a socially elite family, the cops, a couple of seductions, and a young woman falsely accused of murder. In the hard-boiled story the purpose of this kind of bounty has always been to contrast disparate social elements; to provide movement and action; to present occasions for danger, menace, or complexity; and thereby to delineate the hero's world and his character. There's also telling a story, but that has always played a secondary role. Confusion mirrors the hero's world, and clarity and consistency are not necessarily virtues. In *The Godwulf Manuscript*, for instance, there is the business with Terry Orchard's brief residence at the Ceremony of Moloch head-

7

quarters. This has almost nothing to do with what purists would call the plot (it gets us no closer to finding out who murdered Dennis) and it really does nothing to delineate Terry Orchard's character in a fuller or more consistent manner. It's probably there in part to echo a similar incident in Hammett's *The Dain Curse*. It's there in part, too, to add confusion. But that's okay: it's what hard-boiled stories do.

Then there's language. From the very beginning the narrator's language has been one of the defining features of the hard-boiled story. Hammett created it and Chandler made it work. And Parker admires it very much. Traditional hard-boiled language begins with non-standard diction—ungrammatical speech, slang, etc. This shows up more vividly in hard-boiled works written in the 1920s and 1930s when there was a clearer distinction between standard and non-standard diction, when there were clearer and more numerous regional and (for lack of a better term) vocational linguistic differences, and when slang and ungrammatical speech represented a more graphic demonstration of class than they do today. At any rate, this element of hard-boiled style doesn't mean much for Parker or other contemporary hard-boiled writers. They have to look to other characteristic to make their style hard-boiled.

A lot of them look to the simile; Parker certainly does. Chandler made the simile a standard feature of hard-boiled style with gems like "The plants filled the place, a forest of them, with nasty, meaty leaves, like the newly washed fingers of dead men." *The Godwulf Manuscript* is awash in similes: the president's office looked like "the front parlor of a successful Victorian whorehouse," Forbes looked "as if he'd found half a worm in his apple," Tower looked me over "like the weight guesser at the fair," an academic building "looked like the corporate headquarters for White Tower Hamburgers," football players had "necks like pilot whales," there's a voice "almost like a 45 record played at 33," Quirk's voice "squeezed out sharp and flat like sheet metal." That's only a minuscule sample. It's one characteristic way in which Parker tries to evoke the reality of the hard-boiled world. It both reminds readers of the classics of the genre and creates the hero's consciousness in the elements he chooses to make all of the comparisons: whorehouses, worms in apple, weight-guessers, White Tower Hamburgers, pilot whales, records, and sheet metal. Another characteristic element of hard-boiled style resides in his use of the catalog, a feature that Hammett used frequently. Take this passage from Parker's *The Godwulf Manuscript*:

There was a phone bill, a light bill, an overdue notice from the Boston Public Library, a correspondence course offering to teach me karate at home in my spare time, a letter from a former client insisting that while I had found his wife she had left again and hence he would not pay my bill, an invitation to join a vacation club, an invitation to buy a set of socket wrenches, an invitation to join an automobile club, an invitation to subscribe to five magazines of my choice at once-in-a-lifetime savings, an invitation to shop the specials on pork at my local supermarket, and a number of less important letters. Nothing from Germaine Greer or Lenny Bernstein, no dinner invitations, no post cards from the Costa del Sol, no mash notes from Helen Gurley Brown. (63-64)

He is far more restrained in his use of another element of hard-boiled style, hyperbole. Never one of Parker's favorites, there isn't much over-statement until the Los Angeles novel, *A Savage Place,* where there are clusters of these figures: a desk as big as Detroit, a car hood large enough to land small planes one, etc. But catalogs, similes, and hyperbole alone don't make up hard-boiled style. It rests on economy and action, writing based on terse statements of fact and active, often strikingly active, verbs. Parker knows this and puts it into practice from the first book onward.

The other classic element Parker uses so luxuriously in *The Godwulf Manuscript* is the wisecrack. From the very beginning wisecracks play a significant role in the speech and the personality of hard-boiled heroes. Parker loads *The Godwulf Manuscript* with them. In practically every other conversation that Spenser has in the book, he cracks wise:

Look, Dr. Forbes, I went to college once. I don't wear my hat indoors. (2)

Miss Orchard, look at it this way, you get a free lunch and half a million laughs afterward talking to the gang at the malt shop. I get a chance to ask some questions, and if you answer them I'll let you play with my handcuffs. (11-12)

I won't be able to sleep without a night light. (27)

What are you going to do, Sonny . . . sweat all over me till I beg for mercy? (84)

That's only a few. They are all over the place in this book, all over the place because for Parker they serve two purposes. First, they echo the style of Hammett and Chandler—something he wants to do. Also, just as in earlier writers, the hero's wisecracks say something about his character, about the level of his wit, certainly, but about more substantial things as well. Wisecracks demonstrate the hero's refusal to be subservient to artificial social decorum as well as his courage in the face of threats—the Op's reply to Elihu Wilsson in *Red Harvest,* for instance: "And if you don't yell maybe I'll be able to hear you anyway. My deafness is a lot better since I've been eating yeast." It's also linguistic facility, as Chandler makes clear in "The Simple Art of Murder": "He talks as a man of his age talks—that is, with rude wit, a lively sense of the grotesque, a disgust for sham, and a contempt for pettiness." Parker wants to do all of this too. He wants it to be part of Spenser's character. And in the later books this is something he will embellish.

But that happens after *The Godwulf Manuscript*. In that book Parker still needed to establish other parts of his hard-boiled hero. Many of those parts come straight out of Chandler's description in "The Simple Art of Murder":

He is a relatively poor man, or he would not be a detective at all. He is a common man or he could not go among common people. He has a sense of character, or he would not know his job. He will take no man's money dishonestly and no man's insolence without a due and dispassionate revenge. He is a lonely man and his pride is that you will treat him as a proud man or be very sorry you ever saw him. (20)

It's not too difficult to go through *The Godwulf Manuscript* and label Parker's use of these criteria. Start with "relatively poor man." In this first book Spenser drives a beat-up old convertible of unspecified make with a tear in the top and seats mended with duct tape. His office, near Boston's Combat Zone, is "one room with a desk, a file cabinet, and two chairs" (63). He works out at the Boston Y.M.C.A. His wardrobe holds only two jackets:

Went to the front closet and got my other jacket. It was my weekend-in-the-country-jacket, cream colored canvas with a sherpa lining that spilled out over the collar. I was saving it in case I was ever invited down to the Myopia Hunt Club for cocktails and a polo match. But since someone had shot a hole in my other coat I'd have to wear it now. (162)

While Parker does not describe Spenser's apartment, he does include a note of transience in "I was living that year on Marlborough Street, two blocks from the Public Gardens" (18). Later on we get this reflection: "I thought about all the times I'd spent in shabby squad rooms like this. Sometimes it felt like all the rooms I was ever in looked out onto alleys" (33). As did Chandler, Parker reinforces his hero's social status by contrasting him with the affluent. In *The Godwulf Manuscript* much of this comes in Spenser's contact with Mr. and Mrs. Orchard. First the wife with her Palm Beach tan: "I didn't know what to do with her hand, shake it or kiss it. I shook it, and the way she looked made me suspect I'd chosen wrong" (41). And then the husband: "He wasn't being the top-exec-used-to-instant-obedience. He was being the gracious-man-of-affluence-putting-an-employee-at-ease" (44). Spenser's responses to them also reflect Chandler's point about having a sense of character. Parker's hero makes quick and definitive judgments of everyone he meets—cops, university presidents, English teachers, student radicals, mobsters, everyone. With all of them, too, Spenser uses competence and (for want of a better term) naturalness as the bases for his judgments. Take, for instance, the difference in his estimation of the two mobsters, Sonny and Phil. From the first, Spenser sasses Sonny, but he does not mouth off to Phil because he intuits, he feels Phil's competence: "Phil just looked at me and the menace was like a physical force. I could feel anxiety pulse up and down the long muscles of my arms and legs" (80). In much the same way, Spenser feels more than he knows Terry Orchard's innocence: when Quirk asks him why she is innocent, Spenser replies, "I like her" (58). To complete the picture, throughout *The God-wulf Manuscript* common people, average people, respond immediately and helpfully to Spenser, including Belson, Iris Milford, the ruddy faced cop, and the nurse at the hospital who lends him five dollars because "You deserve something for sheer balls" (160).

Then there is Chandler's point about taking "no man's insolence." This hardly needs examination. *The Godwulf Manuscript* like all of Parker's works is replete with Spenser's responses to disrespect whether it comes from individuals or from any of the myriad forms of authority. A more interesting criterion lies in establishing the hard-boiled hero as someone who is alone—Chandler's "he is a lonely man and his pride is that you will treat him as a proud man." It's pretty obvious in the original hard-boiled writers. Take Marlowe's observation in *The High Window*: "Nobody called, nobody came in, nothing happened, nobody cared if I died or went to El Paso." But the danger of sliding from stoicism into pathos is pretty obvious too, and one of the miracles of the best hard-boiled writing is that it frequently prevents that slide. In the first book Parker follows the classic pattern. Spenser lives alone and has no intimate friends. He, too, tries to dance between stoicism and pathos: "In my kitchen I sat at the counter and opened a can of beer. It was very quiet. I turned on the radio. Maybe I should buy a dog, I thought. He'd be glad to see me when I came home" (61). Maybe not the same economy, but we can see that Parker is trying to conform to the established rules of the genre.

There are a couple of other features in *The Godwulf Manuscript* that Chandler didn't put into his description in "The Simple Art of Murder."

Perhaps the most prominent is the hero's age. Hard-boiled heroes are never young bucks. They're all middle aged—or think they are. Parker punctuates *The Godwulf Manuscript* with references to Spenser's years: "I wondered if it was a mark of advancing years when you no longer wanted to neck in the snow" (8). "I'd had about four and a half hours sleep and I needed more. Ten years ago I wouldn't have" (40). "Guile, I thought, guile before force. I had been thinking that more frequently as I got up toward forty" (71). "Sometimes I wondered if I was getting too old for this work. And sometimes I thought I had gotten too old last year" (90). While he does not do it a great deal (and almost invariably associates it with baseball and later with certain Boston landmarks), Parker, following the classic pattern, also includes nostalgia as one of the features of middle age:

When I was a kid it had been Braves Field until the Braves moved to Milwaukee and B.U. bought the field. I remembered going there with my father, the excitement building as we went past the ticket taker and up from the dark understands into the bright green presence of the diamond. The Dodgers and the Giants used to come here then. Dixie Walker, Clint Hartung, Sibbi Sisti, and Tommy Holmes. I wondered if they were still alive. (187)

Part of that nostalgia is an often ironic attachment to the purity of the language. Thus in *Farewell, My Lovely,* Marlowe's "A Harvard boy. Nice use of the subjunctive mood" connects with Spenser's grammatical interchange with Tower:

"Whom," I said.
"What?"
"It's whom, who is employing whom? Or is it? Maybe it's a predicate nominative, in which case . . ." (66)

Then, too, there's booze. Spenser never gets too far away from bourbon: there's a bottle in the desk drawer and an invariable pint in the car. And sex. While in "The Simple Art of Murder" Chandler does comment that the hero is neither a eunuch nor a satyr, imagining the 1970s was beyond his comprehension. Spenser is acutely, even obsessively aware of women's breasts, thighs, legs, and bottoms. Even if he does feel a whiff of guilt, during *The Godwulf Manuscript* Spenser makes love to both Terry Orchard and her mother. This may be a bit kinky, but it's not really that far out of line with the natural development of the form.

A few things in *The Godwulf Manuscript*, however, are out of line with the natural development of the hard-boiled story. For one, Parker is

probably too self-consciously literary—he was, after all, a new Ph.D.
Sure, he follows Chandler in naming his hero for one of the giants of
English literature (although the dark and erratic Marlowe, stabbed
through the eye in what may have been a bar fight, remains a more apt
choice than the establishment Spenser who spent his energies fawning
over Queen Elizabeth), but in this first book there is an awful lot of literary name-dropping: Joyce Carol Oates, *Hamlet*, George L. Kittredge,
Chaucer, *Beowulf*, *Paradise Lost*, Frost, Auden, Dante, *The Play of the
Weather*, *Gammer Gurton's Needle*, and Arthur Conan Doyle. English
majors can become pretty tedious, and Parker learned this in the ensuing
books, where allusions to literature come less frequently and become
internalized in character, or plot, or dialogue. In them, quotations and literary allusions serve to promote Spenser's self-satisfaction and provide
communication with an elite group—a group which consists largely of
Susan Silverman and, of course, the cadre of ex–English majors and
English major wannabes that buy Parker's books.

All the literary stuff, however, isn't as noticeable as the food. Imagine *The Continental Op Cookbook* or *From Mike Hammer's Kitchen*:
Pretty grim. Traditional hard-boiled heroes eat to live. Parker takes a
swipe at this notion in *The Godwulf Manuscript*: "Eating a sub sandwich
with one hand is sloppy work and I got some tomato juice and oil on my
shirtfront and some coffee stains on my pants leg" (89). But he can't sus-
tain it. Spenser's culinary flair and discriminating palate emerge as
defining characteristics, and Parker includes increasingly detailed and
long paragraphs about food and food preparation as the books proceed.
For example, here's dinner at Susan's from *Ceremony* in 1982:

We began by eating hot pumpkin soup and then some cold asparagus with green
herb mayonnaise on a bed of red lettuce. After that we each had half a pheasant
with raspberry vinegar sauce and a kind of saffron pilaf that Susan made from
white and wild rice with pignolia nuts. For dessert we had sour cherry cobbler
with Vermont cheddar cheese, and after we had finished with the last half of the
champagne and I had embarrassed myself with a second serving, we took coffee
and Grand Marnier into the den and drank it. (130)

While not as graphic, *The Godwulf Manuscript* contains a small
hint about a non-canonical approach to clothes. At the same time that he
describes Spenser's sparse and utilitarian wardrobe, Parker calls attention to Spenser's shoes: "They were my favorites, tassels over the
instep" (159). Before too long, this small notation becomes in his books
Parker's need to describe Spenser's attire (as well as Susan's and
Hawk's) and to note the hero's satisfaction with its aesthetic correctness

and sartorial appeal. Indeed, Parker's Spenser books contain strata from which one can observe the evolution of three decades of fashion. The food, the clothes, and other glimpses of sophisticated high-life all connect to the brand-name dropping made fashionable by Ian Fleming's James Bond books in the sixties. And if Parker wasn't getting paid for product endorsements from brewers, vintners, and clothiers, he should have been.

While for many readers they form part of Parker's appeal, these features are really minor digressions from hard-boiled tradition which do not have a great deal to do with altering the direction of the form. To be sure, later hard-boiled writers pay a lot more attention to food thanks to Parker, and even if he does not particularly like fern bars, he serves as the inspiration for and the target of some of the yuppie-bashing that becomes a feature of the genre in the nineties. But this is sport and not substance. Other tentative first steps made in *The Godwulf Manuscript* mean a lot more. First, Parker introduces a minor touch in Spenser's character that he will later interweave into his continuing definition of manhood—self-conscious boyishness or adolescence. This appears first when Spenser gets no response at Cathy Connelly's apartment building and has a brief encounter with the building's super: "I resisted the temptation to ring all the buzzers and run. 'Childish,' I thought. 'Adolescent'" (108). But the temptation is there, the same temptation that moves Spenser to perform a one-handed pushup for Patricia Utley in *Mortal Stakes* and to do pushups on Susan Silverman's chaise in *Promised Land*. It is irrepressible boyish charm, and it is the same motive that changes Spenser's dialogue and narration in later books. The other hint in *The Godwulf Manuscript* of things to come lies in Parker's creation of the Orchard family and with the Haydens, husband and wife. They're screwed up big time. These characters' superficial and artificial definitions of self as well as their confusion about how husband and wife and parent and children relate and should relate to one another potentially lie under all of the trouble in the book. They don't here, but they will.

So, looking back at 1972, Parker could have written the same book again and again and participated in the traditions of hard-boiled fiction in a workmanlike manner. A lot of writers have written the same formula over and over. That's why it's called category fiction. Indeed, later in his career Parker would do it too. But not at the beginning. At the beginning he worked at modifying, perhaps even undermining, the conventions established for the hard-boiled story in the 1920s and 1930s.

As I have noted above, with his attention to food and clothes, Parker moves Spenser out of the world of cold-water flats into one of casual, self-indulgent affluence. And he sloughs off some of the excesses in style. Take similes. Chandler was very good at making similes. They define his hero, his world, and his style. Using them connects a writer with one of the sources of hard-boiled fiction. They are one of the features of Parker's style in *The Godwulf Manuscript*. But it's easy to overuse them, to depend upon them too much. Parker seems to have realized this and in subsequent books used far fewer similes per word foot of prose. But the most significant changes occur in the way in which Parker develops his hero's internal monologue and the way in which he relates to his world.

Captain Shaw, editor of *Black Mask*, codified one of the fundamental tenets of hard-boiled fiction in a letter to Horace McCoy when he said that "my impression is that you agreed that it would have a stronger punch to a character to have his strengths brought out by his acts rather than by the writer's statement." It's very egalitarian, very American, very male: don't talk, do. Virtue resides in action—not thought, not analysis, not description, not feeling, not the opinions of others except those of readers who are to base their judgments on the reality of the world presented to them and what the hero does in that world. Shaw's observation, however, only scratches the surface of what acts mean in the hard-boiled world. Judged by it alone, many action-adventure narratives fall within the terms of the definition. But as it denotes character, action in the hard-boiled world means much, much more. In some respects it's like the complex logic of salvation through faith adapted to the secular realm. The hero engages in good works even though those works by themselves mean little because they do not assure salvation because in a fallen world all are undeserving of the salvation which God alone can grant. His actions, indeed, often appear to be irrational, outmoded, indefensible and unjustifiable in an environment predicated on commercialism and self-aggrandizement. Although the terms chivalric or romantic or even quixotic have become associated with these heroes, none is adequate because their motives lie beyond reason and any attempt to justify them changes, muddles, or betrays both the motive and the hero. Writers show the action and readers interpret its meaning. The most extreme example of this kind of writing is *Fast One,* in which Paul Cain provides neither characters' interior experience nor authorial intervention. He just presents action. Hammett and Chandler occasionally violate this standard, most notably, perhaps, in Spade's defense to Brigid O'Shaughnessy:

Listen. This isn't a damned bit of good. You'll never understand me, but I'll try once more and then we'll give it up. When a man's partner is killed he's supposed to do something about it. It doesn't make any difference what you thought of him. He was your partner and you're supposed to do something about it. (Hammett, *Novels* 439)

But in spite of patches of rhetoric like this, in spite of including spurts of what Shaw would consider authorial interruptions, the first generation of hard-boiled writers made action the rule and authorial interpretation the exception. Otherwise they would have been melodramatic hacks like Carroll John Daly.

But what has this to do with Parker? After he had demonstrated his mastery of the framework of the hard-boiled story in *The Godwulf Manuscript*, Parker moved on to wrestle with his hero's motives and actions and the traditions handed down by Cain, McCoy, Hammett, Chandler, and all the rest. Exactly who pinned whom in this match presents a vexing and probably irrelevant question. What is clear is that Parker set about to change the way of defining the hard-boiled hero.

One of the places this happens is in the picture Parker draws of the inside of Spenser's head. In its purest, most hard-boiled form, the interior monologue of the first-person narrator sets down facts about the world embellished by elements of style—mostly similes and hyperbole—and occasional ironic observations. The rest is description of action and dialogue. Very soon after *The Godwulf Manuscript,* Parker began to work on this. He cranks up his hero's libido, and observations about sex float across Spenser's mind every time he sees a female. I have already mentioned the growing attention Spenser pays to clothes and especially to food and drink, especially beer, after the first book. Then, too, there is the internalized literary reference to which I alluded above. Take this play with *Hamlet*: "Down the corridor a man swore rapidly in Spanish. The typewriter stopped. The rest was silence" (*Mortal Stakes* 72). But as the books progress there is more. First of all, after *The Godwulf Manuscript,* images from the movies play a part in Spenser's narration. In *God Save the Child*, for example, he associates people and actions with Donna Reed in *Ransom*, John Wayne in *The Searchers*, and Lee Marvin—"I looked at him hard as I'd seen Lee Marvin do in the movies" (*God Save the Child* 122). And in *Looking for Rachel Wallace* he does the same kind of comic conversion that he does with literature: "If I weren't so tough, I would have thought about reading glasses. I wonder how Bogie would have looked with specs. Here's looking at you, four eyes" (124). Then, too, Parker works on allusions to detectives. In line with the genre's opposition to the English-style Golden Age detective story, in the first book Spenser notes that "there were no telltale cigar butts, no torn halves of claim checks, no traces of lint from an imported cashmere cloth sold only by J. Press. No footprints, no thumb prints, no clues" (*The Godwulf Manuscript* 122). This kind of comment occasionally recurs in later books—"I looked around the room in case there was a secret panel, or a note written in code and scratched on the window with the edge of a diamond" (*God Save the Child* 14)—but Spenser becomes increasingly ironic about his profession as the books proceed, witnessed by this passage from *Looking for Rachel Wallace*: "I explained to the desk sergeant who I was, and he got so excited at one point he glanced up at me for a moment before he went back to writing in a spiral notebook" (114). In fact what Parker does in the later books in Spenser's internal narrative is to internalize the wise-crack. Each of us, after all, is our own best audience. Without Susan or Hawk around to serve as participants and audience for Spenser's wit, he is certainly his own best audience. Spenser tickles the hell out of himself. Here are a few examples: "I thought about going in and asking them [FAO Schwartz in New York] if they were a branch of the Boston store but decided not to. They probably lacked my zesty sense of humor" (*Mortal Stakes* 69). "Well Spenser, I said, it's your funeral. Sometimes I'm uncontrollably droll" (*Mortal Stakes* 126). "The old phrasemaker. Closing in on the truth. I should have been a poet" (*Mortal Stakes* 133). "I crossed my arms on my chest. After a while I uncrossed them. Always self-amusing. Never without resources" (*Ceremony* 55). It's part of Spenser's self-avowed boyishness or adolescent behavior, but, as is always the case, it's more. Of course Spenser's internal monologue fulfills its traditional role in the hard-boiled story, but through the supplementary content areas, especially food, clothes, books, films, and ironic humor, Parker makes Spenser appeal to new classes of reader, the kind of reader who discovered him in book reviews in *The New York Times* and *The Washington Post*.

It's not so much that it's new, but perhaps that it's slimmed down and simplified that made the content of Parker's books appealing to those new classes of readers. The content mostly focuses on families and relationships between members of families. In *The Godwulf Manuscript* there are the dysfunctional Orchards and Haydens. *God Save the Child* features the Bartletts and run-away Kevin. Spenser searches for Pam Shepard when she leaves her family in *Promised Land*. In *Mortal Stakes* Spenser saves the Rabbs from scandal. The threat in *Looking for Rachel Wallace* comes from the failure of Julie Wells' mother and brother to accept her sexuality. *Early Autumn* introduces the continuing character of Paul Giacomin and his escape from his parents. And *Ceremony* concentrates on Spenser trying to set the adolescent April Kyle on the right track. All of these books revolve around relationships that have failed because one of the partners has become obsessed with material success and the stereotypes imposed on him or her by convention and tradition. The action in these books begins with disruption of the family—someone runs away or someone is kidnapped. They can only end when the people in the book begin to define new roles for themselves as members of a family and as individuals. And Spenser gets in the middle of all of this. He starts off somewhat unwillingly. Thus in *God Save the Child* Spenser sets up guidelines for the Bartletts:

Now, let us establish some ground rules. One, I am not on the Parent-of-the-Year committee. I am not interested in assessing your performance. Yell at each other when I'm not around. Second, I am a simple person. I am looking for a lost kid, that's what I do. I don't reform marriages. (4)

But he's either disingenuous or he can't follow his own rules because in all of the books Spenser involves himself with both solving the immediate and literal threat to the family and the malaise that played a significant role in its creation. "I deal in what it is fashionable to call people. Bodies. Your basic human being. I don't give a goddamn about the sanctity of marriage. But I occasionally worry about whether people are happy" (*Promised Land* 58). And worrying about whether people are happy redefines his role. For the first decade, the Spenser books define the hero as more than a detective. He witnesses and understands the pathos of Mrs. Hayden's passionate attachment to her worthless husband, watches along with Kevin the Bartletts' attempt to fight for their son as well as Marty Rabb's defense of his wife. And then steps in to do what they cannot. In *Promised Land* Spenser has lengthy conversations with both Shepards about their roles and identities. Finally, in *Early Autumn* and *Ceremony*, he, in effect, places Paul and April in foster care. On top of all of this, after the first book and his brief fling with Brenda Loring, Spenser has a guidance counselor who eventually becomes a psychotherapist as his friend, lover, and consultant. Parker identifies this addition to his role as a traditional detective in Spenser's conversation with Slade, the captain of the overworked Plymouth police force:

"I used to be with the States," I said. "Worked out of the Suffolk County D.A.'s office."
"Why'd you quit?"
"I wanted to do more than you."
"Social work," he said. He was disgusted. (*Promised Land* 30)

Perhaps what disgusts Slade is that if there is a profession more tied down by bureaucracy and rules than law enforcement while being faced with similar futile confrontations with the squalid paradox of humanity, it's social work. But not the way Spenser does it.

Spenser uses violence. Parker includes violence in all of the books, especially at their conclusions. Ex-boxer that he is, Spenser engages in fist fights regularly and wins. There is plenty of gun play, too. Whenever Spenser alludes to his skill at violence, whether with fists or guns, he connects it to his view of himself as a professional. Occasionally, as in *Looking for Rachel Wallace*, he bullies weak and pathetic individuals as a means of getting to the truth, but most of the time Spenser directs this toward opponents who are themselves in the profession of violence and whose acts directly or indirectly threaten weak and helpless individuals. But Parker associates violence in part with glamour. With the domestication of Hawk in *The Judas Goat*, Parker increasingly surrounds it with an aura of chic and camaraderie as well as the traditional fascination with process that so often accompanies the perpetration of mayhem in this kind of literature. Not content simply to describe what turns out to be cathartic violence, Parker develops different attitudes toward violence in Spenser and Hawk. Witness the wrap-up in the used car dealership in *Early Autumn*:

> I stepped away from Harry. "Remember what I told you," I said.
> Hawk said, "Spenser you a goddamned fool."
> "I can't kill a man lying there on the floor," I said.
> Hawk shook his head, spit through the open door into the repair bay, and shot Harry in the middle of the forehead.
> "I can," he said. (210)

Hawk is amoral and pragmatic in his view of violence and Spenser is not. Parker has Hawk do things that Spenser cannot. It's a simple pattern writers use to save their heroes' moral bacon. There's Joe Pike in Robert Crais' books, Cowboy and Mimi in W. Glenn Duncan's Rafferty books, Mouse in Mosley, and Max the Silent in Andrew Vachss. Killers all. But Parker recognized the hypocrisy of this character arrangement by *A Catskill Eagle,* which includes the following interchange between the Hawk and Spenser:

> "You spend your life in a mean business, babe, trying not to be mean. And so far you got away with it mostly. But there's stuff on the line that never been on the line before."
> "I found the key for the last door."
> "I know," I said.
> "Gimme the knife," Hawk said.

"No." I turned from the door. "Letting you do it is like doing it myself, only worse. It's doing it and pretending I didn't." (74)

These guys realize and acknowledge through their actions that the perniciousness of human nature makes some problems solvable only through intimidation, force, and ultimately lethal violence. While most of what Spenser and Hawk do in the books is at least extra-legal and all of it falls under the heading of vigilante justice, it serves higher ends. It does this in all hard-boiled books. The difference with Parker lies in the fact that he's not satisfied with describing the process and leaving the rest to his readers. He has to delve into why his hero acts the way he does.

As I noted a bit ago, hard-boiled heroes never used to explain why they did things, they just did them. They either neglect or avoid or refuse explanation. And Spenser sometimes does too. Especially in *Promised Land*, Parker includes a number of instances in which Spenser doesn't come up with an answer to who or why he is what he is:

Explaining myself is not one of the things I do really well, like drinking beer, or taking a nap. Explaining myself is clumsy stuff. You really ought to watch what I do, and, pretty much, I think, you'll know what I am. (117-18)

No, but we're spending too much time on this kind of talk. The kind of man I am is not a suitable topic, you know. It's not what one talks about.
Why?
. . .
It's pointless. What I am is what I do. (143)

Significantly, it's not the hero who needs or chooses to define himself for himself. It's women. First Linda Rabb, then Pam Shepard, then Rachel Wallace, and then Candy Sloan feel the need to know why Spenser is what he is. All of them seek their own definition of themselves as independent persons and as women. Having met a unique individual, they hope that knowing what Spenser is will assist them in knowing who they are and how they can authentically relate to others. The trouble is he doesn't want to talk about it. Parker nevertheless has a go at defining Spenser's motives and credo, and he does this both by using his women characters and by bringing into the hard-boiled story some of the conventions of the love romance. Indeed, the trilogy of *The Widening Gyre, Valediction,* and *A Catskill Eagle* in many ways fits the criteria of that genre—ritual death, commitment, etc. Parker does this because one of the few times that people work hard at definition is when they are building a relationship or when that relationship faces a crisis. It doesn't hurt either that Susan Silverman is a shrink.

So what do these women draw out of the reluctant hero? First of all, Spenser admits in *Mortal Stakes* that he operates according to a system of belief:

See, being a person is kind of random and arbitrary business . . . And you need to believe in something to keep it from being too random and arbitrary to handle. Some people take religion, or success, or patriotism, or family, but for a lot of guys those things don't work. A guy like me. I don't have religion or family, that sort of thing. So you accept some system of order, and you stick to it. (188)

"Jock ethic, honor, code, whatever," Spenser uses these labels just before the passage above. Later on Pam Shepard tosses "machismo" into the mix too. And whatever it is, it's not a personal system of belief. Susan lists some of its adherents in *Looking for Rachel Wallace*:

"You people are like members of a religion or a cult. You have little rituals and patterns you observe that nobody understands."
"What people?"
"People like you. Hawk, Quirk, that state policeman you met when the boy was kidnapped."
"Healy."
"Yes, Healy. The little trainer at the Harbor Health Club. All of you." (193)

Insofar as Parker defines the dogma upon which this system rests, maybe honor comes first:

I don't know if there is even a name for the system I've chosen, but it has to do with honor. And honor is behavior for its own reason. (*Mortal Stakes* 189)

It's an embarrassing question because it requires me to start talking about integrity and self-respect and stuff you recently lumped under John Wayne movies. Like honor. I try to be honorable. (*Promised Land* 133)

Yeah, but machismo isn't another word for rape and murder. Machismo is really about honorable behavior. (*Promised Land* 114)

Sure, Parker twice has Susan quote Shakespeare back to Spenser—"Who has it . . . he that died a Wednesday"—but he keeps coming back to honor, defining it mostly in terms of inherent restraint:

"Maybe he [Macey] did, but he's got no more honor than a toad. He'll do anything. Hawk won't. There's things Hawk won't do."

"Like what?"

"He won't say yes and do no." (*Promised Land* 150)

"Would you do something that would make you ashamed?"

"No."

She poked at her hash some more. "Jesus," she said. "I think you wouldn't. I've heard people say that before, but I never believed them. I don't think they even believed themselves. But you mean it."

"It's another way of being free." (*A Savage Place* 67)

Spenser couples, however uneasily, competition, pride, and violence with honor. Here Parker resorts to a bunch of sports analogies:

You give it all you got and you play hurt and you don't complain and so on and if you're good you win and the better you are the more you win so the more you win you prove you're good. (*Mortal Stakes* 188)

"He likes that part," Susan said. "He's very into tough. He won't admit it, maybe not even to himself, but half of what he's doing all the time is testing himself against other men. Proving how good he is. It's competition, like football." (*Promised Land* 113)

"But the possibility that you'll meet somebody better is part of it"—I gestured with my right hand—"if that possibility didn't exist," I said, "it would be like playing tennis with the net down." (*A Savage Place* 61)

So honor involves being one's best self and proving it through regular testing, and in Spenser's case this means combat, the thread that connects medieval chivalry with the "Be all that you can be" of today's Army. Besides, it has social utility: "there's a need for someone who's good at it. Someone needs to keep that fat guy from smacking you around" (*A Savage Place* 61).

If honor and competition form one part of Spenser's ethos, freedom and independence form another. First there's Spenser to Susan in *Mortal Stakes*: "Whatever the hell I am is based on not doing things I don't think I should do. Or don't want to do" (189). And then Hawk seconds this in *Promised Land*: "Naw, I only do what I want. I never do what I'm told. Same with old Spenser here. You yell your ass off at him, if you want, but he ain't going to do a goddamned thing he doesn't want to do" (145). Allied to, but not quite the same as doing as one wishes, is autonomy. It comes up a lot in definitions of Spenser. Susan, of course, brings it up for the first time in *Promised Land* when she's trying to explain Spenser to Pam Shepard:

"It's autonomy. You are the most autonomous person I've ever seen and you don't let anything into that. Sometimes I think the muscle you've built is like a shield, like armor, and you keep yourself private and alone inside there. The integrity complete, unviolated, impervious, safe even from love." (113-14)

She does it again in *Looking for Rachel Wallace*: "Words can," Susan said. "And tone of voice. You're just so goddamned autonomous that you won't explain yourself to anybody" (23). Then Spenser himself defines it in *Early Autumn*: "Autonomous. Dependent on yourself. Not influenced unduly by things outside yourself" (123). Finally, having learned the lesson, Paul fleshes out the notion of autonomy in *Widening Gyre*:

"Before us you were invulnerable. You were compassionate but safe, you understand? You could set those standards for your own behavior and if other people didn't meet those standards it was their loss, but your integrity was"—he thought for a minute—"intact. You weren't disappointed. You didn't expect much from other people and were content with the rightness of yourself." (72)

In *Promised Land*, in fact, Spenser attempts to underpin the concept of autonomy with a reference to Thoreau—leaving out, of course, the passive resistance part of "Civil Disobedience" and stuff about simple living in *Walden*: "But I believe most of the nonsense that Thoreau was preaching. And I have spent a long time working on getting myself to where I could do it. Where I could live life largely on my own terms" (113). Parker, after all, spent some effort trying to figure out the implied philosophy of the classical hard-boiled hero back in graduate school and put it into Spenser's responses to the women characters in the novels. He also notes the penalty imposed by autonomy when Spenser observes that "he and I are part of the same cold place. You aren't. You're the source of warmth. Hawk has none" (*Ceremony* 127). But it's not simply Susan Silverman that makes Spenser different from Hawk and from the traditional hard-boiled hero. Parker gives him yet one more overpowering male trait.

One of the few biographical bits of background Parker supplies for Spenser is that he was raised by men, by his father and his uncles. This marks him for life. In *Early Autumn* Spenser becomes Paul's surrogate father, and, of course, his parenting is distinctly masculine: sure, at the end there's the dancing, but mostly he teaches Paul carpentry, builds up his strength with weights and punching bag, drinks beer with him (Paul is fifteen), and talks to him about autonomy. But as important, maybe more important than all of this, Spenser demonstrates what for Parker is the primal male trait, the need to nurture and protect. Spenser, then, is not just a social worker with a gun, a do-gooder who knows how to short-cut the system. He's the universal father. Susan pinpoints this in *Looking for Rachel Wallace*:

> "You were brought up with a fierce sense of family. But you haven't got a family, and so you transfer that great sea of protective impulse to clients, and me."
> "Maybe not you, but usually clients need protection."
> "Yes. That's probably why you're in business. You need people who need protection. Otherwise what would you do with the impulse?" (92-93)

Spenser needs to protect people. Parker has Susan set it up in the second novel, *God Save the Child*:

> "You're such a big tough guy, and you think you're funny, but I bet if that fool with the confidence courses got in trouble you'd get him out of it."
> "A catcher in the rye," I said. (95)

And so the novels introduce character after character for Spenser to protect. It's not just Paul and then Susan, it's all of them. He's persistent. Spenser saves April Kyle first in *Ceremony* and then again in *Taming a Sea Horse*. He's intrusive. It's not enough that he save Dwayne Woodcock's basketball career in *Playmates*, but Spenser needs to make sure that he learns to read too. He's sympathetic. Take the finale of *Crimson Joy*:

> "I'll help you," I said.
> I stepped toward him and took his arms and pulled him from the rock. His legs gave way and he sagged. I slid my arms under his arms and around his back and held him up. He sagged toward me and buried his face in my chest and began to cry harder. His arms went around me and held me and he was saying something muffled against my chest. I listened harder.
> "Papa," he sobbed. "Papa." (203-4)

But, hard as it is for him or any father to imagine, he can also be a pain in the ass—maybe even more. This issue forms the core of *Looking for Rachel Wallace*, but Susan brings it up earlier in *Promised Land*: "You can't be everyone's father. It is paternalistic of you to assume that Pam Shepard with the support of several other women cannot work out her own future without you. She may in fact do very well. I have" (75). Parker makes resolving the human paradox of characters' autonomy and their need for protection a central issue in a number of books, most notably those dealing with Susan's temporary abandonment of Spenser. But it's not really a suitable medium to resolve the issue, given that Pam Shepard, Rachel Wallace, and Susan have problems that can only be solved with violence—a capacity they do not possess. So Parker, in effect, glosses over the issue of the conflict between the need for autonomy and the need for protection. Spenser continues to act paternally, protecting and defending people in the books. The only real difference is that he acknowledges and respects others' need for autonomy and, in some cases, after he has saved them advises them of the benefits of counseling.

From the very beginning, Parker supplies Freudian background for characters' actions in his books. Thus in *The Godwulf Manuscript* Marion Orchard suggests an Electral connection between her daughter and husband. Near the beginning of *God Save the Child* Parker has Susan Silverman talking to Spenser about Kevin's unresolved Oedipal conflicts and problems with gender identification. And when we get to *Promised Land* Spenser is making referrals:

"What I do know is that it might be one of your problems. If so, it can be solved. It's one thing to know something. It's another to feel it, to act as if it were so, in short, to believe it."

"And how does one learn to believe something?"

"One talks for a while with a good psychotherapist." (168)

Although in this book Susan is still a guidance counselor at a junior high school, in the later books she has become a psychotherapist. The earlier books, then, mostly emphasize the problems of children and adolescents—Terry Orchard, Kevin Bartlett, April Kyle, Paul. Once Susan has her own practice, the books touch on dilemmas of therapy—Juanita Olmos, the social worker/therapist in *Pale Kings and Princes*, and Susan's sessions with Felton in *Crimson Joy*. And they concentrate on dysfunctional adults: the mother's connection to Felton's serial killings, the father's sexual abuse of Jill Joyce in *Playmates*, Paul's search for his mother in *Pastime*, etc. In spite of Susan's expertise, however, Parker keeps her pretty much in the background. Spenser is the one who makes the diagnoses and Susan confirms them—we're not talking about brain surgery here, after all. It's all predicated on the ideology Spenser expresses in the third book:

I'm sick of movements. I'm sick of people who think that a new system will take care of everything. I'm sick of people who put cause ahead of the person.

And I am sick of people, whatever sex, who dump kids and run off: to work, to booze, to sex, to success. It's irresponsible. (*Promised Land* 10)

And then through the kind of intervention that is anathema to shrinks, he acts to create the conditions that will make successful therapy at least possible—because he is responsible, because he is a detective, because he is a man.

Spenser, of course, is exempt from all of this therapy stuff. Telling tales on the couch, examining one's own behavior, accepting that some-one else might be able to ask more prescient questions or analyze more acutely just isn't done. Besides, as the personal history delineated in *Pastime* makes clear, Spenser had a secure and structured childhood. He was raised by men, real men. So he doesn't need therapy. Parker, how-ever, does float a few clouds through Spenser's psychic sky. There's the affair with Candy Sloan in *A Savage Place* and occasional recurrent guilt about the circumstances of her death. And there's the emotional vacuum created by Susan's departure to Washington and then California in the Susan trilogy, a vacuum that leads Spenser to doubt the center he has created for himself out of his belief in honor: "Maybe it wasn't possible to be a good man and do anything . . . Maybe being a good man didn't amount to anything anyway. It didn't seem to get you much. You ended up in the same place as the bad men. Sometimes with a cheaper coffin" (*Widening Gyre* 54-55).

He does, however, snap out of it in large part because he's just plain lucky. While, like the traditional hero, Spenser says that he accepts the sordid reality of the world, Parker creates a style of living for him which both he and his hero find exuberantly satisfying: there is exquisite food, rare drink, fancy clothes, and never a care about cash. There is a woman who provides energetic sex, witty persiflage, understanding, patience, counsel, and commitment—sometimes even in that order. There are friends and their associated male repartee who provide understanding and support unasked and unrequited. In Susan, Hawk, Quirk, Belson, Paul, and most of all in Spenser himself, Parker provides his hero with an eager and sympathetic audience. That audience—along with his own firmly established view of himself and the absolute rectitude of all of his acts—allows Spenser to find and maintain satisfaction in the delusion that he is an autonomous person, someone like hard-boiled detectives used to be.

Since 1972 Parker has published about a book a year. In the begin-ning he made a real contribution to the evolution of hard-boiled fiction. He understood its form, conventions, and meaning, and transplanted them to the 1970s. Then something happened. Success and the expansive affluence of the 1980s took his hero out of the proletarian tradition of hard-boiled fiction and made him a foppish brand-name-dropping epicure. More importantly, instead of simply having him act as a symbol, Parker also made his hero a spokesman—a superficial exemplar, a glib representative, and a self-consciously suave interpreter of the nature and virtues of modern masculinity. Spenser performs this role in and for a world confronted, confused, and often obsessed by the issues of feminism, sexual identity, and the erosion of the family. This often obscures the core of what he could be, what the hard-boiled character is.

JAMES CRUMLEY

James Crumley began writing with *One to Count Cadence* (1969), a novel about the Vietnam War. To date, he has written five detective novels: *The Wrong Case* (1975), *The Last Good Kiss* (1978), *Dancing Bear* (1983), *The Mexican Tree Duck* (1993), and *Bordersnakes* (1996). There is an epigraph from Ross Macdonald in the first detective book and one from Chandler in *The Mexican Tree Duck*. That's the first clue. Crumley's writing fits right into the tradition of the hard-boiled story. While there are enough psycho-sexual problems in all of the books to justify the little smirk on the conventional picture of Freud, they do not dominate Crumley's fiction as they do Macdonald's. Likewise, while much of the darkness in Crumley's novels takes off from Chandler, his heroes, plots, tone, setting, and atmosphere make the *noir* novels of the thirties and forties seem almost pastel. Crumley's style is also Chandleresque, combining real speech, scraps of literature, and poetry made out of the mundane and the sordid experience of his narrators.

In his detective books Crumley features two heroes, Milton Chester Milodragovitch, III, and Chauncey Wayne Sughrue. Milodragovitch appears in *The Wrong Case* and *Dancing Bear*, and Sughrue in *The Last Good Kiss* and *The Mexican Tree Duck*; *Bordersnakes* combines narration by both characters. Perhaps understandably, neither uses his given name: they use Milo and C. W. And both names mean something. Milo's family name connects him with one of the founding fathers of Meriwether, Montana, a hardy Russian immigrant who made his home and fortune in the rugged American West. Commemorating this heritage, the Milodragovitch name adorns an office building and other sites around the city of Meriwether. The "sugh," in Sughrue, Milo explains in *Bordersnakes*, is pronounced like "sug" in "sugar," and it's "rue" as in "rue the fucking day." Crumley brings Sughrue and Milo together from the second novel by way of several of Sughrue's allusions to "my old partner." Milo is, in fact, older. Additionally, he seems older. In *Bordersnakes* Sughrue tells him, "You're a serious man, Milo . . . and it always made you seem older. And you always took care of people. Like you cared more about that sort of shit than I did" (*Bordersnakes* 42). Sughrue, on the other hand, is "Sonny" to those closest to him. In spite of the difference in their ages, both Sughrue and Milo view themselves, even while in their thirties, as middle-aged, over the hill, washed-up.

Both men, Crumley is at some pains to point out, grew up without fathers, but their pasts affect them differently. Before his death, Milo's father's principal occupation was booze and women. Sughrue's father was possessed by the notion that he was a Native American mystic. Both, too, are veterans, Milo of the Korean War, for which he enlisted before he was eighteen, and Sughrue of the Vietnam War, in which he was a platoon leader and then a victim of the war and the U.S. government.

Sughrue and Milo are detectives essentially because they have nothing else they want to do. Repeatedly they define their vocational choices as either detecting or bartending. While both have some superficial professional experience, Milo as a Meriwether deputy sheriff and Sughrue as an unwilling domestic spy for the Army, they both inhabit the bottom end of the professional food chain—Sughrue chases runaways and repossesses things and Milo does divorce work, smashing down doors and taking dirty pictures to play a part in an even dirtier business. Thus Sughrue describes both himself and Milo in *The Last Good Kiss*:

The only other private investigator I know is my ex-partner here in town, and he's an even worse drunk than I am. I know PI's have conventions, but I've never been to one. They're all about electronics and industrial security and crap like that. I just repossess cars and chase runaways and follow cheating husbands, stuff like that. (171)

So when situations arise that demand more from them as detectives, they have problems. As Milo puts it in *The Wrong Case,* "My major problem, of course, was going to be the fact that I had neither training nor experience as a detective, no matter what it said on my license" (202).

Wanting training and expertise, Crumley's detectives have little left upon which they can rely. Although they try it, neither Milo nor Sughrue can pull off bullying and intimidation as a way of finding facts. And while firearms play a significant role in all of the books, using them doesn't just eliminate bad guys, it creates additional misery for the heroes. Mostly Sughrue and Milo move around relatively blindly and close cases partly because they are obstinate and persistent. In spite of their avowed cynicism, Milo and Sughrue paradoxically close cases because of their longing for ideals; the idea of something beyond their own dingy and squalid lives—love, art, womanhood, the past—keeps them going. Because of their quixotic idealism combined with their lack of experience as detectives, both heroes are manipulated. Indeed, all of the books place the problem which the detective must solve within a larger context of manipulation. For both Sughrue and Milo, discovery of that manipulation is a sadder discovery than the solution to the more mundane problem they had been trying to solve: the recognition that they have been used invades the heroes' selves and diminishes the small store of things that matter in their very dark world. But their dark world grew out of the literary tradition of the hard-boiled detective story. From *The Wrong Case* onward, therefore, Crumley's books possess and refine the criteria—the conventions of character, and theme, and action— which underlie the genre.

One of the most powerful features of the hard-boiled novel, espe- cially the recent hard-boiled novel, is its use of setting. While setting performs a number of functions beyond providing a backdrop for the action—imaging the unweeded garden, the lost past, etc.—in some important ways setting contributes to their status as regional novels, an increasingly important feature of the hard-boiled story. It's almost impossible to imagine Chandler's books being set in any place but L.A., or Burke's any place but Louisiana, or Parker's any place but Boston. The list could go on and on. So Crumley's books never venture further east than Colorado. Idaho, Oregon, Washington, and especially Montana and Texas serve as settings for his books. After all, he knows these places the best. So, in any number of ways Crumley's books are about the West.

First off, the West is the place he describes, often in some detail. Indeed, from a sort of satellite view, the locations in the books are real enough: Crumley is not, after all, making up Denver, or El Paso, or Butte, or Los Angeles—who could? Even Kalispell is on the map over in the northwest corner of Montana. Although he calls it Meriwether, the town that is a magnet in all the books is certainly Missoula, where Crumley has spent his summers. On closer inspection, however, there are a number of places not in the atlas: Milo's cabin is in the canyon of Hell Roaring Creek, the mountains surrounding Meriwether are part of the Diablo Range, the Cathedral Mountains are near the Benniwah Reservation, and Sheba (the queen who wants to investigate about Solomon's wisdom) Peak overlooks Meriwether. In *The Last Good Kiss* Mrs. Trahearne owns the town of Cauldron Springs, Montana, where the spa is "like the entrance to some underground world." And somewhere in the three thousand acres of timber so important in *Dancing Bear* lies Camas Meadow, camas being a western North American variety of lily also called Death-Camas. It doesn't take a Joseph Cambell to work out that setting performs a larger role than simply providing post card local color for background. Setting supplies a symbolic backdrop for the novels.

The places Crumley describes, however, aren't just symbols. First of all, the country he describes is breathtakingly beautiful, and that is important. Indeed, part of the wisdom that Milo's father bequeaths him is teaching him to appreciate the beauty of random Montana scenes. Thus, from the porch of a rural bar, together they look at "lush, verdant green fields," which

grew dark with shadows, nearly as dark as the pine-thick ridges, but the sky above still glowed a bright, daylight blue. A single streak of clouds, like a long trail of smoke, angled away from the horizon, flaming a violent crimson at the far end as if it had been dipped in blood. But the middle was light pink, and the end nearest us was ashen gray. (*The Wrong Case* 237)

In *Dancing Bear*, in fact, Milo has learned the lesson about the beauty of the land and experiences a mini-epiphany on his way to the Benniwah reservation:

But just as I worked myself into an alcoholic's glorious and sober self-pity, as we rolled past the shadowy outlines of the Wilmot Bar, we popped out of the clouds and into the blinding winter sunlight firing back off the snowfields. I locked all four wheels of the pickup, scrambling in my pockets for the new sunglasses. When I had them on, I saw before me the snow-capped towers of the Cathedrals glistening against a sky as blue as the backside of heaven, the sort of vision that makes you forget tire chains and frostbite, makes you remember why you live in Montana until you die. (173)

But the land has value beyond inspiring awe with its beauty and occasionally providing refreshment for the weary soul. It is also a link to the past, part of one's heritage, part of one's person. This comes into the novels with the ex-hippie in *The Last Good Kiss* whose land carries the history of a "great-grandfather . . . born on the Oregon Trail in Applegate's second train, and my grandmother [who] was born in a log cabin that is still standing five miles up the creek" (140). In *The Wrong Case* the link of land and the past becomes the three thousand acres of timber which is Milo's sole tangible inheritance from his grandfather. By the end of *Dancing Bear*, moreover, Milo acknowledges an even older heritage of the land by signing over the timberland and Camas Meadow, "where the bears used to dance," to the Benniwah, the original inhabitants who revere it as sacred.

Beautiful and sacred the land might be, but the smudges and gouges of civilization increasingly mar and profane it. In *Dancing Bear*, Milo looks at Meriwether, the home of three generations of his family, and observes that

The south hills had been gobbled up by developers, the softly rounded slopes layered with rows of ticky tacky houses. Even the pulp mill on half shifts and with millions of dollars worth of scrubbers the mill had installed, the air smelled like cat piss and rotten eggs whenever the wind came out of the west, and the current rage for wood stoves was already filling the valley with a yellowish-brown haze, clotted thickly in the air like something you might cough up, and after a week of winter inversion, you would. (69)

Meriwether, of course, is nothing compared to Butte:

Butte isn't a pretty sight, coming or going. The great maw of the Berkeley Pit is eating the old town off the mountainside, digging for copper they ship to Japan to be smelted. In many ways it's a sad city, a crumbling monument to both the successes and failures of unbridled capitalism, seduced and abandoned first by the copper kings, then by the international conglomerates. (*Dancing Bear* 112)

Through acquiescence or coercion or greed, native westerners of all races may have allowed this to happen, but easterners carry the ultimate blame: "those pimps playing squash in the Yale Club in New York fucking City who are living fat on their cuts" (*Dancing Bear* 145).

For Crumley's heroes, though, the land is also something to travel through. So the novels require more than several glove compartments worth of AAA maps. Thousands of miles, tens, even hundreds of thousands of miles roll by on the odometers of Sughrue's El Camino and Milo's various rigs. In *The Last Good Kiss*, for instance, Sughrue travels from Meriwether, Montana to Sonoma, California; around about greater San Francisco and down to Bakersfield; through Nevada to Cauldron Springs, Montana; then over to Oregon and across to Denver, Colorado; back to Sonoma; over to beyond Polebridge, Montana, and to Meriwether for a spell; on a bender to Elko, Nevada, and "the most depressing place in the West," the bus station in Salt Lake City; then back to Meriwether and down to Denver, around about that city; then back to Cauldron Springs, with only a quick trip to Meriwether and the Polebridge hideout before the conclusion in Cauldron Springs. *The Wrong Case* is the only comparatively sedentary of Crumley's books. Traveling, of course, is what cowboys do. They ride the range. And Sughrue and Milo are both very fundamentally cowboys. *The Six-Gun Mystique* by John Cawelti fits Crumley's books almost as well as it fits *The Virginian* or *Hondo*. The characteristics of the cowboy, of course, play a significant role in the make-up of all hard-boiled heroes. They form part of the background of the urban tough-guy hero. But with Milo and Sughrue, the characteristics of the cowboy are not background. They are foreground.

For cowboys, riding the range has a number of gratifications. Moving on allows them their independence. Nobody tells you what to do. Thus Milo observes that "this is the great American West. Where men came to get away from laws. Almost everything in this state [Montana] is legal. And a lot of things that are illegal are done in spite of the law" (*The Wrong Case* 9). In reality, neither Sughrue nor Milo wants to be anything else but a cowboy. Thus, in a line echoing Steve McQueen in *The Magnificent Seven*, Milo says, "I wasn't about to sell things or clerk in a store or teach children not to suck eggs or even bartend" (*The Wrong Case* 202). The conventional cowboy view of the East helps to define all of this. For Crumley, the East is artificial, alien, and hostile. Milo's "only vision of the East had come from the phony gentility of my mother" (*The Wrong Case* 42). Like the Mafia negotiator in *The Wrong Case*, Easterners talk funny and dress in uncomfortable clothes. In Crumley's description of Butte, we note that Easterners (and this includes all city dwellers) have either conspired to lay waste the land, or, if they do not despoil the land they pester it as tourists in Airstream trailers dressed in Eddie Bauer clothes. To both Milo and Sughrue, the idea of tourists is anathema. They wish them gone, "And a fence built around the state" (*The Wrong Case* 217). Just as Easterners don't belong in the West, moreover, Westerners don't belong in the East. The best example here is Milo's father, who was "asked to leave Harvard for drinking, gambling, and shooting squirrels in the Harvard Yard with a Colt .44 Dragoon pistol" (*Dancing Bear* 19).

When they cannot ride the range, for cowboys there is always the frontier. It's another defining aspect of cowboys and the western. When civilization, the East, catches up with them, cowboys simply move on. Today, however, there is no frontier left, not in Sughrue's Texas or Milo's Montana: "Some of the people who had either been raised in Meriwether or had lived there for years were beginning to drift on, seeking that place they remembered, trying to find it again in British Columbia or Alaska or Australia" (*The Wrong Case* 68).

Sughrue and Milo both possess a wilderness getaway: Sughrue's five acres near Polebridge and the ancestral Milodragovitch timberland. Increasingly, though, neither of them owns anything. The burning of Milo's log cabin in *Dancing Bear*, for example, causes him little sense of loss, and Sughrue ends up in a borrowed double-wide trailer plunked down in the Texas desert in *Bordersnakes*. There is always Mexico. For Crumley's heroes, Mexico means a couple of things. It is the traditional place where outlaws can flee the law. More than that, however, for Crumley's heroes it serves as a frontier concocted by sybaritic fantasy, where, as Milo says, "I could sprawl in the silken laps of luxury, loll grandly about foreign beaches, dawdle with expensive whores, droves of exotic dusky women, maidens with conical breasts and wide, happy mouths, and there were tall, cool drinks I'd never had, a life to live like a king" (*Dancing Bear* 167).

Whether it is British Columbia or Mexico, however, the location of the frontier is not important. Beside the fantasy exists the knowledge of its chimerical nature and the realization that the frontier is just another place to go. In an extended sixties funk, Sughrue muses about

the good times. The parties that last forever, the whiskey bottle that never runs dry, the recreational drugs. Strange ladies draped in denim and satin, in silver and hammered gold. Ah, yes, the easy life, unencumbered by families or steady jobs or the knave responsibility. Freedom's just another word for nothin' left to lose, right, and the nightlife is the right life for me, just keep on keepin' on. Having fun is the fifth drink in a new town or washing away a hangover with a hot shower and a cold, cold beer in a motel room or the salty road-tired taste of a hitch-hiking hippie chick's breast in the downy funk of her sleeping bag. Right on. The good times are hard times but they're the only times I know. (*The Last Good Kiss* 97)

Riding the range and experiencing its beauty gets old. The frontier will forever remain a fantasy. But both are part of what makes cowboys what they are.

And so do guns. Cowboys love guns. Taken to extremes, in *Mexican Tree Duck* Sughrue tells us that

the .50-caliber fires a 500-grain projectile at 2,900 feet per second. It's like being shot at with fishing sinkers. The six-round burst shredded the roof of the school bus and knocked half of the cedar-shake shingles off Norman's front roof. It felt so good bucking against my hands I didn't want to stop . . . That was just pure fun, pure rock-and-roll-automatic fire. (30)

The heavy machine gun here is overdoing it a bit. But every one of the books is filled with lovingly described pistols, rifles, shotguns, and more. The inducement Milo offers Simmons to join him in *Dancing Bear* is "Money, fun, firepower" (122), a phrase repeated in *Mexican Tree Duck*. While violence causes Milo periodic revulsions, he doesn't give up on guns—"just bullets," he says in *Bordersnakes*. Even that resolution, however, does not last too long. And just as cowboys love guns, they love whiskey, fighting, and male companionship. The kind of things found in bars.

For Crumley, bars are an integral part of the West, part of the cowboy's life. *The Last Good Kiss* begins with a tour of the bars of the

West, and the passage about Butte cited above ends with "the old city still lives, filled with perhaps the best bars in a state of great bars." Meriwether, Milo tells us, "could boast of the highest *per capita* ratio of bars in America" (*The Wrong Case* 25). For Crumley, bars mean basic, silly, stupid, juvenile male fun. There is, for instance, the bar fight—not so much the fight itself as savoring recollections of it. Thus Jonas tells Milo, "Goddamn, we usta have some dandy times, didn't we. Seems like ever other night you'd come in here and put knots on my head a goddamned goat couldn't climb" (*The Wrong Case* 231). More importantly, in bars there is the rude companionship of men. In *The Last Good Kiss* Sughrue describes construction workers heading into Rosie's run-down saloon:

The men scrambled out laughing and shouting at Rosie, goosing each other in the butts, happy in the wild freedom of quitting-time beers . . .

I knew the men were probably terrible people who whistled at pretty girls, treated their wives like servants, and voted for Nixon every chance they got, but as far as I was concerned, they beat the hell out of a Volvo-load of liberals for hard work and good times. (32)

These are not yuppie bars with umbrellas in the drinks and micro brews, or franchise bars for tourists with speed guns and bartenders with razor cuts, or biker bars full of hostility and tattoos. Forgetting, for the time being, about the alcohol they dispense, for Crumley bars mean lack of affectation and pretense, they mean acceptance of the failures and weakness and foolishness of others, and they mean a refuge from the road and the insanity of the world. With all of their limitations—bars are, after all, exclusive and peopled by drunks—they mean community.

And in the West and the western, friendship of men is the most apparent aspect of community. The so-called code of the West has mostly to do with the way in which men behave toward one another. Now a lot of Crumley's books have to do with sons and their fathers. But as well they have to do with friendship—unstated, loyal, generous, reassuring, self-sacrificing, forgiving male friendship. In the western, the important idea is that of the partner or the sidekick. The idea of partners is explicit and implicit in all of Crumley's books. Sughrue alludes to his old partner in *The Last Good Kiss*. Milo recruits Simmons in *Dancing Bear*. Sughrue seeks out members of his old platoon in *The Mexican Tree Duck*. And *Bordersnakes*, which finally brings Sughrue and Milo together, is as much about partners as about anything else. In *Dancing Bear* the partners, Milo and Simmons, even adopt the pseudonyms of Mr. Autry and Mr. Rogers, and one can't get much more western than that.

Although in essence his heroes possess all of the cowboy criteria, part of what Crumley is about is the deconstruction of the western myth. Cowboys and the code of the West are, as Gail puts it in *Dancing Bear*, "goddamned romantic affectations" (16). *The Wrong Case*, in fact, runs on deconstruction. At the end of his draft thesis on Dalton Kimbrough, a minor western bad man, Raymond Duffy has scrawled "A fucking klutz," which he was. And in *Dancing Bear* Milo acknowledges that his great-grandfather who captured Kimbrough, mostly through the outlaw's ineptness, was hardly a hero either: "When my great-grandfather was sheriff of Meriwether County, he founded the family fortune on a string of opium dens, gambling hells, and cotes for soiled doves" (169). Thus for all of their attachment to and identification with the idea of the cowboy, Crumley's heroes know that the West of fable never was and that even in its deconstructed form, no one should grow up to be a cowboy. And besides, the West is rapidly being taken over by yuppies. "Trigger's stuffed, love," Milo says, "and Gene Autry owns a baseball team" (*Dancing Bear* 224). All of this, however, is deeply rooted in private eye literature: change or sad knowledge erodes the concept of what is no more—and perhaps never was. An integral part of the hero is his continuing and consciously illogical attachment to romantic ideals and discarded rituals in the face of their dissolution.

In Crumley, the ideal with the most powerful and meretricious attraction is that of home and family. It comes out best in Milo's first description of Helen Duffy:

She seemed like a woman from a simpler, better time, a small-town time when sprinklers graced neat lawns and screen doors smelled like rain or dust instead of plastic, when the seasons changed as gracefully as scenes on greeting cards, when snow was never dirty, when fall leaves were never soggy and damp, and when children never cried, except for brief moments, and then were so gently comforted that they didn't mind crying at all. (*The Wrong Case* 15)

The reverie about family is invariably linked with the past. It is tied to Sughrue's anger when he finds that a strip mall and convenience store have displaced his grandfather's house in south Austin and Milo's caustic descriptions of the modern degradations of Meriwether. But unlike the shock of physical change, the ideal of family comes from pasts Crumley's heroes have never known. In creating the pasts of his characters, Crumley creates for them the most twisted and poisonous of families. Take Mrs. Trahearne, whose son remembers her standing

in the rain, at the window, sometimes touching her dark nipples, sometimes holding the full weight of her large, pale breasts in her hands, always staring into the cold rain. Never in the sunlight, always in rain. Sometimes she tilted her face slowly downward, then she smiled, her gray eyes locked on his through the pane, and hefted her breasts as if they were stones she meant to hurl at him. (*The Last Good Kiss* 75)

The same mother conspires with Trahearne's ex-wife to murder the woman who truly cares for him. Milo's family, chronicled extensively in *The Wrong Case* and *Dancing Bear*, reeks of the charnel house. The son of two suicides, Milo lives through his bitter mother's revenge on her drunken and philandering husband. Hers is vengeance that goes beyond the grave, in her donating her husband's clothes to the Salvation Army "So the drunks and bums could have them, she said, so the whole town could know for certain and remember forever what a drunken bum he had been" (88). Beset with the delusion of Native American ancestry, Sughrue's father abandons his Avon lady wife to chase across the West after spirit visions. Milo's real family, along with those he has seen snapping dirty photos as evidence for divorce cases, leads him to observe that

there ought to be a law against families, or, at very least, children should be given a choice of families or colors of their Skinner Boxes. Families are always a mess: everybody always wants to fuck everybody else and usually finds a particularly vicious substitute. And love doesn't seem to matter either. Too much, not enough—somehow the same unhappy family life comes out. (*The Wrong Case* 17)

This forms the bedrock knowledge of Crumley's heroes. It is the fixed pole of a manic depressive side of Trahearne in *The Last Good Kiss* and more fully of Milo's character.

Milo admits that as the son of two suicides he is subject to depression. That's clinical depression. And Crumley's portrayal of him gives witness to this. Look up the symptoms for manic depression or bipolar illness or affective disorder in the *Diagnostic and Statistical Manual of Mental Disorders*. They start off with depressed mood. Almost as soon as we meet him, Milo observes that "age and sorrow, those were my only assets, my largest liabilities" (*The Wrong Case* 4). Feelings of worthlessness? Simon proposes that he and Milo hold a worthless contest. And *The Wrong Case* begins with Milo sunk in lethargy, unable to do anything, unable to think clearly, unable to communicate—"I haven't been frank with anybody in years, not since I started this grimy racket" (17). At the beginning of both *The Wrong Case* and *Dancing Bear* Milo has withdrawn into himself, and he, admittedly, "hadn't been sleeping very well." While there is no sexual dysfunction, irritability, contentiousness, and hostility show up when Milo talks to anyone—especially Jamison. And he goes over the edge—the "anger beyond irritability" of the DSM—slapping Muffin around in *The Wrong Case*, fighting with the mailman in *Dancing Bear*, and this: "I threw the old man into a parked car. He fell into the gutter, mewling curses, but he looked at me and didn't get up. If he had I think I might have killed him" (*The Wrong Case* 178).

And like anger, poor judgment follows Milo wherever he goes—his five ex-wives testify to this. There are thoughts of suicide, too. After Jamison finds him in a stall in the men's room at the Eastgate Liquor Store and Bar, Milo muses,

Surely in this vale of tears we call life, the ill, the halt, and the lame find it curious that some people with constitutions like bull calves sometimes consider their good health a curse rather than a blessing. It can be, though. In fistfights, even beaten senseless, we don't fall down nearly soon enough; the joys of drug abuse don't seem to take the proper toll; and, sometimes when we try to drink ourselves to death, we fail miserably. Miserably. (*Dancing Bear* 161)

Finally, all of the novels are awash in booze and drugs. All of the criteria are there, and it doesn't even take the whole of a shrink's $90 hour to figure this out.

If it's etiology we want, we can bring in, as Milo does, abhorrent early experience as the cause for manic depression. But for Crumley's heroes, it's not just early experience that's abhorrent. It's most experience. First look at the wars. We hear a bit about Milo's war in Korea in *Bordersnakes*, but it is Sughrue's war in Vietnam that Crumley returns to repeatedly:

We were fighting through a village south of An Ke, a hole in the road called Plei Bao Three . . . and I grenaded a hooch and killed three generations of a Vietnamese family. Both grandparents, their daughter, and her three children. (*The Last Good Kiss* 253)

It's all caught on tape by a Canadian news crew and becomes part of the nightly news. Sughrue calls it "the central trauma of my adult life." In civilian life, too, Crumley's heroes take up a trade founded on disillusionment. Thus Sughrue describes being a detective: "Whenever I found anybody, I always suspected that I deserved more than money in payment. This was the saddest moment of the chase, the silent wait for the apologetic parents or the angry spouse or the laws. The process was fine, but the finished product was always ugly" (*The Last Good Kiss* 8).

Divorce work, Milo's sole occupation, is worse. Hence, "the people who came asking for my help convinced me that the world was just as stupid and filthy and corrupt as I thought it was" (*The Wrong Case* 20). Being detectives, Milo and Sughrue are constantly lied to. More importantly, Crumley bases all of the books on manipulation, on large-scale fraud practiced on Sughrue and Milo for venal ends. Being detectives, they also get beaten up with regularity. Worse, much worse, however, is being a party to violent death:

I knew. At that range, when a bullet enters the human head, the hydrostatic pressure blows the face up like a cheap balloon; the eardrums burst, the eyes pop out, and the head seems to dissolve in a shower of blood. Oh God, did I know, and not want to at all. (*The Wrong Case* 228)

Taken individually each of the above seems more than sufficient reason to drive anyone around the bend. Collectively they ought to be unbearable. Kay Redfield Jamison, the queen of depression and literature, ought to leave her speculations about romantic poets and have a look at Crumley's books—but she is a shrink. And shrinks have no place in Crumley's world.

If not neuroleptic drugs, serotonin re-uptake inhibitors, analysis, therapy, 12-step programs, enhanced self-esteem, and relearned behavior, then what? Crumley's heroes need something beyond the world of degradation and drunkenness in which they exist. And this resides in a number of places. For one thing, as opposed to Milo's fantasy of sybaritic pleasure in Mexico, Crumley's heroes create ideals for women and seek women who possess them. First, they create women who embody the opposite of their bitter and morbid experience with their mothers. While *The Last Good Kiss* reprises Snow White, Cinderella, and the captive princess, the notion of an ideal woman appears first in *The Wrong Case*. It imagines a woman who speaks in the "soft way that good mothers forgive their children, letting them know that they are better children than they know" and who possesses "the compassion, fine and lovely; the forgiveness, eternal. A woman so strong that she could believe in hope and trust and families and love" (81). The idea of women like this, as Milo says, "made me homesick for a childhood I'd never really had, the one I sometimes constructed in odd drunken moments to make me forget the real one" (*The Wrong Case* 15). Now maybe it's because the books after *The Wrong Case* move away from the theme of forgiveness. Maybe it's because one doesn't find a lot of women like this hanging out at cowboy bars. They just don't exist in the world of Crumley's books. Instead there are "gay divorcees, stoned

hippie chicks, and tired barmaids whose emotions were as badly man-
gled as mine" (*The Wrong Case* 21), and "women . . . [who] were so
tough they could chip flint hide-scrapers with their hearts" (*The Wrong
Case* 10). Indeed, when Milo believes he has found a woman who seems
to stand for innocence, loyalty, tenderness, family, and love, she turns
out to be the psycho-sexually twisted Helen Duffy.

Although it does not play a part in their fantasy creations, the ideal
woman in Crumley is more earth than mother. This character type begins
tentatively with Selma Hinds in *The Last Good Kiss,* who resembles "a
pioneer woman standing outside a soddy on the plains." She has turned
"the dry rocky soil of the ridge" into something as rich and "black as
river-bottom land" (147). In that novel, too, Betty Sue often enters
smeared with her potter's clay. In *The Wrong Case* there is Mrs. Crider,
whose "bare feet had seen rough use, suffered badly fitting shoes and
rocky trails, but when they reached the grass and earth, they seemed elegant in their confidence and strength" (219). Tante Marie, the Benniwah
grandmother lady in *Dancing Bear* to whom Milo pays homage in the
form of the deed to Camas Meadow, extends and deepens the connection
of women with the land: "Before I came home to the land," she tells
Milo, she lived mostly in saloons. And all of these elements culminate in
Bordersnakes. There is Nancy Tipton, a naiad on steroids, who almost
overwhelms Milo and Sughrue when they meet her in California. There
is Whitney, Sughrue's wife, who saves his life and tries to make a family
in a double-wide parked on the Texas prairie. Most importantly, though,
there is Betty Porterfield, the veterinarian who unites skill and toughness
and knowledge of the land and attachment to its heritage—"great-great
grandfather and my great-grandmother were born in that barn over
there" (210). So, one of the ways in which Crumley's heroes escape the
pack of black dogs of depression is in finding women who are not like
their imagined mothers—soft, warm, and nurturing—but women who
are like themselves.

Nurturing for Crumley is something men do. Much of *The Last
Good Kiss* revolves around Sughrue babysitting Trahearne—listening to
his self-created guilt and artistic impotence and cleaning up his messes,
without opprobrium or censure. Sughrue extends the same combination
of sympathy and responsibility to Betty Sue. Thus on a trip to the bathroom he gazes at a piece of Betty Sue's pottery:

Usually, on those sleepless nighttime trips to the bathroom, I had to take a long
look at my own battered, whiskey-worn face, searching for a glimpse of the face
it might have been but for wasted years, the bars, the long nights. But this night
I rubbed my thumb over the faces locked beneath the brown translucent glaze,

all the weeping women, and I had no pity left for myself. I had made my own bed and went to it to sleep, then to rise and do what I knew I had to do, to pay what I owed the women. (119)

When we see Milo he is too much of a mess to do much except broadcast his sympathy on the dissolute and downtrodden. He derives some comfort, however, from the fact Jamison is raising his only son. And in a Pyrrhic effort at fatherhood, Milo adopts Muffin and saves him, one supposes, from a worse life than the larcenous life he comes to lead. And in *Dancing Bear* Milo, in effect, adopts Simmons, the shell-shocked Vietnam vet, and makes sure Mrs. Weddington and Cassandra Bogardus set up trusts for the children left orphans by the mayhem in the book. In *The Mexican Tree Duck*, Crumley cranks up the nurturing theme with the introduction of Baby Lester. Soon after Wynona and Baby Lester get into Sughrue's car he feels the baby's head: "I left my hand resting on Lester's little head long enough to feel those shockingly resilient bones, the throb of blood, the bass line pulse of life. Over the years I had worked for blood, pain, bone-ache love, and sometimes money. This was the first time I ever went to work for a baby" (83). Wynona, Lester's mother, has it right about Sughrue when she tells him that "you ain't worldly at all. You just act like that. You're just some good old boy who done forgot where he came from. A sucker for every bird dog pup and shitty-bottomed baby that come down the pike" (85). But it's more than that, or becomes more than that after Wynona's death. By the time of *Bordersnakes* Lester has become both the center of Sughrue's world and has transformed that world: "Loving that boy had washed the cynicism and anger right out of my blood" (156). So caring for another, caring for an innocent, caring for a child becomes a significant way in which Crumley's heroes step out of the dark world they inhabit. But mostly he develops this in Sughrue.

With Milo there is something else. There is caring about the downtrodden—the drunks at Mahoney's, particularly Simon. There is, however, more. This begins with Milo's observation of the purse snatcher who is run over at the opening of *The Wrong Case*. Later on in the same novel Milo recounts the episode that got him mentioned in *Time*, his capture of a mass-murderer. Only the murderer is a "soft, fat honor student" who bursts into tears and throws his arms around Milo when he entered the beauty shop where he was holding out. Later on in the same novel Milo kicks the fight out of a logger who had, unprovoked, assaulted a panhandler. In *Dancing Bear* the incident that ultimately leads to Milo's gift of his timberland runs along the same lines. Here Milo assaults the two men who have shot a convenience store stick-up man and then he and a passing nurse save the life of the robber, who looks like "a malnourished child" (46).

Saved by women, saved by children, saved by compassion, Crumley's heroes are also saved by forgiveness—in the first two books at least. Forgiveness takes up a lot of room in *The Last Good Kiss*. Much of it revolves around Trahearne and his books. Trahearne, the burned-out writer patterned on Roger Wade from Chandler's *The Long Goodbye*, made his name writing books that sound like Mailer's *The Naked and the Dead* and Dickey's *Deliverance*: "fair hack work," Sughrue calls them, "cluttered with literary allusions and symbols . . . The male characters, even the villains and cowards, clung to a macho code so blatant that even an illiterate punk in an east L.A. pachuco gang could understand it immediately" (106). Trahearne bases his books on his experience in World War II, particularly on an incident where he shoots a wounded Japanese soldier in the head: "and then I knew what war was about . . . it was about killing without flinching, about living without flinching" (254). The trouble is that the whole action of *The Last Good Kiss* chronicles one of Trahearne's screw-ups after another, from his half-hearted and inept attempt to break from his mother and ex-wife to his bungling during the rescue of Betty Sue from Hyland. As a consequence of this experience, Trahearne realizes that

all this time, all these years since the war I worried about how tough you had to be to live without flinching, but when it came down to it, when it had to do with living instead of dying, I didn't have the guts to forgive the woman I loved . . . So now I'm through with all that. I'm going to write a novel about love and forgiveness. (255)

But the old fat boy doesn't know the first thing about forgiveness, and never learns. He assumes that it means forgiving someone for breaking a moral code or failing to observe a standard of conduct or behavior. He assumes that there is one who forgives and one who is forgiven. This concept depends on "moral certitude." It depends on "a moral certitude," that, Sughrue tells readers early in the novel, "I no longer even claimed to possess." But another kind of forgiveness surfaces in the novel. Part of it derives from the characters' recognition of their own foolishness. We can see it in this moment between Sughrue and Trahearne: "As we shared the whiskey, I wondered how long men had been forgiving each other over strong drink for being fools" (196). More importantly, Crumley connects real forgiveness with acceptance and refusing to judge. This is what Trahearne sees in Sughrue: "but I watched you go after her with a smile and eighty-seven dollars, and you never judged her, not once, you forgave her without asking anything in return" (255). All of this comes up again in *The Wrong Case*. Wrapped up with Milo's drunkenness and his association with other drunks, Crumley makes a particular case for accepting people and refusing to judge them—although Milo constantly judges himself and finds that he is wanting. As part of the series of incidents and revelations that leads to the solution to Raymond Duffy's death, Milo recalls several bits of wisdom passed on to him from his father. One of them is about accepting both one's and everyone else's foolishness:

"Son," he said without preamble, "never trust a man who doesn't drink because he's probably a self-righteous sort, a man who thinks he knows right from wrong all the time. Some of them are good men, but in the name of goodness, they cause most of the suffering in the world. They're the judges, the meddlers. And, son, never trust a man who drinks but refuses to get drunk. They're usually afraid of something down deep inside, either that they're a coward or a fool or mean and violent. You can't trust a man who's afraid of himself. But sometimes, son, you can trust a man who occasionally kneels before a toilet. The chances are that he is learning something about humility and his natural human foolishness, about how to survive himself." (236)

In addition to this, at the close of the novel Crumley returns to the theme of forgiveness. From her mother, Milo learns that Helen Duffy has manipulated him throughout the entire plot, that she is irresponsible, sexually voracious, promiscuous, indiscreet, and mentally unstable—traits Milo himself has witnessed during the course of the action. Helen Duffy, in fact, is a female version of Trahearne from the next novel. In the final encounter between Milo and Mrs. Duffy, she asks him, "You don't feel betrayed? You can forgive everything?" to which he replies, "Lady, I'm more interested in being forgiven myself" (270). And the final words of the novel are "I sat down, heard the sound of a car driving away, I drank my beer, and forgave her" (272). No bitterness, regret, or blame. Milo's forgiveness does not help Helen Duffy or bring her back. She does not even know about it. But it does something for Milo and it allows him to endure in a world replete with sorrow and injustice.

As much as forgiveness becomes a means of coming to terms with the darkening gloom of life in Crumley's world, it has its limits. Forgiveness as a universal way of life only works in a world in which there are no definite standards and in which equally helpless creatures blunder into one another without reason or motive, subterfuge or conspiracy. The problem is that there are, in fact, some basic moral values and the world is not peopled by equally helpless creatures blundering around. Some are much more vicious than others; some consciously seek to manipulate, use, profit from, and destroy others. In this kind of world, universal forgiveness both makes people suckers and patsys and, worse than that, makes them complicit in destroying the few ideals that survive in the sordid world and makes them unwitting accomplices in causing the suffering of others.

For Crumley, authority is one of the malevolent forces that causes others to suffer. Thus Milo's father's warning about "a self-righteous sort, a man who thinks he knows right from wrong all the time. Some of them are good men, but in the name of goodness, they cause most of the suffering in the world." This kind of person usually winds up in government, and throughout the books, Crumley inserts pieces about the bungling stupidity of government, from its conduct of wars to its refusal to solve the drug problem through decriminalization. Partly as a response to this, Milo and Sughrue have more than a bit of the cowboy outlaw in them. But it's hard to do much about the government besides complain, as Simon does in his scrawled diatribes posted to Washington. There is, however, something his heroes can do about people who conspire to cause the suffering of others.

Thus, although Sughrue asserts that he has no moral certitude, he does possess values. In *Bordersnakes* Milo remembers one of his adages: "anybody who speaks badly of revenge ain't lost nothing important" (29). And Crumley's heroes do lose important things. In *The Last Good Kiss* Sughrue witnesses the destruction of Betty Sue, the ideal of womanhood and personhood he has protected throughout the book. He needs to do something about it. So at the end of the novel he tells Trahearne,

I've got a brand new elk rifle, a 7mm magnum, old man, and some afternoon, some afternoon, you're going to step out on your front deck after a day of scribble, scribble, scribble, and I'm going to put a 175-grain hunk of lead right through your gut. (291)

If revenge is a promise here, the recompense for the death of Wynona is very real with the death of Joe Don Pines at the end of *The Mexican Tree Duck*. Although less spectacular and violent, Milo, too, moves from forgiveness if not quite to revenge then to protest. At the end of *Dancing Bear* he confronts Sarah Weddington, Gail, Carolyn, and especially Cassandra Bogardus. He forces them to give support to the children of the innocents killed during the course of the novel. He then returns the grizzly pelt to Camas Meadow, his grandfather's timberland, which he deeds to the Benniwah. Rather than the forgiveness Milo feels at the end of *The Wrong Case*, *Dancing Bear* ends with "I have learned some things.

Modern life is warfare without end: take no prisoners, leave no wounded, eat the dead—that's environmentally sound" (228).

Rather than continuing this philosophy of cruelty, in *Bordersnakes* Crumley presents a counterpoint of Milo and Sughrue, of revenge and forgiveness. In the novel both characters are wounded—Sughrue has been gut shot and left for dead and Milo's inheritance has been stolen. The action begins as the search for mutual revenge, each character alternately reminding the other of their almost blunted purpose when energy or stamina or determination ebbs. While Sughrue enters the novel having undertaken violent revenge, it is Milo who does the killing in the book. Indeed, the final bloody scene happens because Milo has contrived it in a carefully planned manner. He does not, however, execute the plot for revenge—he has already electronically transferred his money back to Meriwether from the bad guy's account, and Sughrue's assailant is already dead. He does it, rather, to protect his friend.

While it supplies a means of demonstrating the values that Milo and Sughrue depend upon to survive and endure their world, action in itself, doing things, does not provide the kind of value that is often associated with manliness in the action-adventure story. In most cases, at the end of the novels Crumley's heroes are no better off, indeed in some cases they are worse off than they were at the beginning. In *The Wrong Case* Milo begins in lethargy and ends with loss. The same pattern recurs in most of the books. Sughrue loses Wynona at the conclusion of *The Mexican Tree Duck*, and Milo loses one of his last illusions about his childhood in *Dancing Bear*. In *The Last Good Kiss* Sughrue moves from aimless wandering—he and others refer to him as a "saddletramp"—to a future of attenuated anger. Things always seem to go wrong. Stacy accidentally kills Hyland in the rescue of Betty Sue in *The Last Good Kiss*. Milo's boobytrapping his cabin ends with Milo witnessing the surviving interloper blow out his brains in *Dancing Bear*. Whether it is in the incidents in the plot, or in the plot as a whole, action brings only sorrow.

After their experience with this kind of world, in the early novels Crumley's heroes inevitably return to the bars—not as barflies but as bartenders. In this role they can move from patron to patron listening to scraps of bravado and misery, dispensing sympathy without involvement, and offering temporary solace in the form of one more round. They, in effect, become the orderlies in the asylum passing out medication that will block out but not cure the illnesses of their patients and their world. And this is a far more pessimistic vision than most hardboiled writers, even Chandler, allow themselves. In *The Mexican Tree Duck* and *Bordersnakes*, however, the novels end with the heroes, first with Sughrue and then Milo, moving out of the sordid world of other people's problems and into one based on a conscious and focused commitment in Sughrue's case to Lester and Whitney and in Milo's case to Betty Porterfield, commitment to others who represent the ideal they have sought without success when they have tried to solve other people's problems, the ideal that combines love, land, and family.

LOREN ESTLEMAN

When Loren Estleman knocked around the world of small town newspapers and even after he started writing westerns, he must have spent a lot of time reading Hammett and Chandler. It's easy to find them in *Motor City Blue* (1980), *Angel Eyes* (1981), *The Midnight Man* (1982), *The Glass Highway* (1983), *Sugartown* (1984), *Every Brilliant Eye* (1986), *Lady Yesterday* (1987), *Downriver* (1988), *Silent Thunder* (1989), *Sweet Women Lie* (1990), *Never Street* (1997), and *The Witchfinder* (1998)—the Amos Walker books. Clues pop up everywhere. Take Amos' talk about finding people in *Lady Yesterday*: it's really the Flitcraft passage from *The Maltese Falcon*. Or take this passage from *Motor City Blue* describing Ben Morningstar's bodyguard: "His black shirt was painted on and he wore his striped necktie in a knot you couldn't undo with a screwdriver and a pair of pliers" (19). And then consider the way Marlowe describes the Indian's get-up in *Farewell, My Lovely*: "A tie dangled outside his buttoned jacket, a tie which had been tied with a pair of pliers in a knot the size of a pea." So, okay, Estleman knows a good thing when he sees it, and uses it for his own purposes. But this kind of occasional tribute to Hammett and Chandler hardly describes Estleman's relationship with them. He doesn't simply want to borrow bits from the universe they created, he wants Amos Walker to participate in it. Walker dresses right out of the *noir* films of the 1940s—including the regulation fedora. Estleman aims to re-create the wardrobe, office, house, and attitudes—especially attitudes—of the hard-boiled hero of the thirties and forties. Except his hero lives and works in the eighties. Thus, according to the cliché, Amos Walker walks like a duck, and we will return to that topic a bit later. But first I would like to look into the fact that Estleman goes to some pains to have his hero talk like a duck as well.

Although the hard-boiled story has had a continuous existence since the twenties, when writers like Parker, Kaminsky, Estleman, and others "rediscovered" it in the seventies and eighties, one of the things they saw as most worthy of imitation was hard-boiled style, believing—quite rightly—that the way in which the narrator-hero uses words is inextricably linked with the nature of the hero's character and, in fact, the hero's relationship with the world. In discussing Parker I have already gone through the list of elements that make up hard-boiled style: the wise-

cracks, sarcasm, hyperboles, similes, terse utterances, catalogues, etc.
Estleman puts them all into Walker's voice. But of all the elements that
make up hard-boiled style, Estleman, like Earl Emerson a decade later,
fastened on one as his favorite. And that's my justification for the following extended semi-digression on similes.

It's not altogether a digression, since so much in contemporary
hard-boiled fiction depends so heavily on Raymond Chandler. Perhaps
the single most arresting element of Chandler's work is his similes.
Take, for instance, *The Big Sleep*: Chandler uses nine similes in the first
chapter: the first four pages. And on the first page of the second chapter
we get the one I've already cited once: "The plants filled the place, a
forest of them, with nasty meaty leaves and stalks like the newly washed
fingers of dead men." Going back to grammar school, this, like all similes, compares things using "like" or "as." It has the two requisite parts:
something on the left and something on the right. We're not supposed to
know much about the first word or group of words, but we're supposed
to know about what comes after the "like" or "as." So put them together
and, if things work the way the writer wants them to, we get what the
writer is talking about. It has to do with meaning and it has to do with an
essential way humans learn. But in Chandler there's more to it than that.
First of all, his characteristic similes bring things together that don't usually belong together—here it's hothouse plants and corpses. And that
union brings about a vivid and complex insight for the reader about General Sternwood's greenhouse and the way Marlowe feels about being
there. It's intellectual but, in Chandler, it's also verbal pyrotechnics, calling attention, as it does, to the range and originality of the speaker's
imagination. With similes like these, hard-boiled writers say something
else about their world as well. In the second element—the one after the
"like" or "as"—writers posit the world of their audience: they assume
that readers will be familiar with the second term so that, in turn, they
can go back and comprehend the first part of the comparison. They, in
effect, assume the characteristics, or at least the common knowledge, of
their audience, whether it runs to subjects like Proust and the intricacies
of the Albigensian Heresy (as it does in writers like Ellery Queen and
Dorothy L. Sayers) or to knowing how to diagnose a bad CV joint or
about Al Rosen's corked bat episode, or both. Finally, when hard-boiled
writers use similes that bring together disparate elements, they repeat on
a small scale one of the principal themes of hard-boiled literature: that
the world as it is and the world as it should be are two different things
that the actions of the hero make equivalent, or at least coexistent.

All of this, of course, has something to do with how Estleman
writes the Amos Walker books. He loads them with similes. After *Motor*

City Blue, in which he uses fewer than one hundred of them, the simile clearly becomes Estleman's figure of choice. Two of the later books, *Sugartown* and *Never Street*, place at the top of the hit parade, with over two hundred similes each. Rarely extended—most of them contain fewer than five words—the similes are put to various uses. First, and most obviously, they link Estleman's hero to all of the old guys—the Op, Marlowe, Spade, and all the rest of the original hard-boiled heroes. Walker talks the way they talk. By using similes, Estleman both makes Walker a member of the guild and at the same time lets his readers know what they're getting into when they pick up one of the books.

Estleman, of course, uses similes to perform, or seek to perform, the function for which they were designed: to explain things that are difficult to explain. This means emotions (feeling "like the guy who had wandered into his own funeral" [*Glass Highway* 86]) and things experienced by the senses (an aroma "like disinfectant in a public restroom" [*Lady Yesterday* 16]). Since the hard-boiled story, according to the rules, must concentrate on action, it also means employing comparisons to make the action more immediately comprehensible ("Getting the door closed without sacrificing any more of his limbs involved propping him up with one hand and then withdrawing it, slamming the door fast, like closing a closet full of bowling balls" [*Every Brilliant Eye* 22-23]). But Estleman also occasionally ventures into the realm of the disparate simile. Check out the second elements in the following:

a brontosaurus on a whole wheat roll (*Midnight Man* 5)

a Tiffany lamp in a home for the blind (*Angel Eyes* 51)

a Swede on . . . Rosa Parks Boulevard (*Motor City Blue* 227)

Christmas lights at a vigil for the dead (*Never Street* 97)

These similes juxtapose dissimilar things as Chandler's do, but unlike Chandler's characteristic fusions that convey new meaning (his "my cigarette tasted like a plumber's handkerchief," for example), this class of simile in Estleman really simply serves as another form of the wisecrack, thereby reinforcing that facet of character demonstrated when hard-boiled heroes crack wise to people in authority, something Walker does regularly: "Hanging up I felt better. A couple of one-liners off a good straight man and Wiseass Walker was good as new" (*Midnight Man* 72).

If we take it as a given that neither Estleman nor anyone else is likely to supersede Chandler in the form or function of similes in the hard-boiled story, we can still learn something about the form and about Estleman by taking a look at the content of his similes, at the areas of knowledge and experience the writer assumes his readers possess. These are the things that he expects will light up his similes.

There are a number of areas to which Estleman keeps returning when Amos Walker makes similes. Some of these confirm common expectations about a form that began as male oriented. In a number of places, for instance, Walker makes comparisons to things military: "tanks in a motor pool" (*Angel Eyes* 54), "a halftrack" (*Never Street* 174), "weapons at parade rest" (*Downriver* 194), and "walking around a corner into a fire-fight" (*Glass Highway* 55). Not as many of these appear as one would expect, especially given that in several places Walker speaks of his combat experience in Vietnam and Cambodia. He also uses a fair number of similes that refer to industrial or mechanical things or practices. Amos refers to corrugated, molten, polished, coiled, bent, and nickel steel. He compares things to "the head of a Phillips screwdriver" (*Sugartown* 95) and "the bubble in a carpenter's level" (*Never Street* 157). Estleman expects his readers to resonate with similes referring to "a part cast from an imperfect die and then another die made from that part" (*Lady Yesterday* 137), "a Rotomill tearing up pavement" (*Midnight Man* 58), "the coke in the ovens of the foundry" (*Never Street* 337), and "a loose rod" (*Midnight Man* 204). And then there's sports. Al Kaline, Lou Whitaker, Billy Martin, and the sound of "a wooden bat breaking on a fastball" (*Midnight Man* 189) are all supposed to be common knowledge to the readers—or else they won't understand the comparisons Walker makes.

Along with these military, mechanical, and athletic references, Estleman comes back again and again to other kinds of references which connect him with the traditions of the hard-boiled story and which are, perhaps, even more ultimately male than guns, tools, and jock straps. Here is a selection from the first sub-set:

curry combs (*Angel Eyes* 37)
forty acres of unplowed field (*Angel Eyes* 106)
a sharecropper (*Downriver* 36)
a tractor wheel (*Downriver* 112)
thumping a grain barrel (*Downriver* 30)
broiled hog (*Motor City Blue* 22)
a mask carved out of old barnwood (*Midnight Man* 56)
treeing a possum (*Midnight Man* 224)
a mule on a wooden trestle (*Never Street* 80)
a passing cattle truck (*Never Street* 266)
a tired horse returning to the barn (*Never Street* 60)
a big rough farmer (*Sugartown* 17)
a good-natured ox (*Sugartown* 54)
a one-legged milking stool (*Sugartown* 173)
a barn (*Silent Thunder* 55)

a breed bull (*Silent Thunder* 7)
a fence rail (*Sweet Women Lie* 174)
a mule (*Sweet Women Lie* 171)
barn siding (*Sweet Women Lie* 66)

Back in the days of Hammett and Chandler, more than likely a majority of those who read *Black Mask* and the other pulps either lived in or had lived in rural communities. Even Marlowe migrated from a small town to Los Angeles. Similes like these evoked and continue to evoke nostalgia for the pastoral past—hard work, good neighbors, strength, and virtue—a time and place that has nothing to do with the cities in which (or, most likely, near which) readers now live. They possess the same magnetism that attracts male consumers of the 1990s to pickup trucks and sport utility vehicles even though they rarely venture further than the mall. None of them requires more than a superficial knowledge of agriculture (why do they call it a combine? what is barnyard bingo?). But then again, none of the poets who have written pastoral poetry really wants to jump in and lend a hand at sheep shearing. And note that all of the above refer to the things associated with men on farms. Not quite so with the other sub-set in this category of similes, the domestic ones. All of them are commonly associated with women.

More than any other topic, Estleman's hero uses home life as the second, explanatory element in his similes. He assumes that readers will understand what he describes because they know what goes on in the kitchen. Thus actions and feelings are like: "grease on a cheap griddle" (*Midnight Man* 8), "the lid of a pressure cooker" (*Never Street* 67), "a pressure cooker full of red cabbage [that] blew up" (*Sugartown* 17), "a refrigerator in need of a cleaning" (*Midnight Man* 86), and "something forgotten in the back of the refrigerator" (*Midnight Man* 70). Kitchen or bath, it's all the same when things are like "a drop on a faucet" (*Angel Eyes* 68), "a dripping faucet" (*Every Brilliant Eye* 252), or "a faucet dripping itself dry" (*Never Street* 322). From the bathroom proper, Walker compares his experiences to "a wet facecloth" (*Motor City Blue* 72), "a container of shaving cream" (*Never Street* 310), "rubber bathtub stoppers" (*Never Street* 19), a "moldy towel" (*Sugartown* 157), and squeezing "toothpaste through an exhausted tube" (*Sweet Women Lie* 85). And there's the laundry, too: "wet laundry slapping a board fence" (*Midnight Man* 131) and "a silk dress in a steel washtub" (*Sugartown* 2). Walker makes note of moths in the house with comparisons to "moths in a light fixture" (*Glass Highway* 110), "moths seeking a hole in a screen door" (*Every Brilliant Eye* 184), and "a moth caught in a screen door" (*Sugartown* 115). Emery boards, shoetrees, pocket lint, sofa cushions, hot water bottles, fireplace fenders: it's like one of the songs from *The*

Sound of Music. Amos reckons his readers will know what he's talking about if he refers to these and other domestic items. All of this, I think, adds up to a couple of things. First of all, there's the noticing—the hard-boiled hero takes note of minutiae everywhere. It's part of being a detective that doesn't get turned on and off and it also appears in the stylistic element of the catalog in hard-boiled writing. The persistence of domestic references also ties in with those to rural life and suggests a longing for a life that is less complex and less marginal than the one the hero must live. The hero would choose to live in a nice bungalow with music and books and with a spouse and a family, but something in his moral and intellectual make-up puts this out of reach.

The rural and domestic similes in Estleman's books, then, connect him with some powerful traditions implicit and explicit in hard-boiled fiction. So do his repeated references in similes to disease, old age, and death. Similes referring to death ought to be just as routine (and are more chilling by the fact that they are routine) as death itself in hard-boiled stories. And Estleman doesn't let us down. He has lots of references to morticians, funerals, and cemeteries, like

a mortician's handshake (*Angel Eyes* 69)

a mortician lowers the lid on a coffin (*Every Brilliant Eye* 68)

a mortician's workshop (*Silent Thunder* 179)

leaving the chamber where they lay out the corpse (*Midnight Man* 193)

the anteroom to the chamber where they lay out the dead (*Sugartown* 88)

amateur pallbearers (*Downriver* 178)

cemetery monuments (*Downriver* 27)

uniform headstones in a bureaucratic Arlington (*Sweet Women Lie* 65)

And there are references to corpses, too:

dead men's eyes (*Downriver* 145)

skeletal fingers (*Glass Highway* 12)

dead skin (*Lady Yesterday* 14)

a dead man's [hands] (*Motor City Blue* 239)

the groping fingers of men long dead (*Motor City Blue* 156)

Not much going on here that readers should not expect. The figurative language simply reinforces a pretty obvious point about death in the books and in the detective's world. The repetition of words describing disease and old age make the same kind of point, but this time linked to the hero's environment. Of course they connect pretty immediately with every reader's own primal consciousness, but disease and age have also ravaged the world—in Estleman's case, Detroit—in hard-boiled stories, and the ideal world of the hero's youth or his imagination lies in shambles, corrupt and feeble. Thus, Walker's similes summon up "dead cells in an extinct organism" (*Never Street* 269), "cutting into a malignant but dormant mole" (*Downriver* 60), "sticking a boil and pus running out" (*Downriver* 9), "a syphilitic degenerate" (*Angel Eyes* 144), and "a dying cell in a terminal body" (*Silent Thunder* 179). More often than referring to disease, moreover, Walker uses similes to summon up images of decrepit and embarrassing old age:

an old lady shaking her teeth in a glass (*Angel Eyes* 1)

a spinster who'd wasted her youth taking care of an invalid parent (*Silent Thunder* 106)

a hysterical old woman (*Sweet Women Lie* 4)

an old convict trying to cough up a wad of jute (*Sweet Women Lie* 18)

the sparkle in a dirty old man's eye (*Angel Eyes* 37)

a fat old man climbing stairs (*Every Brilliant Eye* 154)

an old man remembering a childhood meal in his sleep (*Glass Highway* 37)

an old man lowering himself to a bench (*Midnight Man* 187)

an old man in an oxygen tent (*Sugartown* 127)

an old man cursing on his deathbed (*Every Brilliant Eye* 36)

The elements in these similes give an undercurrent of despair as bleak as Amos Walker's literal world.

So far, all of Estleman's similes come from pretty much stock sources and function mainly in making his books hard-boiled, but not all that different. As a prelude to talking about the books themselves, a couple of other concept patterns that appear in Estleman's similes, however, do suggest why and how his books stand out from those of others. A couple of times in every book Estleman uses a historical reference as the second element in his similes. These mostly come from the historical periods one sees covered on commercial "learning" channels on cable— ancient Egypt, Rome, and World War II. Estleman's real historical interest centers on Detroit, and little of this resides in common knowledge so it can hardly supply fodder for similes. About once in every book one can find a western simile. Estleman, after all, wrote westerns both before and while he wrote the Amos Walker books. But these references have the feel of using up old stock rather than having any intimate connection with the world of the hero or the novels. The code of the West comes in with Bum Bassett in *Midnight Man*:

Code of the West, huh?

I reckon it sounds sort of funny, put like that. But there's sense behind it.

Women don't get raped and murdered out on the plains because somebody's scared to dial a phone. One scream and the whole neighborhood's out with Winchesters and lynch ropes. (59)

But it pretty much either peters out or gets internalized after that third novel. Not so with movies and music. Estleman does expect his readers to have misspent their youths in the same movie theaters and listening to the same music he did, for he expects us to know names from the films and music of the forties and fifties. Here is the list: Ingrid Bergman, James Mason, the Dead End Kids, Vincent Price (several times), Farina, George Sanders, Sidney Greenstreet, Oliver Hardy, Errol Flynn, Boris Karloff, Gilbert Rowland, Cesar Romero, Jack Warner, Mae West, Clark Gable, Randolph Scott, Dinah Washington, and Nat King Cole. And if we don't know these people, we don't understand the similes, the books, the hero, or the world. In another decade, if anyone wants to read them, they'll have to be annotated with CD-Rom clips of Stan and Ollie pushing the piano up those endless stairs. This lies at the heart of what Amos Walker is all about.

Although his choice of literary style and his multiplicity of similes surely shape the Amos Walker books, perhaps the most significant points about Estleman's style are that it is imitative and that it is old. Before taking on the hard-boiled novel, Estleman's major experience had been in writing the popular sub-genres of the historical novel, the western, and the anachronistic detective story (thus his *Sherlock Holmes vs. Dracula* [1978] and *Dr. Jekyll and Mr. Holmes* [1979]). The natural thing for him to do was to apply the same kind of approach to the hard-boiled story, and this is what he does. In the Amos Walker novels, Estleman places the hard-boiled hero into a number of contemporary realities, and when he does this, he tends to do it historically—he tends to begin by talking about what was.

And this starts with the re-creation of literary history. From the macro point of view, all of the books begin with Estleman's conviction that he is participating in a significant literary tradition. Indeed, *Never Street* centers on a protracted discussion—complete with a fictional professor from Ann Arbor—of the history of the kind of fiction Estleman tries to write. Here he talks about its place in the history of literature:

The allure of the *noir* protagonist to the modern man is he's more approachable than Beowulf or Sherlock Holmes. It takes a Superman to slash away at Grendel or to match intellects with Professor Moriarty, but this guy is an ordinary slob with tall troubles who usually comes out on top, even if it does kill him sometimes. (73)

And later in the same novel, Amos reflects on the particular appropriateness of the *noir*, or hard-boiled story, for contemporary persons:

The narrative spoke to the world after Watergate and Vietnam, sunk in the dreary morass of political correctness and trapped in a society divided along lines racial, sexual, philosophical, dogmatic, and religious, exactly as it had spoken to a world suddenly deprived of an obvious, convenient foreign enemy and forced to look to itself for a substitute. (165)

But more than simply playing a role in the continuation of a significant literary genre, though, Estleman (and his hero) often make it sound like they're resurrecting it from the dead, that we need to hop back to the forties and early fifties to find real heroes and real hard-boiled stories. It's as if the hard-boiled tradition stopped and he's bringing it back. Well, he does note that it hasn't quite stopped. There's Robert B. Parker:

There was nothing on television and I sat up for a while smoking and trying to read a paperback mystery I'd picked up in a drugstore once while tailing someone. It was about a private eye back East who wore expensive running shoes with everything and squawked so much about the things he wouldn't do that you wonder what people hired him for in the first place. His partner was a professional killer and if there was a mystery to it at all I couldn't find it and gave up. To hell with P.I.s with codes they have to keep hauling out and looking at like pocket watches and to hell with cool fresh voices in women's mouths. (*Sugartown* 47)

Rather than stopping, then, the hard-boiled story for Estleman has become effete and self-indulgent. It has lost its hero as well as its connection with the problem-solving core of the detective story. He doesn't say it here, but most apparently Estleman would have us believe that it has also lost both its setting and its essential ambiance.

Robert B. Parker really likes Boston: as Spenser experiences it, contemporary Boston has all that Spenser and Susan require to make life pleasant and fulfilling. The opposite holds true for Estleman's Detroit. Any number of things have made contemporary Detroit a rat hole. And Estleman makes the point that to understand them, one must first understand the city's history. He understands it—indeed has written books that center on it—and lets his readers know about it in the Amos Walker books. Estleman's history of Detroit starts off with the fact that what became the city once formed part of the frontier, the West. Thus his repeated references to historical clashes between settlers and Native Americans. The massacre at the Battle of Bloody Run comes up in the pocket history of Belle Isle in *Lady Yesterday*, and Estleman repeatedly mentions Chief Pontiac's legendary role in the area's past. Here's an example from *Midnight Man*:

Detroit's center of law enforcement is a mammoth block structure designed by Albert Kahn and erected in 1922 at 1300 Beaubein, a street named after a French belle who is supposed to have warned the commander of Fort Detroit that Pontiac's warriors were planning to smuggle sawed-off muskets into the garrison under their blankets and take over. (35-36)

The city may have been born out of Fort Detroit, but the formation of its character waited until the discovery of practical uses for the internal combustion engine. In the following passage from *Midnight Man* Estleman notes the irony of Detroit's origins and its twentieth-century reality in the automobile manufacturing business:

The River Rouge plant. Henry Ford's monument to the Industrial Revolution. One hundred miles of private railroad, a fleet of ships larger than some navies, and enough daily electricity to power two hundred and forty thousand households fire its steel mills, coke ovens, glass plant, paper mill, and assembly operation, all in the name of economic parity with Japan. Cadillac and LaSalle camped on this site two centuries before their names fell to the products of Ford's competitors. (106)

And Ford and General Motors changed the ethnic make-up of the city. In *Sugartown* Estleman focuses on Polish immigrants and notes the mark they continue to make on his community:

Driving down Chene through the old village with its tight rows of identical century-old houses painted in peeling colors, you still catch glimpses of the melting pot: old men loitering in front of the old Round Bar where as children they had packed the balcony along with their fathers to watch the struggling glistening backs of the wrestlers below; a thick-ankled housewife slitting a duck's throat in her backyard and holding it flapping upside-down while her little daughter catches the warm blood in a bowl for the soup they call czarnina; native costumes sagging from a pulley-operated line waiting for the Polish Constitution celebration on Belle Isle. (13)

After the ways in which the automobile industry changed the city and its inhabitants, Estleman fastens on the passage of the Eighteenth Amendment and the geographical anomaly about Detroit that every Trivial Pursuit player knows: there are places where the city is geographically north of the Canadian border. Thus, in *Lady Yesterday*: "The restaurant had been a speakeasy when the Purple gang shot it out with the Coast Guard and their rivals the Licavolis on the river, unlike the current administration it was a proud part of Detroit's past" (23). And Amos makes precisely the same kind of historical reflection in *Silent Thunder*: "The old Detroit, the city of growling trumpets, window-tapping hookers, and contraband Canadian whisky served in smoky cellars, is still visible if you care to look for it and the mayor's contractors haven't gotten to it yet" (32). Maybe more than the automakers or the rum runners, the racial stirrings of the 1960s have changed the city and its fortunes:

When I came to the town it was like a big dumb hunky with a beer keg and a big wide stupid grin. It worked hard, got dirty, swore, told off-color jokes, and laughed a lot and loud. The riots came and then after them the murders and then this new gang took over and threw up those silos on the riverfront and called it the Renaissance Center. Now it's like a hooker that got religion, avoiding old friends, won't laugh at old jokes. (*Sugartown* 84-85)

The history in the Amos Walker books, though, hardly provides a coherent historical account of Detroit—socially, politically, economically, or in any of the other approaches to which historians adhere. Granted, Estleman does give us the kind of things historians despise: tidbits of fascinating trivia like the aside in *Lady Yesterday* about the MacArthur bridge to Belle Isle:

Long before it was renamed for Douglas MacArthur, the Belle Isle bridge had posed a temptation for local barnstorming pilots, beginning in 1913 with William E. Scripps, who later took on more daring journalistic stunts as publisher of the Detroit *News*. (162)

Instead of history, what Walker does is to use the past to beat up on the present. So, he adds things like, "unlike the current administration it was a proud part of Detroit's past," "if you care to look for it and the mayor's contractors haven't gotten to it yet," and "after them the murders and then this new gang took over and threw up those silos on the riverfront and called it the Renaissance Center." The passage about the impact of Polish immigrants on the city cited above ends with the admonition "But you have to look quick, because it's going, going to eminent domain and General Motors' golden ring in the nose of City Hall, its churches knocked to rubble and kindling, the bricks that paved the medieval alleys piled in heaps for the scavengers." Walker summarizes that which has displaced Old Detroit in his repeated references to the travesty of urban renewal symbolized in the sterile futility of the Renaissance Center. And he portrays it in the mean streets of the decayed city that the detective routinely encounters:

Story's After Midnight shared a block of age-blurred buildings with half a dozen similar establishments on the north side of Erskine, a street where business was conducted behind graffiti-smeared clapboard fences and from the back seats of spanking new Caddies and Lincolns, where cops paired up on sticky August nights to patrol on raw nerve-ends, thumbs stroking the oily black hammers of the holstered magnums they preferred . . . ears tuned for the quick scuffling of rubber soled shoes on the sidewalk behind them and the wood on metal clacking of a sawed-off pump shotgun being brought to bear just beyond the next corner, a street where a grunt of uncontrollable passion and stifled scream in the grey, stinking depths of a claustrophobic alley could mean a ten-dollar quickie or a rape in progress. With its stripped, wheelless hunks that had once been cars, and aimlessly blowing litter, it was the kind of street you never saw on the posters put up by the Chamber of Commerce. (*Motor City Blue* 58-59)

Small wonder that Estleman chose the title *Motor City Blue* for the first Amos Walker novel. In that book, Ben Morningstar makes what may amount to a defining statement that exposes the complex personal and racial attitudes characters (including more heroes than just Estleman's) possess about the history of their cities:

This morning I had Wiley take me down Twelfth Street where I grew up. Rosa Parks Boulevard they call it now. It made me sick. They burned down the house I was born in. Burned it to the ground during the riots. Same thing with all the places I used to work to help support the family after my pa got killed. Nothing but black holes in the ground with here and there a chimney or a cast-iron sink sticking out of them. I remember thinking as a kid how ugly it all was, that neighborhood, how it would be a blessing if somebody put a match to the whole thing. I was wrong. It's worse. (33)

As much as the old gangster crystallizes a semi-pervasive attitude toward the past latent in many hard-boiled stories, the past isn't so bad for Estleman's detective hero. In fact, it's much, much better than the present. For Amos, the past supplies ideals of romance, a stock of prejudices, and a role which provides an alternative (albeit a singular and most difficult one) to the close to universal corruption and decay of the present.

The romance comes in the synthetic form of cinematic images embedded in the hero's consciousness. Recall the people to whom Amos refers when he makes similes: Ingrid Bergman, James Mason, Vincent Price, George Sanders, Sidney Greenstreet, Errol Flynn, Boris Karloff,

Gilbert Roland, Cesar Romero, Jack Warner, Mae West, Clark Gable, Randolph Scott, Dinah Washington, and Nat King Cole. These people (except maybe Randolph Scott) dressed for dinner. Sex was a sultry suggestion instead of a ten-day-free-trial offer. Villains were just villains and not subjects for study by eager undergraduate social work students. They spoke suavely and correctly—Walker shares the same concern for finical grammatical correctness with most hard-boiled heroes. They had class; they had style. Corruption, vulgarity, and commercialism has displaced it. Thus Walker's repeated references to rampant political corruption in Detroit; his outrage at the feminine hygiene product commercial that interrupts his channel surfing in *Never Street*; and his conviction that owning a Big Wheel can never be the same as having a tricycle: it was "one of the new plastic jobs that no one will ever find affectionately preserved in a middle-aged citizen's garage" (*Silent Thunder* 137). Throughout the books there's a constant yearning to return to the fifties:

"A great big slice of nineteen fifty-five," he said. "That's what you can get me. I ate it too fast the first time." (*Lady Yesterday* 21)

"This was a nice place nineteen years ago." Mayk said.
"Everything was nicer nineteen years ago." (*Sugartown* 31)

"They [cars] get much smaller we'll be wearing them instead of driving them. There's not a lot you approve of about this part of the century, is there?"
"Nothing since the polio vaccine." (*Midnight Man* 110)

And returning to Errol Flynn, George Sanders, and the rest, Estleman writes this bit of dialogue in *Glass Highway*: "She was watching me with a look I've seen a couple of times, too far apart. 'I don't think I ever knew anyone like you,' she said. 'There used to be a lot of us'" (169). So Walker savors the bits of the halcyon past that remain, like jazz and the restaurant he happens on in *Midnight Man*:

The music was subdued, and though the lights were low you could see what was on your plate without having to set fire to a napkin. They ought to declare those places national treasures while there are still a few left. For all I knew this was the last one. (43)

And Amos, too, sees himself as a national monument, a throw-back to better times and better people whose values and demeanor he treasures and imitates.

Of course, a lot of this puts the hero in conflict with the present. This happens on the plot and theme level with Estleman's attempt to return to the narrative in which "You've got your good guy, your heavy, your good girl, and your tramp. Upon examination the *noir* landscape makes more sense than ours" (*Never Street* 74). It extends, as well, to the area of personal taste, and here Amos almost always comes in conflict with the mores and folkways of the eighties: in almost every social change of the last two decades, Amos sees overwhelming evidence that American society is going straight to hell. Liquor comes in skimpy liters instead of quarts, and Bogie and George Sanders stamp their feet in chilly doorways with the rest of the pariahs when they want to have a smoke. Coins are made from alloys not real metal, and nowadays, criminals get "recycled" not punished (*Glass Highway* 88). While he rumbas around the racial issue and tosses in John Alderdyce and Iris as two of Amos' three friends (the third being reporter Barry Stackpole), the new racial make-up of Detroit clearly disturbs a lot of people in the books. Walker also frets about the current status of American manhood: "The man was a representative specimen of middle-aging American manhood: sad-eyed, hesitant in the jaw, hairline in retreat" (*Never Street* 278). And he's not too happy about gays either. A number of Estleman's characters flaunt their homophobia:

We used to shop in some of the same stores, and I don't mean the kind with fairy floor-walkers and end-of-the-season discounts. (*Midnight Man* 67)

I went past bakeries and butcher shops with names as long as your belt and the municipal tennis courts that turned out this country's best pros before the kids and dykes took over the sport. (*Sugartown* 14)

Swishes I can take or leave, but swishes that buy muscle I don't like lots. (*Sugartown* 164)

The blame for at least part of what Walker views as the rapid decline of American life he places on Affirmative Action. Thus in *Glass Highway*, although the African American detective to whom he refers turns out to be one of the only honest cops in Iroquois Heights, Amos observes that "telling tales out of school wouldn't bother him, standing as he was on the solid gold of Affirmative Action" (81). The application of Affirmative Action to women bothers Walker even more. In *Lady Yesterday*, instead of the hero, Estleman uses a woman, Lieutenant Mary Thayer, to articulate the cliché argument against women's rights: "I was against them from the start. All those women running around fulfilling themselves while some poor schnook couldn't get a job to feed his family, or hers" (57). Amos, in fact, holds strong views about women—the kind of views common to the fifties:

Hats on women were coming back, and that was okay with me. It meant the end of utility hairstyles and everything that went with them, from lime-colored slacks with front zippers to colorless lipstick and men's tuxedoes in women's sizes and stone-washed denims with designer patches, all the dumpy fashion paraphernalia of the unisex society. (*Silent Thunder* 165)

Walker's feelings about women, however, extend beyond the aesthetic. And, in part, this comes from Estleman's adherence to the classical hard-boiled form, which, in many cases, was tainted by the misogyny and anti-feminism of the twenties that extended from the cinematic portrayal of the vamp and the backlash against the Nineteenth Amendment to *The Maltese Falcon* and *The Big Sleep*. He creates for Walker a marriage destroyed by the peccadilloes and infidelity of an arrogant and worthless woman. Indeed, part of what his mentor, Dale Leopold, teaches Walker about being a detective goes back to the inevitable mendacity and duplicity of women, all women:

Sweet women lie, kid. Dale Leopold had said, a long time ago, when he found out his partner was going to be married. *Men lie to get something or get out of something. Women lie because they're good at it. The sweeter the woman the better the liar. They're so good at it they hardly ever have to pull the trigger. Somebody always does it for them.* (*Sweet Women Lie* 108, author's italics)

Here Leopold just dresses the old stereotype of the *femme fatale* in stone-washed denims with a front zipper. And Estleman puts plenty of this kind of woman in the Amos Walker novels. The series starts off with Marla Bernstein in *Motor City Blue,* who "never knew what it was like to have a conscience" (240), and ends with a wife who murders her husband in *Never Street*, with plenty of deceiving, predatory women in between. All of this, though, seems almost laudatory when placed against Walker's observation about Fern in *Glass Highway*: "She smelled of the usual cosmetics and that scent that the female of the species exudes when she's in season" (14).

The next thing you know, Walker will be talking about our mommas —actually he is talking about our mommas. And this raises the question of why Estleman deliberately makes the hero of these books say things so antithetical to the values that have shaped public life in the last two decades of the twentieth century. In other words, is he serious? The Walker books don't seem like satire or irony. Estleman writes burlesques—*Peeper* (1989), for instance—but his comic drawing of Ralph Poteet in that novel bears little resemblance to the way he presents the hero in the Amos Walker books. He also knows about and uses the idea that stress can cause individuals to adopt different personalities and constructs *Never Street* on the notion that the missing man has taken on the persona of the detective from all of the *noir* films he watches. And I suppose one can also raise the possibility of a science fictionish scenario in which the hero gets zapped out of his own time and inserted in a dreary and degenerate future: in reverse it's what the Dixon Hill episodes of *Star Trek: The Next Generation* do. But this also seems pretty unlikely. The most likely motive, though, given Estleman's proclivity for literary juxtapositions (i.e., his *Sherlock Holmes vs. Dracula* and *Dr. Jekyll and Mr. Holmes*), is putting together characters from different fictions and trying to make interesting and entertaining reading out of the synthesis. The problem is that moving the hard-boiled hero from the forties into the eighties without significantly altering his consciousness makes life even more bleak than it was back when women struggled with zippers in the back, when gays stayed in the closet, and when the only African Americans most white people knew were the Kingfish, Calhoon, Andy, and Amos—the cab driver after whom Walker's father ironically named the hero of these books.

Well, taking all of this into account, what is Walker all about? Mostly he despises everything about contemporary society and would prefer to be back in the fifties. But that's not going to happen. During the course of the novels he does have three friends, but even of them he's never sure, and their friendship slips away. Iris, the junkie hooker with whom Walker has a continuing semi-intimate relationship in several novels, returns to Jamaica and marries someone else. He has a falling out with Barry Stackpole in the middle of the series. And, although it continues through all of the books, Walker's relationship with John Alderdyce always teeters on the brink of breaking down. So there's not much satisfaction for Walker in close human relationships. There's not much he gains from possessions either. He does have a house in Hamtramck:

Just three rooms, a garage, and a dandelion patch with some grass in it, but the surrounding houses were still standing with lights on and when you woke up in the morning it was to the sound of the neighbor's power mower . . . and not a two-ton ball punching holes in the brick house across the street. So far General Motors hadn't whistled at the mayor and pointed my way. (*Sugartown* 43)

And even though a glint of the domestic appears in the reference to the lawnmower, his house barely ekes its way past minimal and Walker uses it mostly as a place to flop. With no one else there, not much makes it a home. Walker does have booze; he has booze everywhere, at the office, at home, everywhere. Amos views liquor as an adjunct, even one of the essentials, of his profession: "Too much scotch on an empty stomach brings out the detective in me" (*Midnight Man* 139). All of this taken together seems pretty pitiful: a person with no friends living in marginal conditions comforted and aided only by alcohol. Layer on top of this profound pessimism about the state of society and a profession in which betrayal, duplicity, and physical abuse are accepted as normal working conditions. Why does this guy persevere? Surely there's something else he could do with his degree in sociology.

For one thing, Estleman has his hero say he does it because there's something besides the social critic in Walker. Something of the philosopher lurks behind his vocation: "I'm a curious man, Sergeant. It's one of the reasons I sit here day after day on my college degree and take jobs a cat wouldn't bury for no money to speak of. I get to study the human condition, and I don't even have to sign up for a night course" (*Sweet Women Lie* 158). Then, of course, there's toughness. Walker defines this as an essential American trait in *Sugartown*:

You can be born tough . . . or you can acquire toughness like a callus from what life bounces off you . . . We set a lot of store by it here ever since a small group of misfits in Boston stuck their tongues out at King George and made him like it. That's what tough is really all about, bucking the odds and coming out with all the important things you had going in. (108)

And real toughness has a lot to do with devotion to justice whether on the large or small scale: "Let's just say I'm the patron saint of little men in funny clothes who take jobs outside their aptitudes and get killed for it" (*Sweet Women Lie* 118). This, however, always carries with it a price, and usually in the working out of the plots in the Walker novels this price has something to do with discovering the betrayal or perfidy of a woman.

Finally, Amos Walker lives and works as he does because he wants to be Sam Spade or Marlowe. But he can't make it. The hard-boiled detective of the thirties and the forties can't be transported. Spade and Marlowe would end up sucking on cigarettes in the same doorway with Bogie and Sanders, cast out by a society just as sorely in need of what the hard-boiled hero can do as that of the middle of the century. But it remained for others to show how the most essential traits of the hard-boiled hero can be adapted to the needs of the eighties and nineties.

SARA PARETSKY

V. I. Warshawski: she's nearing forty, she's a Chicagoan, she's a detective, she's Polish, she's a woman, she's usually mad as hell, and she's something new. Sara Paretsky knows it, too. In her introduction to *A Woman's Eye* (1992), after a brief homage to Dorothy Sayers, she noted that in 1982 "Sue Grafton and I flung Kinsey Millhone and V. I. Warshawski on an unsuspecting world." But it's not just that the world was unsuspecting. In 1982, in a whole lot of ways, hard-boiled fiction was inimical, even hostile to women. Take a look at Robert Leslie Bellem's Dan Turner stories published with risqué drawings in *Spicy Detective* or consider Spillane's *The Erection Set*. It's no coincidence that the beginning of the form in the 1920s coincided with the popularity of the vamp, Theda Bara. Misogyny lingers near the surface in even the best of the original hard-boiled writers. Not only that, writers built the hard-boiled hero upon traditional male stereotypes—the knight and the cowboy—and created his character and actions to show fulfillment of supposedly male fantasies of power and stoicism. Then, too, style is so important, style compounded of slang, wisecracks, and violence—the kind of language ladies do not use. But then again, some of the essential features of the hard-boiled story have as much, and maybe more, to do with women's experience as they do with men's—work, anonymity, quixotic idealism, small town values, and so forth. It's hard to imagine, however, anyone creating a credible woman hard-boiled detective much before the 1980s—and even in the eighties it wasn't that simple. But Sara Paretsky did.

To start with, nobody has a monopoly on shabby quarters. But even this standard hard-boiled feature Paretsky makes more than subtly different. Take offices. Chandler depicts the standard detective's office in *High Window*:

I had an office in the Cahuenga Building, sixth floor, two small rooms at the back. One I left open for a patient client to sit in, if I had a patient client. There was a buzzer on the door which I could switch on and off from my private thinking parlor. I looked into the reception room. It was empty of everything but the smell of dust. I threw up another window, unlocked the communicating door and went into the room beyond. Three hard chairs and a swivel chair, flat desk with a glass top, five green filing cases, three of them full of nothing, a calendar and a framed license bond on the wall, a phone, a washbowl in a stained wood cupboard, a hatrack, a carpet that was just something on the floor, and two open windows with net curtains that puckered in and out like the lips of a toothless old man sleeping. (17)

He does not mention them here, but the self-portrait of Rembrandt in *Farewell, My Lovely* and the inevitable office bottle complete the setting. On top of the realistic catalog of the thrift-shop furnishings, Chandler's description adds self-deprecating irony ("if I had a client"; "three of them full of nothing") and the striking image of poverty and mortality contained in the simile to convey the essence of Marlowe's office. Now it's not quite fair to compare anyone to Chandler, but we can notice a few things if we compare Warshawski's office with Marlowe's. Warshawski works out of the Pultney Building near the Loop. The Pultney's electricity, plumbing, and elevator work only fitfully, and the building eventually succumbs to urban renewal in *Tunnel Vision*. But the office V. I. (aka Vic) works in is a bit different from the building itself:

With the lights on my office looked Spartan but not unpleasant and I cheered up slightly. Unlike my apartment, which is always in mild disarray, my office is usually tidy. I'd bought the big wooden desk at a police auction. The little Olivetti portable had been my mother's, as well as a reproduction of the Uffizi hanging over my green filing cabinet. That was supposed to make visitors realize that mine was a high-class operation. Two straight-backed chairs for clients completed the furniture. I didn't spend much time here and didn't need any other amenities. (*Indemnity Only* 2)

In spite of some overt similarities, this is not the same kind of pathetic place that Marlowe hangs out in. Warshawski has made it orderly and pleasant, and part of making it so comes from items associated with her family, with her mother. Indeed, Vic's emotional investment in the Uffizi print becomes clear from the role it later plays in *Tunnel Vision*. And Vic makes her office orderly and pleasant in spite of the best efforts, indeed in spite of the conspiracy of Tom Czarnik, the super, and the Culpepper brothers, owners of the Pultney Building. In the face of Czarnik's sloth and overt anti-feminism—typified by his refusal to repair the women's restrooms in the building—and the Culpeppers' greed and indifference, Vic teaches herself how to fix the plumbing and the electricity in order to make this small part of her world tenable.

The case of Vic's apartment is somewhat different. She usually highlights the stacks of papers and the refrigerator that serves as much as a petri dish as it does to store edibles. Even though she spends a lot more time in the bathtub, and may shun housework as a stereotypical female role, the apartment and its "mild disarray" belong in pretty much the same category as the digs and housekeeping habits of most hard-boiled detectives. But with her hero's home Paretsky includes significant differences here as well. For one thing, Vic has neighbors and lives in a neighborhood, something not typical of hard-boiled heroes. One of the reasons Vic objects to yuppies—a constant theme in most hard-boiled works—has to do with their impact on her neighborhood, displacing neighborliness with materialism. It's why Hattie Frizell and her dogs, for instance, form one of the plots in *Guardian Angel*. And from *Bitter Medicine* onward, Mr. Contreras plays an increasingly important role in the books and her life first as her neighbor and then as more. The other thing about Warshawski's apartment that differs from the norm lies in the fact that Paretsky's bad guys repeatedly violate it. In *Indemnity Only* goons ransack the place, a would-be intruder chisels at the deadbolts in *Deadlock*, conspirators destroy it by fire in *Killing Orders*, and bad guys ransack Warshawski's new co-op in *Bitter Medicine* and attempt to enter it forcibly in *Blood Shot*. Vic purchases successively serious deterrents—the solid oak door, the three deadbolts, the steel door, and finally an electronic security system. And in spite of the threats she does not move.

Some of this, the affection for and adaptation of place, adheres in Paretsky's treatment of the city in her novels. All of the novels take place in Chicago. No stockyards, but she gives us the Loop, Lake Michigan, expressways, government and corporate offices, shipyards, chemical plants, and machine shops that are definitely in Chicago—or ought to be. Typical of hard-boiled works, Vic experiences nostalgia for the way things used to be. First there's the shock of revisiting childhood scenes—here a visit to the savings and loan company used by her parents: "When I walked up to the grimy stone building at Ninety-third and Commercial, it seemed to have shrunk so with the years that I checked the name over the entrance to make sure I was at the right place" (*Blood Shot* 208). And then the wistful realization of what a realigned economy has meant to industrial Chicago:

I could remember when eighteen thousand men poured from those tidy little homes every day into the South Works, Wisconsin Steel, the Ford assembly plant, or the Xerxes solvent factory. I remembered when each piece of trim was painted every second spring and new Buicks or Oldsmobiles were an autumn commonplace. (*Blood Shot* 1)

Along with contrasting past and present, in typical fashion Paretsky presents the contrast between the world of the detective and that of the affluent—the Grafalks in *Deadlock*, the P;cioreks in *Killing Orders*, the

Felittis in *Guardian Angel*. Compared to these places, Chicago is a "sprawling, graffiti, garbage-ridden city" (*Burn Marks* 336), and "during the day it looked like Beirut" (*Burn Marks* 165). Indeed, in *Guardian Angel* Warshawski feels "a twinge of envy, mixed with anger that someone could live the happy, blissful life not needing two or three deadbolts between himself and the rest of the world" (195). In spite of the crime and squalor of the city, however, Chicago forms a vital part of Paretsky's detective's character. Just as Vic makes the office in Pultney Building her own, Paretsky connects her detective's attachment to the city with Uncle Remus' Br'er Rabbit and his briar patch:

I feel like Br'er Rabbit out here in suburbia—I need to get back to my briar patch. (*Deadlock* 8)

Back in the comfort of my own briar patch, the ugly images of Consuelo receded. (*Bitter Medicine* 24)

Chicago looked decrepit and useless. I wondered if my beloved briar patch was as tired as I was. (*Tunnel Vision* 211)

Not cunning like Br'er Fox, or possessing Br'er Bear's brute strength, Br'er Rabbit's understanding of character enables him to survive the plots and threats of the world. And, of course, he makes the most inhospitable place his home.

Just as Paretsky's treatment of these standard accouterments adds new dimensions to the hard-boiled character, so does her treatment of her hero's age. Like every other hard-boiled hero, Warshawski has some miles on her—in the books she edges closer and closer to forty. She notices the flap of flab that droops from other women's upper arms, and exercise instead of being fun becomes a necessity: "When thirty is a fond memory, the more days that pass without exercise, the worse you feel getting back to it" (*Indemnity Only* 9). Not only that, mounting years bring with them different attitudes toward excitement: "The thrill was less than overwhelming: the razor edge of excitement that comes from chasing and being chased seems to diminish with age" (*Guardian Angel* 35). "Incipient middle-age was making me risk-averse" (*Tunnel Vision* 26). But unlike the middle-aged men who inhabit hard-boiled stories, Paretsky includes in her hero's dilemmas those of family. This doesn't mean the urge to nurture children that becomes so important to Spenser and Robicheaux and Rawlins—although Vic does share some of this inclination. It means something more difficult than children. It means the burden of sorting out and recognizing one's obligations toward aging family members, a burden that too, too often falls upon women. Most clearly this comes with Vic's memories of her parents' dissolution:

I'd held glasses of water for Gabriella when her arms were too weak to lift them herself, emptied wheelchair pots for Tony when he could no longer move from the chair to the toilet. I've done enough, I kept repeating, I've done enough. But I couldn't quite convince myself. (*Burn Marks* 197)

But it's not just obligations to Gabriella and Tony, there are others. *Killing Orders* starts off with Vic's querulous Aunt Rosa and her mother's deathbed request, *Burn Marks* revolves around the problems caused by Aunt Elena's picaresque life, and *Blood Shot* starts off with yet another of Gabriella's dying wishes. The demands of her family become acute just when Vic really becomes an adult and an accomplished professional. And if the obligations don't come from her family—demands that include her cousin Boom Boom's death in *Deadlock*—they come from her friends, from Lotty in *Bitter Medicine*, and from Mr. Contreras in *Guardian Angel*. Yet the demands placed upon Vic by others often become the fulcrums that set the novels going.

Along with the tendrils of family that become increasingly suffocating in middle age, Paretsky creates for her hero a past that shapes what she has become and carries with it its own set of imperatives. Like every hard-boiled detective, Paretsky makes up the past that causes her hero to choose to be a detective. First comes law school, then the frustrations of serving as an attorney in the Public Defender's office:

Then I got disillusioned with working for the Public Defender. The setup is pretty corrupt—you're never arguing for justice, always on points of law. I wanted to get out of it, but wanted to do something that would make me feel that I was working on my concept of justice, not legal point-scoring. (*Indemnity Only* 141)

Part of the motive for becoming a private investigator comes from Vic's need for justice and drive for independence. "'Anyway, I solved a case for a friend and realized it was work I could do well and get genuine satisfaction from. Plus I can be my own boss.' I should have given that as my first reason—it continues to be the most important with me" (*Burn Marks* 95). Additionally, "some of it was curiosity, but a big chunk came from my old street fighter's resentment of rich, powerful people who tried to spin me around" (*Tunnel Vision* 212). Hence Vic has a background similar to every other hard-boiled detective.

But this, perhaps, is the least important past that Paretsky creates for Vic. What happened to her at the University of Chicago holds far more significance for her character. In *Tunnel Vision* Paretsky tells readers that during her student days Vic helped to organize the first women's union at the University (13). She reflects on this fact in *Indemnity Only* when she visits Chicago's women's center of the 1980s: "It was clearly not large, but better than nothing at all, which was what we'd had in my college days when even women radicals treated women's liberation as a dirty phrase" (47). Along with helping to organize the women's union, Vic also assisted with an abortion underground: "My friendship with Lotty goes back a long way, to my student days at the University of Chicago when she was one of the physicians working with an abortion underground I was involved in" (*Killing Orders* 65). It goes without saying that all of this serves as one of the foundations for Vic's feminism. But Paretsky also uses it in *Killing Orders* to present a quick survey of the decline of ideals and idealism. It begins during Vic's college years—"the Golden Age of the sixties, when we thought that love and energy would end racism and sexism" (97). But the dream does not last long: "Then the dream started falling apart. We had Watergate and drugs and the deteriorating economy, and racism and sexual discrimination continued despite our enthusiasm. So we all settled down to deal with reality and earn a living" (106). And in *Blood Shot* Paretsky extends the history of defeat into the Reagan years: "Americans have never been very understanding of poverty, but since Reagan was elected it's become a crime almost as bad as child molesting" (11). In addition to this personal and political background, Paretsky creates for her hero a pre-history which serves as precursor to Vic's immersion in women's causes during her college years.

Dead before the novels begin, Gabriella Warshawski in many ways dominates her daughter's world and influences her character. Paretsky gives readers Gabriella's earliest history a couple of times in the novels: she was trained as an opera singer in her native Italy but fled the country before World War II in order to avoid persecution as a Jew. Somehow, as Paretsky sketches it out in *Killing Orders*, Gabriella ends up in Chicago living with Rosa Warshawski:

My father had told me more than once how he met my mother. He was a policeman. Rosa had thrown Gabriella out on the street, an immigrant with minimal English. My mother, who always had more courage than common sense, was trying to earn a living doing the only thing she knew: singing. Unfortunately, none of the Milwaukee Avenue bars where she auditioned liked Puccini or Verdi and my father rescued her one day from a group of men who were trying to force her to strip. (*Killing Orders* 10-11)

As the novel unfolds Paretsky reveals that Rosa had thrown Gabriella out because she had had an affair with Rosa's husband. Later in *Killing Orders* Vic interprets Tony's rescue of Gabriella in a somewhat different light: "The middle-class dream. My father protecting Gabriella in a Milwaukee Avenue bar. My mother giving him loyalty and channeling her fierce creative passions into a South Chicago tenement in gratitude" (215-16). And much later, in *Tunnel Vision*, Paretsky gives a more serious interpretation of the formative event in Gabriella's life: "Gabriella had been like some wild bird, choosing a cage as a storm haven, out of bewilderment, then beating her wings so fiercely she broke herself against the walls" (121). Between *Killing Orders* and *Tunnel Vision* Paretsky sheds light on Gabriella's experience when she introduces Ms. Chigwell and tells her story in *Blood Shot*. It makes clear that the kind of achievement in medicine denied to Chigwell because of her gender parallels the potential lost in Gabriella because of the role as wife and mother imposed on her by the times and the culture.

A young woman, however, could not have a better mother than Gabriella. Vic retrospectively sees her mother as an early feminist. In *Burn Marks* Vic realizes that her mother, too, had connections with an abortion underground (30). As Paretsky would have it, many of her hero's personal traits come from Gabriella. Thus, "she would never let me slouch at the dinner table grumbling it wasn't turning out right" (*Indemnity Only* 66). "In my mind's ear I could hear my mother chewing me out for self-pity. 'Anything but that, Victoria, Better to break the dishes than lie about feeling sorry for yourself'" (*Deadlock* 139). On top of this, Vic believes that she has inherited her mother's ardor: "But she was a fighter, and I got my scrappiness from her, not my big, even-tempered father" (*Indemnity Only* 70). More importantly, though, Vic recalls her mother's belief in her: "Fierce, intense, prickly, she'd been difficult to live with, but my earliest memories included her strong belief in me and what I could achieve with my life" (*Blood Shot* 173). This belief, moreover, had a specific shape and form: "I could hear her saying, 'Yes, Vic, you are pretty—but pretty is no good. Any girl can be pretty—but to take care of yourself you must have brains. And you must have a job, a profession. You must work'" (*Indemnity Only* 10).

Throughout all of Paretsky's books Gabriella permeates her hero's consciousness. Vic hears her voice giving counsel, and her dreams (a standard feature of hard-boiled fiction going back to the Continental Op's dreams in *The Red Harvest*) return again and again to her mother. Lotty often characterizes herself as Gabriella's surrogate: "You are the daughter of my heart, Victoria. I know it's not the same thing as having Gabriella, but the love is there" (*Blood Shot* 187). In *Blood Shot* Louisa mistakes Vic for her mother and in *Bitter Medicine* Vic pretty much becomes Gabriella. Thus, with Lotty

I took her with me to the living room, away from the unmade bed, to a big chair like the one Gabriella used to hold me in when I was a child. Lotty sat with me for a long while, her head pushing into the soft flesh of my breast, the ultimate comfort, spreading through giver and receiver both. (26)

He's no Gabriella, but Paretsky does give Vic a father as well. Tony Warshawski, a big, easy-going cop, teaches his daughter how to shoot a pistol and how to play basketball: "When I made the team, my dad tacked a hoop to the side of the house and played with Nancy and me . . . He'd taught us how to fade, how to fake a pass then turn and dunk, and I'd won the game in the last seconds with just that move" (*Blood Shot* 134). One wishes that Paretsky knew more about the game than a probable women's basketball background of three dribbles and pass provided her with, and that she included a few more details about Vic's father. But she didn't. Vic does wear her father's old steel watch (*Tunnel Vision* 174), but his name has a greater impact on her life than anything else about him. Warshawski, of course, is Polish. As a police officer Tony was "Polish in an Irish world." Paretsky repeats this phrase in *Indemnity Only* (10) and again in *Killing Orders* (102). Vic identifies "immigrant inferiority complex" in *Burn Marks* (162) as one of the things that motivated her to marry Richard Yarborough—"the complete WASP" when she was young and foolish. Having attained reason, Vic accepts, even relishes her Polish background—as in her encounter with Masters at the end of *Indemnity Only*. And in *Tunnel Vision* she does not protest when Murray tries to buck her up by saying "Come on, Warshawski. You can't play Achilles—that's a role for a Greek nobleman, not a Polish gutter fighter" (427).

And in almost every dimension of her life, Paretsky draws Vic as a fighter. Literal fighting—fisticuffs, karate, kick-boxing, etc.—tapers off after *Indemnity Only*. In that novel Vic can go toe-to-toe with almost anybody, but she rarely does so in the later novels. What Paretsky doesn't change is the threats Vic faces. We've already seen the violence directed at her apartment in many of the books, but there's also a lot of violence directed at her person. Bad guys throw acid at her in *Killing Orders*, they sabotage her car in *Deadlock*, they abduct her and throw her into a toxic lagoon in *Blood Shot*, they knock her unconscious and leave her in a burning tenement in *Burn Marks*, and they try to squash her with a tractor trailer in *Guardian Angel*. Vic has to be paying hefty health insurance premiums because in every novel either Lotty has to patch her up or she ends up in a hospital. A lot of this comes from the hard-boiled convention of the battered hero, a convention that focuses on the personal virtues of bravery and determination. And Paretsky certainly endows her hero with plenty of these things. Increasingly in the novels, though, it turns out that the physical violence inflicted on Vic is merely an adjunct to much larger and often untouchable sources of societal violence and evil. This comes from Paretsky's use of the master criminal. These Napoleons of crime start out on a small scale with Yardley Masters in *Indemnity Only,* who uses both gangsters and the Knife Grinders Union to defraud Ajax Insurance. But they get bigger. In the next book, *Deadlock,* she works up the scale with the charming and magnetic Neils Grafalk, who paralyses Great Lakes shipping in order to save his struggling shipping line. In *Killing Orders* Xavier O'Faolin heads an international conspiracy traveling under the guise of a religious organization. Alan Humphries in *Bitter Medicine* acts as the agent for another kind of large conspiracy—one focused on squeezing profits from health care. Gustav Humbolt in *Blood Shot* with his empire of chemical industries could step into any of John Buchan's novels. In *Burn Marks* Paretsky has two of them—a millionaire and a politician. *Guardian Angel* has its evil tycoons in the Felitti family. And, finally, in *Tunnel Vision* we get Senator Gantner, who brings together the worst of two corrupt worlds, politics and international business. After Yardley Masters in the first book, Paretsky cuts all of these characters from the same cloth. All possess superficial charm, public recognition, social position, and the accouterments of wealth. They all have multiple layers of goons to do their dirty work: in *Guardian Angel*, for instance, there are garden variety thugs and a middle manager in Milt Chamfers. In every case profit motivates them to either break the law or to operate in its cracks and fissures. Their victims are ultimately the powerless or the dispossessed: ordinary workers, retirees, the homeless, women. And at least from *Blood Shot* onward, at the end of the novels while the goons and middle managers take the fall, it's not entirely clear whether those really responsible—captains of industry and politicians—have been defeated or merely inconvenienced.

If greed and power provide the ground rules for the economic world of Paretsky's books, the same forces conspire in the social realm to maintain a perpetual underclass, conspire to keep women from achieving their full potential. And Vic notices this constantly. She notices it in words when people call her a "broad," or a "girl," or address her as "young lady." She highlights its ingrained bias when in *Burn Marks* Vic notes that the State of Illinois Building is "one of the worst monstrosities known to woman" (163). She finds it too in women's names: "Cindy,

Kerry, Kim—all those cute, girlish names parents love to bestow on their daughters, which don't suit us when we're middle-aged and grief-stricken. I thanked my mother's memory for her fierce correction of anyone who called me Vicky" (*Guardian Angel* 305). Even more, because she often deals with businesses, Vic notices the blight imposed on women by the corporate world. Here again it starts out with names: "Starting to write Janet's name on top, I realized I didn't know her last name. Women exist in a world of first names in business. Lois, Janet, Mr. Phillips, Mr. Warshawski" (*Deadlock* 76). From there it extends to roles. Women are supposed to be either subservient: "I thought of Ollie North and Fawn Hall. Men like Dick always seem to find women so enthusiastic in their devotion that they consider their bosses more important than the law" (*Guardian Angel* 324); or they are decorative: "Women were sprinkled along the table like poppies among penguins. They, too, may have been distinguished jurists or business owners, but they looked as though they had been invited strictly as decoration" (*Tunnel Vision* 48). And if they don't fall into any of these categories, in one way or another they pay:

"Camilla's just telling me about her introduction to sexual harassment back in the mills. They kept leaving rust-coated tampons in the bathroom sink when she was the only woman on the shift. Why do you think all successful women have a bathroom story as part of their initiation experience?" (*Tunnel Vision* 22)

Especially in the early books, Paretsky pays attention to the wasted potential of women in the generation preceding Vic's. She begins with Vic's repeated memories of her mother, whom she portrays as a "wild bird, choosing a cage as a storm haven," and adds to this the recurrent theme of Gabriella's intelligence, independence, drive, high personal standards, and determination that her daughter become an independent person. After Gabriella, in *Killing Orders*, Vic reluctantly visits her Aunt Rosa, an embittered, fanatical old woman. It occurs to her, upon their first meeting, that "she might have been less angry if she had channeled her energies into a career. She would have made a good corporate financial officer" (18). Instead Rosa serves in a marginal position at the monastery and adopts the unquestioning servitude that Vic will associate with Fawn Hall in *Tunnel Vision*. Paretsky, however, gives the most extensive picture of the invidious effects of anti-feminine bias with Ms. Chigwell in *Blood Shot*. When Vic first visits the Chigwell residence in Hinsdale, Paretsky introduces her this way: "An old woman in a severe navy dress stood frowning in the doorway. The scowl seemed to be a habitual expression, not aimed at me personally" (50). The scowl is like

Aunt Rosa's: "She didn't stand up, didn't smile—I couldn't remember ever seeing her smile" (*Killing Orders* 3). But Ms. Chigwell's pluck does not come from Aunt Rosa. Ms. Chigwell both provides the documents that help unravel the conspiracy of Xerxes Solvents' knowledge of the toxicity of their manufacturing process and facilitates and takes part in the action close of *Blood Shot*. Along the way she unburdens herself to Vic:

> "In my day young ladies did not have lives of their own outside the household," she said abruptly . . . "We were supposed to marry. My father was a doctor out here . . . I used to help him out. By the time I was sixteen I could've set a simple fracture, treated a lot of fevers he saw. But when it came time for college and medical school, that was Curtis's [her brother's] role." She looked at me fiercely. "I see you're an active young woman, you do what you want, you don't take no for an answer. I wish I'd had your backbone at your age, that's all." (172)

At the end of the novel after Ms. Chigwell fulfills her ambition to visit Italy and buys out her brother's share in their house, Paretsky introduces another theme:

> "How do you like living alone?"
> "Very much. I just wish I'd done it sixty years ago, but I didn't have the courage to do it then. I wanted to tell you, because you're the one who made it possible, showing me how a woman can live an independent life." (274)

And the theme of independence comes to subsume all of Paretsky's other points.

Most of the classic hard-boiled writers purposely chose to portray their heroes as loners, and recent writers make nods in that direction as well—it's why Parker goes on at such lengths about "autonomy." But a lot of them really focus on the issue of male friendship: Spenser and Hawk, Easy and Mouse, Milo and Sughrue, Dave and Clete, Hiaasen's heroes and Skink, and plenty more. And plenty of writers use the old Tommy and Tuppence, male-female "friendship" adventure story pattern: most of Hiaasen, Earl Emerson's Thomas and Kathy Birchfield, Jeremiah Healy's Nancy Meagher and John Cuddy, just for starters. Vic Warshawski doesn't have any one. Sure she has friends—Lotty, Murray, Max, Mr. Contreras, and a succession of relatively wimpy lovers before Conrad—and they play changing and increasingly important roles as the novels proceed. But the idea of independence dominates Vic's thinking throughout all of the books.

Throughout Paretsky's books independence means a number of things to her hero. Some of it comes in from Vic's refusal to fit traditional stereotypes of women. This appears in a number of forms, most frequently in Vic's confrontations with her parents' old friend, Lieutenant Bobby Mallory, who bristles at Vic's profession as an investigator and wants to see her settled down as wife and mother. Bobby, trapped by a dying tradition, refuses to recognize Vic's right as a person to make her own decisions. She gets a concentrated dose of this, too, from her relationship with Michael Furey in *Burn Marks,* who wants her to be "smart and sweet at the same time" (317) and who interprets her independence as evidence of both abnormality and hostility: "You're not interested in the things a normal girl is—you just play the odds and wait your chance to jump on a guy's balls" (316). Subjected to this kind of primitive fascism, it's small wonder that Vic gets angry and approaches relationships with caution. Business and politics are much the same. In the world of organizations, independence connects Paretsky's hero with the traditional hard-boiled aversion to authority. It lies under Vic's whole motive for being self-employed: "It makes an enormous difference. I'm the only person I take orders from, not a hierarchy of officers, aldermen, and commissioners" (*Indemnity Only* 163). Independence also connects to the tradition of the hard-boiled detective's perseverance—of not wanting or not letting others do one's work. Vic gets fired at some point in every book but refuses to give up her investigations. She also consistently refuses to share her discoveries with the police, for to do so would both impugn her professionalism and limit her independence. Independence also means accepting the consequences of one's acts without whining. A couple of times during the novels Paretsky quotes the classic jock adage: "Quitters never win, and winners never quit." She may as well have included the one about "when the going gets tough," because that's what Warshawski does. Every time she's beaten, blasted, or burned, she bounces right back to continue her work. Part of independence in Paretsky also comes from pride in one's abilities and self-sufficiency. Thus in *Killing Orders* she tells her current lover, "No one protects me, Roger. I don't live in that kind of universe" (215). Independence also lies under Vic's need for the security that comes from sole ownership. In *Indemnity Only* she makes the association: "But the real problem is my independence. I guess you could call it a strong sense of turf" (141). Thus she finds comfort in being alone: "But today I felt a catlike languor envelop me, a sense of well-being that came from having my castle to myself" (*Burn Marks* 86). This kind of solitude and security provide a contrast to the hurly burly of Vic's daily life and make the repeated break-ins at her apartment an even more graphic violation. Some of Vic's need for independence rests upon personal preference, some rests on principle, and some is the result of garden-variety stubbornness. She admits as much and acknowledges its childish motives in *Deadlock*: "At that point a stubborn decision to keep the rest of the information to myself overtook me. If they were going to be so damned pigheaded, I would be too" (206). In all, Vic's assertion and defense of her independence is an admirable part of her character and one that has a number of connections with the conventions of the hard-boiled hero. Those same conventions, though, also dictate that the hero's choice of independence make life difficult and even potentially desolate. It certainly makes Vic's life difficult, but, in the end, not desolate.

Not that she looks for it here, but Vic doesn't find much comfort or fulfillment in the men she meets. She does have an eye for male posteriors: "I appreciated his narrow waist and the way his Brooks Brothers trousers fit" (*Indemnity Only* 18) and she has a succession of lovers: Ralph in *Indemnity Only*, Roger in *Killing Orders*, Bledsoe in *Deadlock*, Burgoine in *Bitter Medicine*, Robin and Furey in *Burn Marks*, and Conrad in *Guardian Angel* and *Tunnel Vision*. Of course, Dick Yarborough played the role of self-aggrandizing prig before the books begin. Vic's marriage to Dick persuaded her that "some men can only admire independent women from a distance" (*Indemnity Only* 24). And Murray functions as much as her newspaper source of information as her sometime lover. From first to last, Vic assesses her relationships in terms of the impact they might or will have on her independence. Thus, in *Indemnity Only*, wary of his intent, "I studied Ralph's face, but all I saw was friendly concern" (71). And even injured and exhausted she refuses even to ask his help with the stairs to her apartment: "If I asked Ralph to, he would carry me up. But it would alter the dependency balance in the relationship too much. I set my teeth and climbed the stairs" (67). She does virtually the same thing with Conrad in *Guardian Angel* when she thinks about getting help: "I could call Conrad, but it would be a mistake to start a relationship in a state of dependency" (237). On top of this, most of the guys she associates with possess increasingly glaring defects. The R guys, Ralph, Roger, and Robin, are basically ineffectual; Vic suspects Bledsoe of complicity in her cousin's murder and Burgoine actually participates in a conspiracy; Furrey tries to kill her. Conrad is the pick of the litter—masculine, understanding, sensitive, and patient. But at the close of *Tunnel Vision*, after Vic has saved his life, Conrad backs off of their relationship because of her single-mindedness: "I think you and I need to cool things off for a while. The last month has taken a real toll on my love for you. You don't have enough room in your breast for compromise" (414). Compromises mean a degree of abdication of one's independence.

If her relationships with men do not offer much, some of Vic's other relationships do, but not without a struggle and not without compromise. Mostly this has to do with Lotty. Lotty Herschel embodies most of Vic's ideals. A woman by herself, Lotty has both entered and distinguished herself in a profession—the same profession denied to Ms. Chigwell in *Blood Shot*. She has both escaped persecution, leaving Nazi-controlled Austria, and overcome prejudice: "When Lotty first opened her clinic she'd been 'esta judia'—'that jew'—first, then the doctor. Now, the neighborhood depended on her" (*Bitter Medicine* 14). Further, Lotty lends her energies and talents to making life better for women and children and her community. Always there to patch Vic up after her confrontations with goons and thugs, always ready to let Vic use the guest room to convalesce or to lie low, Lotty serves as Vic's ultimate source of comfort. Indeed Lotty acts as both Vic's surrogate mother and as a representation of her ideals and aspirations. In *Killing Orders* their relationship becomes strained when Vic uses Lotty's brother, Stefan, to help make her case against Corpus Christi. At the end of that novel Vic gives Lotty a *mea culpa* for the danger in which she placed Stefan and the implications of her acts upon others:

Lotty, I have been so alone this winter. Do you know the torment I have been through? Agnes died because I involved her in my machinations. Her mother had a stroke. My aunt has gone mad. And all because I chose to be narrow-minded, pig-headed, bullying my way down a road the FBI and the SEC could travel. (338)

The same kind of thing happens in *Guardian Angel*, but this time to Lotty. Because she happens to be driving Vic's car, thugs mistake Lotty for Vic and beat her up. Once again, what Vic chooses to do affects her friends' lives. And it happens, too, with Lotty's friend Max in *Tunnel Vision*: he accompanies Vic to act as translator and INS agents mistakenly arrest him and put him through an experience that revives his memories of Nazi persecution as Lotty's experience had in the previous novel. In *Killing Orders* and *Guardian Angel*, Vic's first response is to blame it on crossed stars or on fate or on her middle name, Iphigenia, who at the temple at Tauris was forced to sacrifice all strangers who came to the country. The distance between Vic and those for whom she cares that results from these disasters, however, focuses more on the dangers of her profession, on her single-mindedness, on the nature of self-regarding acts, on independence, and on interdependence. In *Guardian Angel* Carol Alvarado's summary comment on all of this is "You and Lotty don't understand. Leaning on people who love you isn't a sin. It really isn't, Vic" (359).

As the novels proceed, moreover, Paretsky makes Vic confront a number of people and issues that provide further challenges to her hero's notions of independence. We've already seen the family obligations that Paretsky drops on Vic during the course of the books—avenging Boom Boom's murder in *Deadlock*, investigating for Aunt Rosa in *Killing Orders*, and finding new lodgings for homeless and indigent Aunt Elena in *Burn Marks*. Except for investigating Boom Boom's murder, the incursions of her family inconvenience, irritate, even infuriate Vic, but she interrupts her life to deal with them. The same thing happens with victims—from Jill in *Indemnity Only* to Tamar Hawkings and her children in *Tunnel Vision*—because she perceives that they have no one else, they complicate Vic's life. All of them make explicit or implicit demands. Some of them, like Elena, invade Vic's space. Some of them are unpredictable. All of them limit the hero's independence. That's people, but there is the dog, too. Vic and her neighbor adopt Peppy at the end of *Bitter Medicine*. And while Vic manages to avoid most of the inevitable intrusions pets make into the lives of their owners, still she has to sneak out of her own apartment building and consciously ignore the fact that Peppy sits on the other side of a door doggily anxious for her company and companionship. Inanimate things, too, limit Vic's independence—the beater she drives in the first few books, car payments for her new car, the rising cost of her co-op apartment, income taxes, and a lot of the other things that intrude into everyone's life. She has the interesting and absorbing cases she pursues in the novels, sure, but since along the line her employer almost inevitably fires her she worries about income: "I'm almost forty. I can't afford to get fired" (*Tunnel Vision* 16). And she has to pay attention to the humdrum chore of tracking down financial chicanery—Vic's avowed specialty. The weight of human experience intrudes as well. Intimations of her own mortality occasionally weigh Paretsky's hero down—dream images of her mother dying tangled in the tubes of resuscitative technology combine with the dismal prospects provided by the old age of Aunt Elena in *Burn Marks* and Mitch in *Guardian Angel*: "I thought gloomily about my own old age. If I lived that long, and probable end. Would it be like this, in a derelict boardinghouse, with nothing but an old TV and some threadbare jeans for an ungrieving landlady to pick through?" (127). Along with the siege of mortality, in spite of the fulfillment her work gives her, doubt occasionally descends upon her. Thus, in *Tunnel Vision*: "I'm helpless too . . . The amount of misery is overwhelming and I'm not brave enough, smart enough, or rich enough to know what to do about it" (51).

More than any place else, the issue of independence comes in with Vic's relationship with her neighbor, Sal Contreras. A retired machinist,

Mr. Contreras lives by himself on the ground floor of Vic's co-op building. Although his daughter, Ruthie, wants him to live with her, Mr. Contreras prefers, in fact, insists on living by himself. He putters in a small garden, he fusses over Peppy, the dog—and later her pups—and he does a number of things that drive Vic up the wall. He invariably calls her "doll" and "cookie," is solicitous—often over-solicitous—of her well-being, is anxious to help her with her cases, keeps tabs on her visitors, and doesn't think that any of her men friends are good enough for her. With Mr. Contreras Paretsky makes up for the dearth of references to Tony Warshawski in the books. Just as Lotty becomes Vic's surrogate mother, Mr. Contreras gives Vic as much or more concerned, doting, interfering attention as any father gives his daughter. To his credit, however, Mr. Contreras also knows when to back off when Vic wants to or needs to be alone. As the books proceed he also becomes more engaged in the action. It starts when Mr. Contreras and his friends volunteer to defend Lotty's clinic in *Bitter Medicine*. More importantly, he saves Vic's life when he rescues her from certain death in *Blood Shot*. In *Guardian Angel* he assists Vic in burgling Dick Yarborough's office. And in *Tunnel Vision* Mr. Contreras and Vic save the Hawkings and the Messenger children. Even though he does save her life in *Blood Shot*, her attitude toward him stays the same until *Guardian Angel* and *Tunnel Vision*. Before these books she sees Mr. Contreras as an occasionally irritating but essentially neat little old man—leave out the irritating part and she views Lotty's companion, Max, the same way. In *Guardian Angel* Vic finds that he actually means something to her when he helps her to understand the larger context of the events that led to the mistaken attack on Lotty: "He slapped my knee again for emphasis. I patted his hand and thanked him for the pep talk. The odd thing was, I really did feel better" (182). In *Tunnel Vision* Vic comes to even more understanding of her neighbor and what he means to her. In the rescue of the children from the flooding tunnels she recognizes his tenderness: "As I trotted further up the tunnel Mr. Contreras began crooning to the child in the soothing tone you usually hear only from women" (291). And earlier in the novel Vic recognizes what had been implicit since *Guardian Angel:*

Nothing made the old man happier than to feel I needed him as caretaker. I leaned back in the chair. It smelled of must, as any chair that hasn't been cleaned in two decades will, but after the traumas of the morning I was too tired to mind. The smell even seemed soothing, like the embrace of the old man himself. (*Tunnel Vision* 103)

This is the same woman who in *Killing Orders* says, "No one protects me . . . I don't live in that kind of universe" (215). Do the assumed roles and attitudes connected with the prospect of sleeping (and waking up) with someone make these responses different or has Paretsky changed the way in which Vic views her need for other people? It's probably the latter. Vic's relationship with Conrad may have to contend with her independence, the rock upon which it founders, but unlike the departure of all of her previous lovers the loss of her relationship with Conrad causes Vic real pain at the end of *Tunnel Vision*. And almost as a precursor to the pain occasioned by emotional attachment, at the end of the previous novel, *Guardian Angel*, Vic articulates her feelings for Mr. Contreras: "Please don't cut me out of your life, or take yourself out of mine, I'm not going to say something stupid, like I know you'll come around in the end. Maybe you will, maybe you won't . . . It would bring me great pain to lose you" (356). At the end of *Guardian Angel* Carol introduces the topic of independence and friendship with her suggestion that "Leaning on people who love you isn't a sin. It really isn't, Vic" (359). And proof of this comes at the end of *Tunnel Vision* when Vic finds all of her friends gathered to celebrate her birthday and realizes that "good friends are a balm to the bruised spirit" (432). Like her reinterpretation of many of the essentials of the hard-boiled story and its hero's character, here, too, Paretsky takes the motifs of the scarcity of authentic people in a sordid world and the inclination toward the "buddy book" and makes them into something larger, something about community.

From the very beginning Paretsky aimed to reinvent the hard-boiled story. Just as Parker's books emerged from academic study, so did Paretsky's. Her thanks to Stuart Kaminsky, author of the Toby Peters books, appear before anything else in her first novel. And in *Deadlock* Paretsky initiates her custom of acknowledging those who assisted with the research upon which she bases details of her books. In her books, too, one finds the conventional practice in detective and in hard-boiled fiction of allusions to other genre characters and writers. Taken together, in the books Paretsky includes occasional references to Sam Spade, Mike Hammer, Spenser, Kinsey Millhone, and Gervase Fenn as well as to Tom Clancy and Ross Macdonald. *O tempora, O mores*: she even alludes to Magnum, P.I. several times. Most often, however, Paretsky brings in references to Sherlock Holmes, Marlowe, and Peter Wimsey. Further afield, but still literary, from the first book onward Paretsky plays with her chapter titles—making allusions in them to books, literary phrases, song and film titles, etc. that are reminiscent of Golden Age writers like Sayers. *Blood Shot*, for example, has chapters entitled "Bringing Up Baby," "The Old Folks at Home," "The Mill on the Calumet," "In

Grimpen Mire," "The Game's Afoot," "Humbolt's Gift," and "Toxic Shock." In making her books Paretsky surely uses the conventions of detective and hard-boiled fiction as patterns. In making them, however, Paretsky realized and made manifest that the essential truths about character and the world contained in the best hard-boiled fiction are not exclusive. Indeed, in her books she demonstrates that hard-boiled fiction is one of the best ways to examine and explain the experience of women in the last quarter of the twentieth century.

SUE GRAFTON

Sara Paretsky and Sue Grafton get lumped together fairly frequently. Indeed Paretsky herself does it in her introduction to the anthology *A Woman's Eye,* when she says that "Sue Grafton and I flung Kinsey Millhone and V. I. Warshawski on an unsuspecting world." While they published their first detective novels at the same time, the succeeding years have witnessed these two writers developing along very different lines. For one thing, there is the cult of Kinsey: Grafton's character has achieved many of the accouterments of commercial success—fan clubs, web sites, souvenirs attached to the books, and mobbed book tours for her creator. Then, too, while all of Paretsky's books properly fall into the hard-boiled category, Grafton has gradually inched her way either out of the subgenre or at least to its edges. And while both writers use the "independent woman" as the major focus of their books, Grafton and Paretsky demonstrate either that Kinsey Millhone and V. I. Warshawski wouldn't like each other very much or that feminism, or maybe sisterhood, is a tolerant and flexible concept. That's as good a place to start as any.

And where it starts in Grafton is in the accumulation of myths and stereotypes built up as a pattern for women's roles, behavior, and aspirations. One of the places in which this comes through most forcefully is in Kinsey's ruminations about ladies' magazines—found particularly in *J* and *K*. Take this passage from the latter novel:

For the next fifteen minutes, I read outdated issues of *Family Circle* magazine: articles about children, health and fitness, nutrition, home decorating, and inexpensive home building projects for Dad in his spare time—a workbench, a treehouse, a rustic shelf to support Mom's picturesque garden of container herbs. To me it was like reading about life on an alien planet. All the ads showed perfect women. Most were thirty years old, white, and had flawless complexions. Their teeth were snowy and even. None of them had wide bottoms or kangaroo pouches that pulled their slacks out of shape. There was no sign of cellulite, spider veins, or breasts drooping down to their waists. These perfect women lived in well-ordered houses with gleaming floors, an inconceivable array of home appliances, oversize fluffy mutts, and no visible means of support. (95-96)

Men, of course, invented and seek to perpetuate the stereotype. They invented it to keep women at home with their children even though, as Kinsey says, "All this talk about women being nurturing is crap. We're being sold a bill of goods so we can be kept in line by men" (*B* 83). They invested the stereotype with their own artificially concocted concepts of beauty, a concept that included high heels—"I figure if high heels were so wonderful, men would be wearing them" (*I* 216). Then there's oppression in the workplace. Sure, Grafton notes in a couple of places, women constitutionally make good detectives: "The basic characteristics of any good investigator are a plodding nature and infinite patience. Society has inadvertently been grooming women to this end for years" (*A* 34); and "There's no place in a P.I.'s life for impatience, faintheartedness, or sloppiness. I understand the same qualifications apply for housewives" (*B* 34). But women are never recognized or compensated for their abilities. It's an issue Kinsey confronts in *I* when she realizes that a semi-competent male P.I. gets paid more than she does: "Morley was getting fifty? I couldn't believe it. Either men were outrageous or women were fools. Guess which, I thought" (23). On top of this comes the whole fish without a bicycle motif, Kinsey's frequent castigation of the idea that single women are a kind of monstrous anomaly. Again and again in the novels she asserts that as a single woman she does not need a man to make her life rich and fulfilling. Here are a few samples:

I don't experience myself as lonely, incomplete, or unfulfilled, but I don't talk about that much. It seems to piss people off—especially men. *(B* 64)

I love being single. It's almost like being rich. (*D* 17)

I like being single. I like being by myself. I find solitude healing and I have a dozen ways to feel amused. (*E* 6)

The notion of changing times and recognition of and pride in competence runs under the shedding of male-imposed stereotypes for women in Grafton's books. As in Paretsky, this comes out most forcefully when she describes Kinsey's responses to older women. It appears in the first novel with Ruth, who made herself into a crack secretary in her seventies: "Her husband had left her for a younger woman (fifty-five) and Ruth, on her own for the first time, despaired of ever finding a job, as she was then sixty-two years old" (28). The more telling passage comes in Kinsey's thoughts about Sufi in *C*: "Maybe, like many single women her age, she reached that point where the absence of a man translates into dripping faucets and rain gutters in need of repair. A single woman my age would haul out a crescent wrench or shinny up the down spout, feeling that odd joy that comes from self-sufficiency" (164). The home repair stuff simply articulates what Grafton presented in the character of carpenter Becky, who, tool belt and all, reveals the mystery of sash weights to Kinsey in the previous novel. Like carpentry, women can do everything, and more and more women recognize this—that they can do everything men can do. But men make this really hard. It's what Kinsey experienced during her brief career as a police officer:

I was frustrated by the restrictions, and frustrated because back then, police-women were viewed with a mixture of curiosity and scorn. I didn't want to spend my days defending myself against "good-natured" insults, or having to prove how tough I was again and again. (*B* 1)

If Kinsey believes that quitting the police department will relieve her of the constant burden of "having to prove how tough I was," she has another thing coming. It's something that follows her, follows many women, everywhere. Thus the theme comes again up late in the series in Kinsey's conversation with her landlord and friend, Henry, in *N*:

"Don't go. You don't have anything to prove."
"Of course I do, Henry. I'm a girl. We're always having to prove some-thing."
"Like what?"
"That we're tough. That we're as good as they guys, which I'm happy to report is not that hard."
"If it's true, why do you have to prove it?"
"Comes with the turf. Just because we believe it, doesn't mean guys do."
"Who cares about men? Don't be macha."
"I can't help it. Anyway, this isn't about pride. This is about mental health." (207-8)

Shrugging off male stereotypes involves a couple of other things as well. First come the conventions of dress. In every novel Grafton makes it clear that Kinsey's wardrobe consists mainly of jeans, sweaters, and sneakers. She owns but one dress, the black number made of a miracle fabric. In only a couple of places in the fourteen novels does Kinsey sully her face with make-up, and she cuts her own hair with nail scis-sors—although Grafton seems to back off of the nail scissors in later novels. Then come the conventions of deportment. Especially notable in the first novel, Kinsey has casual sex—just like guys are supposed to do. Throughout the series she periodically speaks about ogling men. She also openly mentions bodily functions: Grafton includes urination more frequently in the Kinsey Millhone books than in the works of any writer I have (and maybe anybody has) ever read. Then, too, Kinsey doesn't talk "like a lady." Again Grafton places particular emphasis on this in *A*, where Kinsey uses the word "fuck" four times: "Oh fuck. Who are you?" (165); "I don't want you fuckin' up my case" (193); " 'Fuck off,' I said mildly. 'Just go fuck yourself' " (220); " 'Don't fuckin' smart mouth me,' I snapped" (249). And *A*, of course, ends with Kinsey's matter-of-fact statement about violence: "I blew him away" (274).

While she never learned to behave quite like this from her Aunt Gin, as in Paretsky, Grafton introduces an independent woman from the last generation who serves as a model for her hero's concept of self. Late in the series, Grafton tries to fill this role with Kinsey's mother:

Rita Cynthia was the oldest. She was Grand's favorite, probably because they were so much alike. I guess she was spoiled . . . [*sic*] or so the story goes, a real hell-raiser. She *totally* refused to conform to Grand's expectations. Because of that Aunt Rita's become like this family legend. The patron saint of liberation. The rest of us—all the nieces and nephews—took her as a symbol of independence and spirit, someone sassy and defiant, the emancipated person our mothers wished they'd been. (*J* 170)

But Kinsey's real model is Virginia, her "no nonsense aunt," a character Grafton gradually makes into a foremother for Kinsey's independent character. Aunt Gin starts in *A* as someone who tries to teach Kinsey needlework and warns her about the dangers of the world, like "raging gangrene, perilous infections, or blood poisoning—dangers my aunt had warned me about every time I skinned my knee" (*A* 175). In *B*, however, it's Aunt Gin who teaches Kinsey to shoot a pistol when she is eight years old. By the time *D* rolls around, Grafton makes Virginia the source of sound feminist doctrine:

Rule Number One, first and foremost, above and beyond all else, was financial independence. A woman should never, never be financially dependent on anyone, especially a man, because the minute you were dependent, you could be abused . . . My aunt believed that a woman should develop marketable skills and the more money she was paid for them the better. Any feminine pursuit that did not have as its ultimate goal increased self-sufficiency could be disregarded. "How to Get Your Man" didn't even appear on her list. (82)

Taken together, all of these reactions to and demonstrations of the roles women have played and can and should play gave Paretsky ample justification for coupling her hero with Grafton's and noting the shock experienced by an unsuspecting world upon their simultaneous arrival in 1982. Nevertheless, Paretsky and Grafton's heroes are at least as different as they are the same. And a large measure of this resides in the ways in which each of them defines feminism. Take gender neutral language, for example. Warshawski makes a point of emphasizing the irony and mendacity of the suffix "man" that has been attached to so many terms. Grafton, however, seems to find the whole issue amusing, and makes Kinsey ridicule it in *L*, first with "The girl stewardperson moved down the aisle behind her, snapping the overhead bins shut with a series of small bangs" (86); and then with "There didn't seem to be any bell-humans on duty" (95).

There are other things on the linguistic level as well. Although she casually uses coarse language fairly frequently in the first novel, Kinsey cleans up her speech in most of the later books. Instead of recording them for her audience, Kinsey simply says, "I gave vent to a string of expletives" in *D*, and in *J* she actually describes people as "cads" and "bounders," and uses "poot" as an expletive. Throughout all of the books, too, Kinsey is far more aware of women's bodies than is V. I. Warshawski. The only thing V. I. worries about in Paretsky's books is the tendency of women's triceps to become flaps of flab. Kinsey, on the other hand, thinks a lot about breasts and buttocks and the perverse workings of time on women's bodies. "What is it about middle age," she asks in *B*, "that makes a woman's body mimic pregnancy?" (74). And she finds that warding off the effects of gravity becomes a constant chore: "I hadn't jogged for three weeks and I could feel my ass getting bigger with every bite I ate" (*N* 107). More problematic than these points, Kinsey seems to back off somewhat from the notion of gender-specific roles. Thus in spite of Becky the carpenter and Kinsey's statement in *C* that "A single woman my age would haul out a crescent wrench or shinny up the down spout, feeling that odd joy that comes from self-sufficiency (164)," when we get to *J* Kinsey tells her readers that "Boys know about these things: guns, cars, lawn mowers, garbage disposals, electric switches, baseball statistics. I'm scared to take the lid off the toilet tank because the ball thing always looks like it's on the verge of exploding" (206). In fact, Kinsey even eventually admits to sort of liking housework in *I*: "Cleaning house is therapeutic—all those right-brain activities, dusting and vacuuming, washing dishes, changing sheets. I've come up with many a personal insight with a toilet brush in my hand" (93). Indeed, looking at the similes throughout all of the books reveals a writer, character, and probably readers extensively versed in traditional women's subject matters, like clothing and fabrics—for example, there are comparisons to "a crepe de chine dress" [D 21], "a taffeta skirt with a ruffle of white" [D 10], "a fur muff" [B 155], "a pair of cotillion gloves" [E 53], "tissue thin kid leather" [E 53], and "a percale bedsheet" [D 25]) There are household items as well: comparisons to "a crumpled brown grocery bag" [D 87], "a faulty garbage disposal" [F 161], "a convection oven" [E 143], "dark gray vacuum cleaner fluff" [D 29], "the torn lining on the underside of an old box spring" [E 49], and "a Playtex rubber glove" [D 19]).

The idea of guns and violence, however, may be even more problematic. V. I. Warshawski goes toe to toe with men in a couple of places in Paretsky's books. Almost every one of Grafton's novels ends with physical danger from which Kinsey extricates herself. But while in the first novel and again in N Grafton plots an ending that requires Kinsey to use a gun to save herself in a violent confrontation with a man, she is not the street fighter that Warshawski is. Additionally, Grafton seems in places to concede that physical violence is a male province. Thus, in G she makes Kinsey hire Robert Dietz to protect her.

In addition to the association of men with proficiency in violence, Kinsey's association with Dietz also brings up the larger issue of self-sufficiency. In G Dietz moves in with Kinsey, becomes her lover, and then leaves at the end of the book. Later in the series he makes appearances in M and N. But even before Dietz, Kinsey finds meaning and value in physical and emotional relationships with men. Although she is badly mistaken about the individual, in A Kinsey observes, "But far from feeling trapped, I felt comforted and safe, as though nothing could ever harm me as long as I stayed in the shadow of this man, this sheltering cave of heat and flesh" (190). But instead of rejection and bitterness after discovering her lover's real nature and motives, Kinsey continues to find substantial meaning in relationships with men. Thus in L she says, "There's something about love that brings a focus to life. I wouldn't complain about the sex, either, if I could remember how it went" (68). The problem she has with Dietz does not come from Kinsey's fears about loss of self or independence in their relationship. It comes from the fact that, so far in the series at least, Dietz is a rolling stone who does not want to stay in one place for long.

The differences in Paretsky's and Grafton's heroes come in part from the changes Grafton makes in her character over the course of a lot more books. In part, too, they come from Kinsey's all too human uncertainty about how people create and recreate themselves in response to the vagaries of the present and skeletal fingers reaching out from the past. And they exist because feminism, or maybe sisterhood, is a tolerant and flexible concept which allows women to be individuals instead of stereotypes.

Along with Kinsey's role as an independent woman, Grafton also spends considerable time defining Kinsey in terms of her past. She includes a recounting of the death of Kinsey's parents in almost every book. As the books proceed, this event gains increased significance, until in *J* Kinsey tells her readers that, "In many ways, my whole sense of myself was embedded in the fact of my parents' death in an automobile wreck when I was five" (132). In the previous book Kinsey describes in some detail the aftermath of her parents' death:

After the death of my parents, when I first went to live with my maiden aunt, I established a separate residence in an oversize cardboard box. I had just turned five and I can still remember the absolute absorption with which I furnished this small corrugated refuge. The floor was covered with bed pillows. I had a blanket and a lamp with a fat blue ceramic base and a sixty watt bulb that heated the interior to a tropical pitch. I would lie on my back reading endless picture books . . . Fantasies within fantasies. I don't remember crying. For four months, I hummed and I read my library books, a little closed-circuit system designed to deal with grief. I ate cheese-and-pickle sandwiches like the ones my mother made . . . Some days I substituted peanut butter for the cheese and that was good. My aunt went about her business, leaving me to work through my feelings without intrusion. (*I* 48-49)

The most apparent use Kinsey makes of this story is to account for her affection for small, cozy spaces—like her apartment. A point that almost does not have to be made, though, is that while this kind of early experience would in reality probably lead to a severely dysfunctional adulthood, Grafton uses it as precursor for Kinsey's later independence and self-sufficiency. Nevertheless, in spite of Grafton's use of Kinsey's aunt to make points about independence and self-sufficiency, she also includes a number of Kinsey's recollections of her childhood that paint a pretty grim picture. She, of course, is dragged to church and to grown-up social functions by her aunt, and these are arid enough occupations for any child. Worse than this, however, are Kinsey's other recollections of childhood. She sometimes recalls the awkwardness of not belonging to a group: "I was overcome with the same self-consciousness I'd felt once at a birthday party in the sixth grade when I realized that all the other little girls had worn nylon stockings and I was still wearing stupid white ankle socks" (*A* 185). And she includes a long passage in *G* about the horrors of school:

I hadn't liked school. I'd always been overwhelmed by the dangers I sensed. Grade school was perilous. There were endless performances: tests in spelling, geography, and math, homework assignments, pop quizzes, and workbooks. Every activity was judged, graded, and reviewed. The only subject I liked was music because you could look at the book, though sometimes, of course, you were compelled to stand up and sing all by yourself, which was death. The other kids were even worse than the work itself. I was small for my age, always vulnerable to attack. My classmates were sly and treacherous, given to all sorts of wicked plots they learned from TV. And who would protect me from their villainy? Teachers were no help. If I got upset, they would stoop down to my level and their faces would fill my field of vision like rogue planets about to crash into the earth. (*G* 42)

Subsequent to this, as Kinsey tells readers a number of times, in high school she began hanging out with the wild boys. She usually connects this with her use of foul language—even though this is not the first association one makes about the single girl who hangs around with the bad actors in high school. But while she mentions these things about Kinsey's youth Grafton does so to make more vivid through comparison certain moments in her adult life rather than to present them as building blocks for Kinsey's self.

This is not the case with Kinsey's family. In the tenth book, *J*, Grafton discovers her hero's lost family for readers. All the time Kinsey lived with her aunt as an orphan, her Kinsey grandparents, aunts, and cousins enjoyed a comfortable, extended-family existence up the road in Lompoc. And why doesn't Kinsey know about them until she is an adult? Grafton has yet to make this clear. She, however, does make clear that Kinsey's cousins make pretty strenuous efforts to make up for lost time, get to know her, and bring her back to meet the rest of her family. It's hardly that Kinsey resists associations. Grafton builds for her the pseudo-domestic circle of Rosie, Henry, and Henry's assorted siblings with whom Kinsey finds comfort and pleasure. Nevertheless, Kinsey wants to have nothing to do with the relatives up in Lompoc. And it seems odd or discordant. Well, yes, her grandparents did not approve of her mother's marriage, but there was a reunion in the making. And Grafton has not shown Kinsey as being so psychologically frail as to blame her family for her parents' death. It's also difficult to believe that she fears that her late-onset family could pose a threat to her independence—more of a threat to her independence than Dietz, with whom she goes to bed. Unlike Paretsky's hero, Grafton's hero worries little about threats to her independence. Most likely, though, Grafton is saving the family unraveling for a later book. It depends, after all, on something that happened almost four decades ago. And this kind of situation mirrors that which readers find in almost all of the novels.

In part it's her past and in part it's a convention of the hard-boiled story, but another of the characteristics Grafton includes in her hero is minimalism. One of the ways in which Grafton defines her hero is with her car and her apartment. A couple of the dust-jackets of the novels—*F* and *G*—feature Kinsey's VW Beetle: *F*, in fact, has a photo of Grafton sitting on the rear bumper of a Beetle with the vanity plate KINSEY M. Anyway, she presents Kinsey's bug as pretty basic transportation. The same holds true of her lodging—she once lived in a trailer and now lives in a one-car garage converted into an apartment. And in the first five books, at any rate, Spartan may be a generous way to describe it. Indeed, until the place gets blown up and cunningly remodeled in *E*, Kinsey doesn't even have a proper bed. I've already mentioned Kinsey's limited wardrobe—one dress, jeans, sweaters, boots, sneakers, sweats, and the underpants she mentions fairly regularly. Indeed, in *J* Kinsey herself alludes to her "Spartan, stripped-down life-style" (191). One also can find little evidence of a discriminating palate in Kinsey Millhone. Her most constant meal consists of a Quarter Pounder with cheese and fries. And when she dines at Rosie's, Kinsey rarely even knows precisely what she's eating—as if she had a choice. She's also never flush. In all of this Grafton makes her hero fit the traditional mold of the P.I. found in hard-boiled fiction. In the genre, minimalism brings with it a number of associations. Hard-boiled detectives tend to be proletarian heroes for whom wealth and luxury mean corruption, they tend to be romantics for whom surroundings are mundane or corrupt, and they tend to be idealists for whom abstract values mean more than concrete distractions. And here— because Grafton has other intentions for her hero—Kinsey doesn't quite make the grade as a hard-boiled hero.

Take luxury to start with. Sure, Kinsey prefers her apartment as it is rebuilt by Henry after the bombing in *E*. Who wouldn't? After all, she doesn't have to flop the sofa bed open every night. But she does derive a great deal of pleasure from its amenities—like the skylight in her bedroom. This, however, is a quibble. There are, however, other more serious indications that she hankers to belong to the white wine (from a bottle with a cork, not a jug) set. In *J*, for example, we get this: "She used a pair of silver tongs to lift cubes of ice, which she dropped, clinking, into her old-fashioned glass. I always wanted to be the kind of person who did that" (267). And in *I* she snuggles into a Rolls Royce Corniche III at the dealership. She murmurs that "it's beautiful" rather than taking issue with the fact that Rolls uses fourteen hides in every Corniche interior. Indeed, Kinsey comes right out once in a while and says things like: "What I love about the rich is the silence they live in— the sheer magnitude of space" (*E* 52). And then there's authority: it's something Kinsey almost likes. She does not quit her job as a police officer for the usual reasons—insubordination, unwillingness to follow rules, disillusionment with official, corporate justice. She leaves the Santa Teresa force because of her unwillingness to make an issue of the sexism displayed by fellow officers. Late in the series, in fact, Kinsey speaks of her deep-seated attachment to police officers based on her early childhood memories of being rescued at the age of five from the car wreck in which her parents were killed. In the one case in which she turns to extra-legal means to accomplish justice—using mob hit men in *K*—she goes to the extreme of turning herself in to the cops: "I spent a long time in conversation with Lieutenant Dolan and Cheyney Phillips and, for once, I told the truth. Given the enormity of what I'd done, I felt I had to accept the responsibility" (285). Of course, what she had done was to follow natural versus statute law, and save her own life in the bargain. But it shows how wired in to authority Kinsey really is.

In terms of those mean streets that so often help to define the hard-boiled hero, there aren't very many of them in Grafton. *H* takes Kinsey into the Hispanic ghetto, and in *F, L* , and maybe *N,* she works mostly in lower-middle-class environments, but in a lot of the books she works for the affluent and in affluent surroundings. And she likes it. Then, too, Grafton imposes a severe handicap on herself by writing about Santa Barbara, or Santa Teresa as it were. While Grafton admittedly finds little pleasure in scenery or landscapes (although in some of the books she takes some pains to describe them), she really likes Santa Barbara. There is little not to like about the place. Like other writers enthusiastic about their locales, she gives snatches of local history in several of the books, particularly in *J.* And "Santa Teresa," Kinsey tells us in *M,* "was one of the few towns that looked more elegant as time passed" (127):

There are no flashing neon signs, no slums, no fume-spewing manufacturing complexes to blight the landscape. Everything is stucco, red tile roofs, bougainvillea, distressed beams, adobe brick walls, arched windows, palm trees, balconies, ferns, fountains, paseos, and flowers in bloom. Historic restorations abound. It's all oddly unsettling—so lush and refined that it ruins you for anyplace else. (*B* 7)

On top of this, there's not even a sleazy politician or corrupt cop on the horizon.

On the last count, Kinsey sort of makes the grade. She is the idealist for whom values hold ultimate meaning. Most obviously, the truth ranks right up there as a value to be honored and pursued. That's what detectives do, and it is something that Kinsey works assiduously to find. It lies behind Grafton's choice of returning again and again to plots based on reopening old cases, cases, as in *A* and *F,* in which there has been a miscarriage of justice. Indeed in some of the later books her zeal for finding the truth threatens to make her a harridan. However in a couple of cases, *D* and *J* in particular, Kinsey finds that truth provides neither solution or solace to profound human misery. But, then again, most hard-boiled heroes find this out sooner rather than later. But it is not just truth or justice that motivates Kinsey. In a number of cases she makes a substantial and continuing emotional investment in one of the characters. This occurs first in *C,* where Kinsey quite literally dedicates her narrative to Bobby Callahan: "This report is for him, whatever it's worth" (1) and persists through *M,* where, after the conclusion of the action,

Guy Malek came to me in a dream. I don't remember now what the dream was about. It was a dream like any other, set in a landscape only half familiar, filled with events that didn't quite make sense. I remember feeling such relief. He was alive and whole and so like himself. Somehow in the dream I knew he'd come to say good-bye. (299)

So Kinsey's detecting holds for her something other than the quixotic pursuit of justice that lies at the very center of the hard-boiled vision.

The most accurate way in which we can describe Kinsey, then, is as a hybrid. All of the material above reflects on her character, and some—but not all—of it falls into or at least on the edges of the hard-boiled character type. Although aggression and zeal form part of her character, the ways in which she pursues the truth—and the ways in which Grafton locates the revelation of the truth in her plots—don't really belong to the hard-boiled genre. First of all, Kinsey makes a lot of noise about systematic thinking. She, in fact, sometimes talks like a character out of a golden age plot: "I didn't want to form a hypothesis too early for fear it would color the entire course of the investigation" (*A* 25). Hard-boiled stories usually run on plots in which the bad guy is obvious and known from the start or they present a muddle that the hero only solves by determination, not by sophisticated thinking. Indeed, Grafton repeatedly puts the Golden Age shibboleth into Kinsey's mouth—the puzzle metaphor; for example, we get statements like "There were pieces missing yet but they would fall into place and then maybe the whole of it would make sense" (*A* 172), and "Eventually, I would realize how all the pieces fit together, but at that point the puzzle hadn't even been dumped out of the box" (*H* 9). Kinsey purportedly solves her puzzles by being a logical and systematic thinker. Everywhere she goes, her index cards go with her. Kinsey uses them like this: "I started making lists, systematizing the information I had, along with the half-formed ideas that were simmering in the back of my head" (A 221). Sometimes she uses another logical routine to find the facts: "Basically, in my investigation, I was mimicking the spiral method of a crime scene search: starting at the center, moving outward and around in ever-widening circles" (K 141). Whatever the method, however, logical analysis does not enable Kinsey to solve the enigmatic facts presented to her by the case. In fact, it usually fails as in L: "Something wasn't right, but I couldn't figure out what it was. I shifted some cards around and pinned them up in a new configuration. It was something I'd read" (58). With this, of course, Grafton gratifies readers who have an appetite for the classical "whodunit." And she appeals to them, too, with the endings of her plots. The Kinsey Millhone books (with only a couple of cases like G and L where Grafton experiments with other forms) almost always end with the revelation that someone the detective (and the reader) has largely overlooked committed the crime. She began using this "least likely character" pattern in A, where it has a romantic/sexual spin, and it influences even books like I where the culprit is the most likely suspect. Indeed Grafton's usual practice depends on plots taken from the inventory of classic detective stories. Even before the plotting, Grafton is demonstrably punctilious about her facts. Every book begins with acknowledgments. They, however, are not the usual authorial nods to spouses, agents, and editors. Taken at random, in I Grafton acknowledges the assistance of seventeen people (including four lawyers, a private investigator, two Sheriff's officers, a coroner's investigator, two broadcasters, and two people connected with firearms sales and manufacturing). While it may not be an absolute test, this insistence on verifiable accuracy belongs more to the subgenre in which readers incline to base their objections upon factual inaccuracy rather than character inconsistency. More to the point, Grafton uses many of the favorite plots and plot devices of writers like Christie and Marsh: the plot in which the villain has assumed a false identity, the plot in which the murder weapon has been cleverly hidden, and the confused chronology plot, to list only a few of her favorites. And since this kind of plot cries out for the use of red herrings, Grafton repeatedly encourages fishy suspicions. Then, too, the light-heartedness of some of Kinsey's exploits, while not quite in the same class as the influence of Golden Age plotting, have a certain kinship to the tone of all those books written between the wars. Thus Kinsey tells her readers things like "It's fun to snoop in other people's dresser drawers" (C 154) and "I dearly love being in places I'm not supposed to be. I can empathize with cat burglars, housebreakers, and second-story men" (E 45). In a lot of ways, it's very Christie.

In a lot of ways, too, Grafton is much attracted by romance motifs. An independent, rational, modern woman Kinsey may be, but as much as she says she focuses on facts, her feelings and intuitions also sometimes go into overdrive. Thus we get things like: "I felt a sudden chill. There was something odd about that, something off" (*A* 144); "I was beginning to feel a low-level anxiety, the sort of sensation you experience when you know you're having major surgery in a week" (*B* 180). In one place, late in the series, in a creaky old house Kinsey even gets the willies, much like those to which romance heroines have always been susceptible:

The ringing in my ears went on, mounting in intensity like the howling of the wind. I was weighted down with dread. Occasionally in nightmares, I suffer from this effect—an overpowering urge to run without the ability to move. I struggled to make a sound. I would have sworn there was a presence, someone or something, that hovered and then passed. I tried to open my eyes, almost convinced I'd see Guy Malek's killer passing down the stairs. My heartbeat accelerated to a life-threatening pitch, thrumming in my ears like the sound of running feet. I opened my eyes. The sound ceased abruptly. Nothing. No one. The ordinary noises of the house reasserted themselves. (*M* 190)

Like romance writers, in fact, Grafton finds no shame in attaching the "had-I-but-known" formula to Kinsey's storytelling. Even though Grafton starts the series using the case report—facsimile page and all—as a superficial frame for the narrative, she's also right up front in the prologue to *B* about her stories' connections with the classic "ladies' mystery" formula: "After it's over, of course, you want to kick yourself for all the things you didn't see at the time. The Had-I-But-Known school of private investigation perhaps" (1). And she quite literally works the formula into the beginning of several books. Thus,

I went after him for the money and the next thing I knew, I was caught up in events I still haven't recovered from. (*D* 1)

I don't mean to bitch, but in the future I intend to hesitate before I do a favor for a friend. Never have I taken on such a load of grief. (*L* 1)

Here in the blank and stony present, we're shielded from the knowledge of the dangers that await us, protected from future horrors through blind innocence. (*N* 1-2)

For readers this portends not just a story about logic and rational detective work, but also gothic terror.

Like Eberhart and other golden age writers, Grafton tends to center her plots on families. So in *C* readers learn a lot about the Callahans, in *F* it's the Fowlers, and so on all the way through the Maleks in *M*, and the Newquists in *N*. Hmmm: the choice of the family names can hardly be coincidence. They actually start with Elaine Bodt in *B*. That's the first clue. And sometimes the books' advertisements give us another clue: the dustjacket to *E* says "As Kinsey begins to unravel the frame-up she finds that her fortune is intimately tied to the family's past and to the explosive secret it has protected for almost twenty years." And, sure enough, Kinsey spends a lot of time in the novels getting to know families and their members. In *F*, in fact, she moves in with the Fowlers and helps to tend the ailing Mrs. Fowler, just as in *N* she stays at the Newquists' house and endures Jell-O and brownies made from a mix. It's all right out of the classic closed-environment, limited-suspects plot. The implication of this kind of plot, like the classical detective story itself, is basically conservative. Its workings—what the detective does—ensure the maintenance of wealth and privilege and the succession of that wealth and privilege to the proper heir and the next generation. There's nothing wrong with that; it's just not hard-boiled.

Indeed, Sue Grafton is not really a hard-boiled writer. After she gave her hero some of the traits commonly associated with the hard-boiled hero in *A*, Grafton in some respects domesticated Kinsey Millhone. Granted, Kinsey remains an independent woman from start to finish. As the books proceed, though, she curses less, engages in less violence, and even gets a salon haircut once in a while. As the books proceed, Kinsey often works for or around affluent people, and, unlike the typical hard-boiled set-up, her clients don't usually lie to her or fire her when the going gets tough. As the books proceed Grafton also confronts her hero with intrusions into her personal life designed to make things more complicated and less secure for Kinsey—the termination by California Fidelity, the contract on her life, the appearance of her "lost" family, and her on-and-off relationship with Robert Dietz. Pretty clearly, the Kinsey in the later books admits to far more uncertainty about herself and about life than the Kinsey in the early books. In *M*, in fact, she talks of serotonin levels and bouts with depression—hardly the kind of thing one would expect from the character introduced in the first novel. Then, too, while Kinsey only ages three years and change (she says she's thirty-two in *A* and almost thirty-six in *N*), sixteen years have gone by for Grafton and her readers between the first and *N*, years in which fashions and attitudes have changed—some more radically than others. On top of that, people act differently when they're thirty-two than when they are forty-eight—or they have not learned very much or else there's something wrong with them. Besides, since Grafton has chosen (with a couple of exceptions, like the treasure-hunt book *L*) to stick with Santa Teresa and make it a peaceful, safe and static setting, and since after the early books she has chosen classical plots as her meat and potatoes, developing Kinsey's character offers one area in which Grafton is not confined by the conventions she has chosen.

If Sue Grafton isn't a hard-boiled writer, she's certainly a successful one. Her books have ever-larger first printings and one rarely passes a bookstore that does not carry most or all of Kinsey Millhone's alphabetical cases. While some very good hard-boiled writers never make the best-seller charts, Grafton keeps hitting them. Partly this may have something to do with the gender make-up of her audience—on entirely unscientific grounds, I would guess that it's heavily female. Partly, though, it has something to do with the fact that Grafton has chosen to write a hybrid form based on detective story formulas popular for almost a century. And maybe it has something to do with the fact that maintaining the vitality of the hard-boiled character and hard-boiled vision over the course of more than a few books is very, very difficult to do.

CARL HIAASEN

There's not much to deconstruct about Florida history. There are all kinds of sordid human episodes—the extinction of the Tequestas, Apalachees, and Calusas; the Seminole Wars; the city of Miami's murder rate; the overturning of the Miami mayoral race because of widespread fraud. There are plenty more to choose from. And there are also the assaults on nature: the Army Corps of Engineers first shortening and now lengthening the Kissimmee River; large parts of the Everglades being drained for agricultural, commercial, and residential development; the fouling of the existing ecosystem with toxins (like those to which the U.S. Sugar Corporation pled guilty to dumping in 1991); and claiming second place (to California's first) in the number of endangered species in the continental United States. Plenty of good arguments exist to suggest that people just aren't supposed to live in Florida, especially below Orlando—heat and humidity, traffic on I-95, lots of people with guns, perennial dangers of water shortages, roaches as big as hamsters, miscellaneous drug traffickers, annual invasions by uninhibited college students, people wearing white belts and shoes, Caribbean revolutionaries, and random visitations by hurricanes.

It's a common notion that in the first half of the twentieth century the United States tilted toward the Pacific Ocean and a force akin to gravity pulled most con men, grifters, charlatans, get-rich-quick artists, shills, hookers, snake oil salesmen, shady tycoons, and crooked politicians, along with every known variety of screwball and nut case, to California. From the middle of the century onward, though, abetted by Social Security, air conditioning, and the interstate highway system, the same thing happened to Florida. Except Florida has a lot less room than California. And if you think about this long enough, you become like Skip Wiley, or Clinton Tyree, or Mick Stranahan, or Molly McNamara, or JoLayne Lucks. Or maybe you create them. Carl Hiaasen did.

To date Hiaasen has written seven detective novels: *Tourist Season* (1986), *Double Whammy* (1987), *Skin Tight* (1989), *Native Tongue* (1991), *Strip Tease* (1993), *Stormy Weather* (1995), and *Lucky You* (1997). And he has also kept his day job—first as an investigative reporter and now as a columnist for the Miami *Herald*. In fact, in a lot of important ways, it's difficult to separate Hiaasen's books from his vocation as a journalist. The hard-boiled detective story, after all, began with

101

journalism: before he began to write, Hammett took a course at Munson's Business College to learn newspaper reporting; Chandler worked for the London *Daily Express;* James M. Cain wrote for both the Baltimore *American* and *Sun;* Raoul Whitfield reported for the Pittsburgh *Post;* and Horace McCoy worked on the Dallas *Journal.* A pretty impressive list of newspaper men who went into writing detective stories. Journalism held out the promise of three things to that first generation of hard-boiled writers—exposure to the corrupt and brutal underside of life; training in how to write succinct, readable prose; and a code of ethics that focused on the individual's responsibility to the truth. But writing for newspapers did not deliver on any of the promises. Thus William Randolph Hearst instructed his papers to

> *Make a paper for the best kind of people.* The masses of the reading public are better and more intelligent than newspapermen think they are.
>
> Don't print a lot of stuff that nice people are supposed to like and do not, but omit things that will offend nice people.
>
> Avoid *coarseness* and *slang* and a *low tone.*

Newspapers, and not just the Hearst papers, hired bright, skeptical, talented, and honorable people, and then made it difficult for them to do their job. They could not describe many of the things they saw and they couldn't write about them using their own diction and syntax. That, of course, was when there were two or more papers in every city. Now there is cable, and only a handful of papers that can measure up to those of the last generation. Although permissible language has become a bit more casual than it used to be, being a reporter is just as difficult and just as frustrating as it was in the twenties and thirties. And that's where Hiaasen starts.

It's hard to miss that newspapers and reporting play a significant role in Hiaasen's books. Most feature reporters of one kind or another: *Tourist Season* has reporter Brian Keyes and columnist Skip Wiley; *Double Whammy* has news photographer R. J. Decker; *Skin Tight* has Christina Marks and the Reynoldo Flemm show; *Native Tongue* has ex-reporter Joe Winder; and *Lucky You* has reporter Tom Krome. And even in *Strip Tease* and *Stormy Weather* (which do not feature newspaper people) Hiaasen comments on news, newspapers, and the media. Talking about them is a significant motif in all of his books.

In much the same way he treats Florida, Hiaasen describes the newsroom as paradise lost. Given his penchant for the aberrant and loony, the newsroom is Hiaasen's great good place. Thus in *Tourist Season* the publisher of the Miami *Sun* can't "imagine anyone trying to manage so many deeply disturbed individuals as there were in a news-room. It was a disorderly place where eccentricity, torpor, petulance, even insubordination were tolerated" (242). It's a place, as Brian Keyes observes, where "Some of the smartest people I know work . . . And some of the screwiest. That's what happens when you chase the truth for too long; you finally catch up with it and you're never the same. Screwed up for life" (223). There are the reporters, cynical, skeptical, driven, and aberrant in one way or another who become Hiaasen's heroes. In *Lucky You,* Sinclair wishes this were not so: "Good reporters were temperamental and impulsive; this Sinclair learned from newspaper management school" (84). "Those temperamental and impulsive people," however, find identity in their writing. Thus, Carrie's plea to Joe Winder in *Native Tongue* is that he "Write about important things, whatever pisses you off. Just write something" (318). And in *Skin Tight,* it's the reporter in Christina Marks that most attracts Mick Stranahan to her: "Unlike the others he had loved and married, Christina avidly pur-sued that which was evil and squalid and polluted. Her job was to expose it" (311). After reporters, Hiaasen lists editors, old-fashioned editors like Cab Mulcahy in *Tourist Season* or the managing editor in *Lucky You.* Here's Mulcahy:

Cab Mulcahy was a patient man, especially for a managing editor. He had been in newspapers his entire adult life and almost nothing could provoke him. Whenever the worst kind of madness gripped the newsroom, Mulcahy would emerge to take charge, instantly imposing a rational and temperate mood. He was a thoughtful man in a profession not famous for thoughtfulness. (*Tourist Season* 23)

A notion that newspapers serve the truth and the public good binds them all together in a weird fraternity which, by turns, is public and private, zany and intimate.

But this kind of newsroom, this kind of paper is rapidly becoming an anachronism, and that's part of Hiaasen's sardonic lament. First, he looks at the economic realities of the contemporary newspaper:

The downsizing trend that swept newspapers in the early nineties was aimed at sustaining the bloated profit margins in which the industry had wallowed for most of the century. A new soulless breed of corporate managers, unburdened by a passion for serious journalism, found an easy way to reduce the cost of publishing a daily newspaper. The first casualty was depth. Cutting the amount of space devoted to news instantly justified cutting the staff. At many papers, downsizing was the favored excuse for eliminating such luxuries as police desks, suburban editions, foreign bureaus, medical writers, environmental specialists and, of course, investigative teams (which were always antagonizing civic titans and important advertisers). As newspapers grew thinner and shallower, the men who published them worked harder to assure Wall Street that readers neither noticed nor cared. (*Lucky You* 21)

As a result of these economic realities,

The nineties had brought a boom in celebrity journalism, a decline in serious investigative reporting and a deliberate "softening of the product" by publishers. The result, he said, was that daily papers seldom caused a ripple in their communities and people paid less and less attention to them. (*Lucky You* 235)

As a consequence, Hiaasen has Joe Winder writing press releases for the Amazing Kingdom of Thrills, Christina Marks doing research for the Reynoldo Flemm show, and Bonnie Lamb as assistant corporate publicist for Crespo Mills, "required to use the word 'tasty' in fourteen consecutive press releases" (*Stormy Weather* 155).

And more pervasive than all of the recent corporate throes of the newspaper industry—unions, the loss of cold type, Watergate, downsizing, etc.—Hiaasen makes the personal and ethical dilemmas of the journalist a central concern of many of his characters. With journalists it's hard to know what goes first, a facility with words and mastery of a set style, or dedication to objectively finding and reporting facts. In *Lucky You* Hiaasen lists reporting as the principal tenet of journalism: "Honest reporters could always make a good-faith stab at objectivity, or at least professional detachment" (204). For Hiaasen's heroes, however, "professional detachment" causes problems. For one thing, as with Brian Keyes in *Tourist Season,* professional detachment carries with it an enormous personal cost:

The first happened a year after his arrival, when a fully-loaded 727 fireballed down in Florida Bay. Keyes had rented an outboard and sped to the scene and he'd filed a superb story, full of gripping detail. But they'd damn near had to hospitalize him afterward: for six months Keyes kept hallucinating that burned arms and legs were reaching out from under his bedroom furniture. (17-18)

Professional detachment, too, sometimes means inflicting pain on others. This is the whole point of the story about Callie Davenport in *Tourist Season.* Assigned to cover the kidnapping and murder of a four-year-old girl, Keyes creates a fictional interview with Callie's parents rather than intrude on their grief. It's an act that Skip Wiley in journalistic terms calls "the ultimate impiety" (*Tourist Season* 372), a judgment with which the reporter in Keyes agrees.

For the journalist, the proper alternative to nausea or creative avoidance of sordid reality lies in doing

what he had trained to be—a professional bystander, an expertly detached voyeur who was skilled at reconstructing violence after the fact, but never present and participatory. For reporters, the safety net was the ability to walk away, polish it off, forget about it. It was as easy as turning off the television, because whatever was happening always happened to somebody else; reality was past tense and once removed, something to be observed but not experienced. (*Tourist Season* 311-12)

In *Double Whammy,* R. J. Decker's means of achieving this state is his camera: "Certain things were easier to take if you were looking through a camera; sometimes it was the only protection you had, the lens putting an essential distance between the eye and the horror" (86). For Hiaasen's people, however, none of this works. It's an old adventure story scheme, but here he places it in the context of journalism. Their experience—people, events, and facts—changes his heroes from observers to actors. Thus Keyes quits his job at the *Sun* and becomes a private investigator, Decker packs his camera with "fourteen ounces of malleable plastic explosive" and blows up Thomas Curl, Joe Winder authors guerrilla press releases before invading the Amazing Kingdom of Thrills, and Tom Krome's adventures with JoLayne Lucks take him beyond journalism:

Joining JoLayne Lucks meant Krome couldn't write about her mission; not if he still cared about the tenets of journalism, which he did. Honest reporters could always make a good-faith stab at objectivity, or at least professional detachment. That was now impossible . . . Too much was happening in which Tom Krome had sway, and there was more to come. Absolved of his writerly duties, he felt liberated and galvanized. (204)

Although he portrays a fairly broad spectrum of commitment, something invariably draws Hiaasen's heroes into action. Usually it's Florida.

The big problem with Florida is people. Thus, in *Tourist Season* Hiaasen gives us guidelines for estimating the worth of the population of any place in the country. Here Skip Wiley calculates that

the quality of life declined in direct proportion to the Asshole Quotient . . . Miami had 134 assholes per square mile, giving it the worst A.Q. in North

America. In second place was Aspen, Colorado (101), with Malibu Beach, California, finishing third with 97. (167)

And the classes of people subject to this equation? From the very beginning Hiaasen includes tourists. First of all, they are downright unattractive. So in *Skin Tight,* Stranahan observes "a typical Miami-bound contingent—old geezers with tubas for sinuses, shiny young hustlers in thin gold chains; huge hollow-eyed families that looked like they'd staggered out of a Sally Struthers telethon" (214). In *Native Tongue* Joe Winder notes that "a high percentage of the Amazing Kingdom's tourists were clinically overweight. Was this a valid cross-section of American society? Or did fat people travel to Florida more frequently than thin people?" (300). And tourists dress badly as well. Hiaasen refers to them as "polyester manatees" in *Tourist Season,* and like every other recent hard-boiled writer he condemns their addiction to mail order outfits from L. L. Bean and Banana Republic. In spite of their offenses against good taste, however, Hiaasen largely portrays tourists as innocuous. Therefore the Shriners in *Tourist Season,* the visitors to the Amazing Kingdom of Thrills in *Native Tongue,* and the busloads of religious pilgrims in *Lucky You* are mostly middle American heroes and boobs. They are more victims than villains. Thus, "To lifelong Floridians it was a dream concept: fleecing a snowbird in such a way that he came back for more" (*Native Tongue* 32).

The real problem for Hiaasen doesn't lie with visitors, it lies with those who stay in Florida. In *Double Whammy* Decker labels this group "The Human Sludge Factor" (151), and Hiaasen finds that those who profess to practice professions comprise the main ingredients of the sludge. Take, for instance, Hiaasen's lawyers: Kipper Garth in *Skin Tight* and Mordecai in *Strip Tease* are scarcely even ambulance chasers. And when lawyers ascend to the bench, they get worse. There's larcenous Judge Goomer in *Skin Tight,* the libidinous, Bible-thumping divorce judge in *Strip Tease,* and Judge Battenkill who almost makes it to the Bahamas in *Lucky You.* Psychiatrists? There are Drs. Remond Courtney and Vibbs in *Tourist Season* and *Skin Tight* respectively, neither of whom knows or cares about human nature. Of course Hiaasen spends a lot of space in *Skin Tight* hammering the medical community from Rudy Graveline's rampant malpractice to the collusion of the state's licensure board: even after seeing manifest proof of Graveline's cavalier incompetence,

The board immediately reinstated Rudy's license and sealed all the records from the public and the press—thus honoring the long-held philosophy of Florida's medical establishment that the last persons who need to know about a doctor's incompetence are the patients. (102)

Whether they are physicians, lawyers, or judges, however, none of them is very bright. Indeed, all of them engage in shady and illegal practices with scarcely a thought to subterfuge or cover-up. And all because of Florida: "One of the wondrous things about Florida, Rudy Graveline thought as he chewed on a jumbo shrimp, was the climate of unabashed corruption: There was absolutely no trouble from which money could not extricate you" (101).

In addition to the chronically corrupt members of the professions, regular criminals infest South Florida in great numbers. Thus when offered relocation by the Witness Protection Program, Francis Kingsbury blithely chooses Miami, but "What Frankie did not know was that Miami was the prime relocation site for scores of scuzzy federal snitches (in the theory that South Florida was a place where just about any dirt-bag would blend in smoothly with the existing riffraff)" (*Native Tongue* 39). Hiaasen regularly brings up Miami's sky-high murder rate. In *Strip Tease,* for example, Sergeant Garcia researches vacation spots and "found out that Montana, for all its Wild West lore, was a safe and tran-quil place; there were traffic intersections in Dade County with higher murder rates" (85). Not only that, in *Tourist Season,* Miami's head coro-ner determines "that Greater Miami had more mutilation-homicides *per capita* than any other American City" (31). Furthermore, while drugs do not play a significant role in any of his plots, Hiaasen occasionally reminds readers of the dominant role of drugs and drug dealers in South Florida:

Half the new Miami skyscrapers had been built with coke money and existed largely as an inside joke, a mirage to please the banks and the Internal Revenue Service and the chamber of commerce. Everyone liked to say that the skyline was a monument to local prosperity, but Stranahan recognized it as a tribute to the anonymous genius of Latin American money launderers. (*Skin Tight* 310)

Whether they come from the professions of law or medicine or from the lower end of the criminal food chain, Hiaasen characterizes his South Florida criminals as inept and hapless felons. This is especially the case with the minor criminals of which he is so fond. Hiaasen introduces this character type with Jesus Bernal in *Tourist Season,* followed by Chemo in *Skin Tight,* Thomas Curl in *Double Whammy,* Darrell Grant in *Strip Tease,* Edie Marsh and Snapper in *Stormy Weather,* and Chub, Bode, and Shiner in *Lucky You.* Screwing up is their major occupation: Bernal can never get his bombs to go off at the right time or right place, Chemo repeatedly misses murdering Mick Stranahan, Thomas Curl spends a quarter of the book with a pit bull's head attached to his arm,

Darrell Grant gets caught stealing wheelchairs, Edie Marsh and Snapper have trouble pulling off a simple insurance scam, and the three hapless members of the White Rebel Brotherhood don't even know the shape of a swastika.

Hiaasen says each of them is a member of a diminished gene pool. This being the case, the dominant gene is the sloth gene. It's the case with Chemo: "Once Chemo was free of the Amish, the foremost challenge of adulthood was avoiding manual labor, to which he had a chronic aversion. Crime seemed to be the most efficient way of making money without working up a sweat" (85). Likewise, Snapper in *Stormy Weather* "had neither the ambition nor the energy to be a predator in the classic criminal mold. He saw himself strictly as a canny opportunist. He wouldn't endeavor to commit a first-degree felony unless the moment presented itself. He believed in serendipity, because it suited his style of minimal exertion" (60). And in *Lucky You,* Hiaasen shows the same thing in Chub's family background: "All of Onus' siblings made it to Georgia State University, and Onus himself could have gone there, too, had he not by the age of fifteen already chosen a life of sloth, inebriation and illiteracy" (72). What with the climate and wholesale corruption of the state, Florida acts as a magnet for this kind of people.

But these minor felons serve Hiaasen another way. In addition to the role of his sardonic comments about their backgrounds, depicting these characters and portraying their antics provides Hiaasen with an opportunity to employ a variety of comic techniques. For one thing, he almost always portrays their sheer incompetence to do anything right in a comic manner, exemplified best in Jesus Bernal's long history of inept bombs and bombings. For another, a lot of them are simply funny looking. There's Chemo, six foot nine with a Rice Krispies face; Snapper with his misshapen jaw; and Chub with a tire patch over one eye and Amber's Hooters shorts over his head. He puts more than a bit of Laurel and Hardy into some of their relationships, as with that of Bud and Danny in *Native Tongue.* Hiaasen also creates disparate elements in their backgrounds, like Bernal the Dartmouth-educated New Jerseyean Cuban liberation fighter, or Chemo the Amish gay bar bouncer. The sheer absurdity of their crimes, too, serves a comic purpose with Darrell Grant's stolen wheelchair business and Chub's counterfeiting of handicapped parking permits. And then there is Hiaasen's fixation on extremities. Most of his minor criminals have something happen to their hands or arms: Thomas Curl with the pit bull head on his arm, Chemo and the weed whacker prosthesis, Bud Schwartz's gunshot hand and Danny's gunshot foot, Pedro Luz and his gnawed-off foot, Darrell Grant's golf club splinted arm, and the blue crab claw on Chub's hand. With most of them, once more, it is disparate element comedy, but this time with added ridicule of the simpletons who go on with their nefarious schemes oblivious to their ostentatious deformities.

Hiaasen does, however, give his readers several characters who are more than buffoons—individuals whose desire for wealth or power drives them to create or participate in monumentally destructive acts. This is the case with Reverend Charles Weeb in *Double Whammy,* Rudy Graveline in *Skin Tight,* Francis Kingsbury in *Native Tongue,* and Malcolm Moldowsky in *Strip Tease.* Each of them is involved with wholesale fraud and consciously dupes large numbers of credulous and unsuspecting people, mostly tourists. With Weeb it's the Outdoor Christian Network and Lunker Lakes, with Kingsbury it's the Amazing Kingdom of Thrills, with Graveline it's his plastic surgery clinic, and with Moldowsky it's Congressman David Dillbeck. Each represents a characteristic Florida institution—fundamentalist religion, Disney World, medical quackery, and the sugar industry. In each case, too, they understand the sham they are perpetrating on the public—ersatz religion, youth, entertainment, and statesmanship. Weeb, Kingsbury, Graveline, and Moldowsky's principal occupation is creating and sustaining a wholesome image that belies the base reality of their creations. Lunker Lakes are polluted and are not lakes; the Amazing Kingdom's animal attractions are both puny and mendacious; Rudy hires other surgeons to perform his operations; and Congressman Dillbeck is hardly either a statesman or even a politician. They depend on images built with publicity and manipulation of the media. Hence Weeb has his own cable network, the Amazing Kingdom has Charles Chelsea and an entire publicity department, and Moldy is the model of a spin doctor. Bound together by hypocrisy, in typical Hiaasen fashion, they are also united by execrable taste. In his first appearance in *Double Whammy* Charles Weeb wears "an expensive maroon jogging suit he'd bought for cash on Rodeo Drive in Beverly Hills" (46) which "looked like K-Mart pajamas" (48); Rudy lives near the Bee Gees; Moldowsky's cologne nauseates people throughout *Strip Tease;* and "even to two men who had spent most of their adult lives in redneck bars and minimum-security prisons" the appointments of Kingsbury's house (including the nude portrait of his wife) are "unspeakably crude" (*Native Tongue* 137). Perhaps most significantly, none of these characters is unmasked or defeated by the scrutiny of the media. Something else causes their downfall.

There is, however, another class of villainy in Hiaasen's books—a class that is both ubiquitous, largely faceless, and far more dangerous than the larger than life charlatans Hiaasen depicts. The developer. While most of his works center on Miami or the Keys, Hiaasen shows the hand

of developers extending even to northern Florida and the hamlet of
Grange in *Lucky You*. Their works come in a number of varieties. It's difficult to say which is more offensive to Hiaasen, the trailer park (especially in *Stormy Weather*) or the commercial franchise. Thus, "Heading
west, Keyes could chart the march of the chain saws and bulldozers.
What once had been misty pastureland and pine barrens were now golden
age trailer parks; medieval cypress stands had been replaced with 7-
Elevens and coin laundries" (*Tourist Season* 86). Worse even than these
blots on the Florida landscape is the condominium: "And spreading like a
spore across the mottled landscape was every developer's wet dream, the
condominium cluster" (*Tourist Season* 86). There are condominia for
every pocketbook. There is the basic unit, such as Otter Creek—

Otter Creek consisted of three cheerless buildings set end to end at mild angles.
Each warren stood five stories high and was painted white with canary yellow
trim. Every apartment featured a tiny balcony that overlooked a notably
unscenic parking lot. (*Tourist Season* 86)

—and there is the exclusive and luxurious unit, such as Osprey Island—

there'll be four air-conditioned racquetball courts, a spa, a bike trail, a tennis
complex, a piazza, two fountains, and even a waterfall. Think about that: they're
going to bury the natural spring and build a fiberglass waterfall! . . . It says here
they're also planting something called a lush greenbelt, which is basically a
place for rich people to let their poodles take a shit. (*Tourist Season* 363)

These are bad enough when people live in them, but worse when lots of
people live in them as the euphemistically named "Interval-Ownership
Units" that come up in *Double Whammy* (168). And since the principal
occupation of the residents of these places is the pursuit of leisure,
developers inevitably find ways to provide it. So there are tennis courts
and restaurants: "The county had hired him [George Graveline] to rip
out the old trees [two full acres of virgin woods] to make space for some
tennis courts. Before long a restaurant would spring up next to the tennis
courts and, after that, a major resort hotel" (*Skin Tight* 269). But golf
courses attract the most attention for Hiaasen's guerrillas—Jesus Bernal
plants a bomb that actually works in the twelfth green of the Palmetto
Country Club in *Tourist Season*; Joe Winder sabotages the bulldozers
about to gouge out fairways and greens for Falcon Trace and the Mafia
hit man mistakenly shoots Jake Harp, the prospective pro, in *Native
Tongue*; and Skink drops a scorpion in the cup of the eighteenth green at
the Key Biscayne course in *Stormy Weather*.

Behind all of the golf courses, condominia, and commercial franchises (including the strip clubs featured in *Strip Tease*) stand a variety of base motives. Sometimes it is a simple get-rich scheme like the one that creates Gables-on-the-Bay in *Stormy Weather.* Sometimes it's a financial shell-game as with the savings and loan financing of Lunker Lakes in *Double Whammy.* And, worst of all, sometimes it's a cynical plot not to build something but to lose money, as with the investment of funds from the Central Midwest Brotherhood of Grouters, Spacklers and Drywallers International "pension fund in such a way as to conceal the millions of dollars being skimmed annually by organized crime, specifically, the Richard Tarborne family of Chicago" in *Lucky You* (102).

Hiaasen embodies a lot of what this means to him in two of his omnipresent kidnappings. First consider Skink's kidnapping of Max Lamb in *Stormy Weather.* Max represents many of the things Hiaasen considers anathema: voyeuristic tourism, advertising, and naiveté. Among other things, Skink gives Max Florida lessons. These start with the charge that "You people come down here—fucking yupsters with no knowledge, no appreciation, no interest in the natural history of the place, the ancient sweep of life. Disney World—Christ, Max, that's not Florida!" (72) and Skink follows with a short quiz:

> "Who was here first," Skink asked, "the Seminoles or the Tequestas?
>
> "I, uh—don't know." Max gripped the branch so hard his knuckles turned pink.
>
> Skink, replacing the artificial eyeball, retrieving the remote control from his pocket: "Who was Napoleon Bonaparte Broward?"
>
> Max Lamb shook his head helplessly. Skink shrugged. "How about Marjory Stoneman Douglas?"
>
> "Yes, yes, wait a minute . . . She wrote *The Yearling!*"
>
> Moments later, regaining consciousness, he found himself in a fetal ball on a mossy patch of ground. Both knees were scraped from the fall . . . Opening his eyes, Max saw the toes of Skink's boots. He heard a voice as deep as thunder. "I should kill you."
>
> "No, don't—."
>
> "The arrogance of coming to a place like this and not knowing—." (73-74)

Here, in capsule, Hiaasen demonstrates that tourists and developers alike have acted toward Florida in a typical colonial fashion. They have invaded a place oblivious to its culture and its past. So that his readers do not repeat the same error, Hiaasen includes passages in his books on the real history of Florida—background on the Seminole Wars and Fort Dallas (the precursor to Miami) in *Tourist Season*; and bits about the

slaughter of Huguenots in *Native Tongue.* And he shows, too, how it has
been bowdlerized, as in the pageant performed at the Amazing Kingdom
of Thrills: "As the history of Florida unfolded in song and skit, Joe
Winder imagined that the Stations of the Cross could be similarly
adapted and set to music, if the audience would only forgive a few minor
revisions" (306).

But learning about the state's past is only a small lesson compared
to learning about the region's delicate ecosystem which cannot support
the tide of humanity that has descended on it. This is the point of Skip
Wiley's various kidnappings in *Tourist Season,* and Hiaasen makes this
point in book after book. In *Tourist Season* Wiley kidnaps Kara Lynn,
the Orange Bowl Queen, and intends to leave her on a small island about
to be dynamited to make room for an exclusive residential community.
He wants to make a point about the rampant indifference of developers
("idiots who couldn't tell an osprey from a fucking parakeet," *Tourist
Season* 372) to the natural world:

To the creators of the Osprey Club, that precious eagle up there is not life, it has
no real value. Same goes for the wood rats and the herons. Weighed against the
depreciated net worth of a sixteen-story condominium after sellout, the natural
inhabitants of this island do not represent life—they have no fucking value.
(*Tourist Season* 364)

It's the same point Wiley makes earlier in the book when he tosses Mrs.
Kimmelman into the water with Pavlov, the salt water crocodile. He
wants to call attention to human indifference to the ninety-two endangered or threatened species indigenous to Florida (U.S. Fish and
Wildlife: www.fws.gov). All of South Florida belonged and belongs to
wildlife. This is Wiley's platform and his constituency:

Relax . . . just a raccoon. My constituency, Brian. Along with the eagles, the
opossums, the otters, the snakes, even the buzzards. All this belongs to them,
and more. Every goddamned acre, from here west to Miami Beach and north to
the big lake, belongs to them. It got stolen away. (103)

It's the reason that one of Hiaasen's characters will eat only roadkill (and
miniature poodles) and quixotically wears the radio collar of a dead
Florida panther. These guys speak for the animals.

And they speak for the land. One of Hiaasen's favorite juxtapositions is contrasting crass development with pristine nature: it's the case
with Otter Creek Condos in *Tourist Season* and with this passage
describing Lunker Lakes in *Double Whammy*:

Water glistened on both sides of the dike. Under a thin fog, Lunker Lake Number Seven lay as flat and dead as a cistern; by contrast, the small pool on the Everglades side was dimpled with darting minnows and waterbugs. The pocket was lushly fringed with cattails and sawgrass and crisp round lily pads as big as pizzas. (279)

While he pays attention to destruction of Florida's Keys in several books—*Native Tongue* and *Stormy Weather,* in particular—Hiaasen concentrates, as anyone concerned about the fate of the state must, on the past, the present, and the future of the Everglades. On this topic he includes what amounts to a summary lesson in *Lucky You*:

The Everglades empties off the Florida peninsula into a shimmering panorama of tidal flats, serpentine channels, and bright mangrove islets. The balance of life there depends upon a seasonal infusion of freshwater from the mainland. Once it was a certainty of nature, but no more. The drones who in the 1940s carved levees and gouged canals throughout the upper Everglades gave absolutely no thought to what would happen downstream to the fish and birds, not to mention the Indians. For the engineers, the holy mission was to ensure the comfort and prosperity of non-native humans. In the dry season the state drained water off the Everglades for immediate delivery to cities and farms. In the wet season it pumped millions of gallons seaward to prevent flooding of subdivisions, pastures and crops.

Over time, less and less freshwater reached Florida Bay, and what ultimately got there wasn't so pure. When the inevitable drought came, the parched bay changed drastically. Sea grasses began to die off by the acre. The bottom turned to mud. Pea-green algae blooms erupted to blanket hundreds of square miles, a stain so large as to be visible from NASA satellites. Starved for sunlight, sponges died and floated to the surface in rotting clumps. (246)

Q.E.D.: Hiaasen demonstrates again and again the depredations done by people to Florida's environment. In all of it, there is as well a layer of the nostalgia that so typically appears in the hard-boiled novel—the grimy present of middle-aged heroes inevitably compares badly to recollections of their idyllic boyhoods. But here it's not an incidental feature of the books. In many ways the issue of the destruction of Florida's environment dominates Hiaasen's books. But what to do about it?

What to do about the destruction of Florida's environment becomes a major part of the depiction and development of Hiaasen's characters. He creates a number of characters defined by their concern for Florida's environment. First comes Skip Wiley in *Tourist Season*. A writer for the Miami *Sun*, Wiley becomes increasingly virulent on the subject of

Florida. With Tommy Tigertail, made rich by legal Seminole bingo parlors, Viceroy Wilson, former Miami Dolphin running back, and Jesus Bernal, Wiley forms *Las Noches de Diciembre*. *Las Noches* kidnap tourists, dump shopping bags of snakes on a cruise ship, and kidnap the Orange Bowl Queen during half-time of the football game.

In *Double Whammy* Hiaasen introduces Clinton Tyree, who appears again in *Native Tongue* and *Stormy Weather*. Hiaasen gives readers a number of biographical portraits of Tyree. This is the first:

In the mid 1970s a man named Clinton Tyree became governor of Florida. He was everything voters craved: tall, ruggedly handsome, an ex-college football star (second-team All-American lineman), a decorated Vietnam veteran (a sniper once lost for sixteen days behind enemy lines with no food or ammunition), an eligible bachelor, an avid outdoorsman—and best of all, he was native-born, a rarity at that time in Florida. At first Clinton Tyree's political ideology was conservative when it was practical to be, liberal when it made no difference. At six-foot-six, he looked impressive on the campaign trail and the media loved him. He won the governorship running as a Democrat, but proved to be unlike any Democrat or Republican that the state of Florida had ever seen. To the utter confusion of everyone in Tallahassee, Clint Tyree turned out to be a completely honest man. (*Double Whammy* 92)

Stymied by developers and bought politicians in his efforts to save Florida from ecological disaster, Tyree simply leaves office and, going by the names of "captain" or "Skink," retreats with only his library to the remaining patches of wilderness left in the state to live a Thoreauvian existence. Along with occasionally shooting at airliners, busses, and rental cars, Skink sabotages Reverend Weeb's televised healing service and the Lunker Lakes bass tournament, sets fire to the Amazing Kingdom of Thrills, and attaches the Club to Snapper's disfigured jaws.

The last of Hiaasen's ecoterrorists is Molly McNamara in *Native Tongue*. Leader of the Mothers of Wilderness—"Of all the environmental groups fighting to preserve what little remained of Florida, the Mothers of Wilderness was regarded as the most radical and shrill and intractable" (*Native Tongue* 31). She is the mastermind behind the theft of the mango voles from the Amazing Kingdom of Thrills. And with Danny and Bud, she has much to do with undermining the Amazing Kingdom of Thrills and the prospective golf course, Falcon Trace.

Each of these characters, Wiley, Skink, and Molly McNamara, uses violence and illegal means to change a way of life that will inevitably destroy what remains of a pristine natural world. Before violence, though, Hiaasen's characters use publicity in the hope that it will prevent the pestilential influx of tourists and homesteaders that compounds and accelerates ecological disaster in the state. Thus in his columns in the *Sun*, Skip Wiley almost re-creates the plagues of Egypt in order to frighten tourists away: "'Rats as Big as Bulldogs Stalk Condo.' 'Snakes Infest Bathroom Plumbing at Posh Resort.' 'Mystery Disease Sweeps Shuffleboard Tourney'" (*Tourist Season* 63). Joe Winder, in his press release duel with Charles Chelsea, also uses infectious disease and the threat of snakes to frighten customers away from the Amazing Kingdom of Thrills in *Native Tongue*. Neither one causes a mass exodus from Florida. But perhaps something else will work. From the very beginning, Hiaasen's characters wish for something apocalyptic to save the state. Thus Mick Stranahan in *Skin Tight* "wondered what it would be like to wake up and find the city vaporized, the skies clear and silent, the shoreline lush and virginal! He would have loved to live here at the turn of the century when nature owned the upper hand" (210). In Florida, however, one does not have to dream vague dreams about apocalyptic forces, because the state has always been subject to hurricanes. Thus Skip Wiley's "infamous hurricane column":

What South Florida needs most is a killer hurricane, sudden and furious, an implacable tempest that would raze the concrete shorelines and rake away the scum and corruption . . .

The tidal surge, a swollen gargoyle of a wave, is born in the Gulf Stream. Gaining size and thunder by the minute, it races under a deafening wind toward Florida's sweeping coastline. In the purple darkness it pulverizes Miami Beach with a twenty foot wall of water, flooding Carl Fisher's billion-dollar island of muck. Picture it: corpses upon corpses, clogging the flooded lobbies of once-majestic condominiums; dead dreamers, swollen, blue-veined, carplike.

They will die in bewilderment, in the fierce arms of the beloved ocean that brought them here in the first place. Fools! the wind will scream, fools all. (293)

But like the force of publicity, hurricanes don't work either. In *Stormy Weather*, in fact, Hurricane Andrew brings people in rather than driving them out:

It hadn't been the cataclysmic purgative he had hoped for and prophesied. Ideally a hurricane should drive people out, not bring people in. The high number of new arrivals to South Florida was merely depressing; the moral caliber of the fortune seekers was appalling—low-life hustlers, slick-talking scammers and cold-blooded opportunists, not to mention pure gangsters and thugs. (170)

If not hurricanes, then what? Throughout most of the books, Hiaasen uses another process of nature to make the point about people and the land—survival of the fittest. He starts this when Wiley pits Ida Kimmel-man against Pavlov, the crocodile: "This is not murder," Wiley declared, "it's social Darwinism. Two endangered species, Pavlov here and Mrs. Kimmelman, locked in mortal combat" (115). In the next book, Skink arranges a combat between Queenie, the large-mouth bass, and Dennis Gault, a combat that Queenie wins. Then there is Chemo and Liza the barracuda in *Skin Tight,* and both Churrito and the baboons and Pedro Luz's encounter with Dickie the Dolphin in *Native Tongue.* The theme of people versus nature persists through *Stormy Weather* and *Lucky You,* both of which end with the villains abandoned in wild nature where they will not survive. All of these incidents, though, are more in the way of poetic justice than a solution to the problems people have inflicted on Florida's ecosystem.

While individual acts of ecoterrorism may be satisfying to the per-petrators (and to the readers), they accomplish little and do not stop the violation of the land that, as Hiaasen repeatedly says, once was paradise. One alternative Hiaasen provides for his characters is that traditionally associated with the American frontier: when a place becomes civilized, just move on. In *Lucky You*, for Tom Krome it's dreams of emigrating to Alaska. Augustine and Bonnie move to Chokoloskee "a fishing village on the edge of Florida's Ten Thousand Islands" at the close of *Stormy Weather*. Danny Pogue in *Native Tongue* becomes a game warden in Tanzania. Christina Marks buys a second-hand Boston whaler in *Skin Tight* to search for the remote spot that Mick Stranahan has taken up res-idence. And in *Strip Tease*, Erin Grant notes that "Tasmania was looking pretty good as an alternate homeland" (254). But not everyone has the option or the desire to move whenever the land has become corrupt.

And even if one moves, the politicians, developers, and every other variety of deviant will show up sooner or later. So, there's plenty of reason for pessimism. Thus in *Native Tongue*: "'We're all doomed,' said Joe Winder, 'if you really think about it.' Which he tried not to" (18). And on a slightly brighter note, Hiaasen gives us this conversation in *Strip Tease*:

The lieutenant pulled his feet off the desk. "I remember what you told me a long time ago—"

"The world is a sewer and we're all dodging shit."

"Very uplifting, Al. I'm surprised Hallmark hasn't bought up the copy-right."

"Words to live by," Garcia said.

"You know what's sad? I'm beginning to think you're right. I'm beginning to think there's no hope."

"Of course there's no hope," Garcia said," but don't let it get you down."
(245)

And on the brighter side of hopelessness, throughout all of the books, Hiaasen portrays average people who have not been tainted and cannot be diminished by the incessant stupidity and the rampant corruption of their environment.

In all of the books, of course, Hiaasen uses the old adventure story pattern of initiation, of an innocent awakened to his or her own potential and virtue when caught up in events of the larger, corrupt world. Thus there is the succession of Brian Keyes and Kara Lynn, R. J. and Catherine Decker, Christina Marks, Joe Winder and Carrie, Augustine and Bonnie Lamb, and Tom Krome. As the books progress Hiaasen's ecoterrorist heroes become less flamboyant and less revolutionary. Skink appears in the books principally to help innocents who have become involved in catastrophes created by others. And the old and frail Molly McNamara quickly assumes a subsidiary role once Danny, Bud, Winder, Carrie, and Skink decide that they must take part in the action. In *Native Tongue,* in fact, Hiaasen moves from ecoterrorists to begin to add focus on other characters whose objectives are different and much more limited.

First there is Jim Tile, the state police officer formerly attached to Governor Clinton Tyree. At first he appears as the former governor's guardian angel. But with the addition of a love interest in *Stormy Weather* Jim Tile's role becomes somewhat larger than playing Tonto to an erratic and mercurial Lone Ranger. Perhaps more importantly, a group of mildly larcenous but admirable characters appears in the later novels. This group begins with Bud and Danny in *Native Tongue.* For one thing, Bud differs from the yuppie world:

Bud Schwartz had been a two-bit burglar since he was seventeen years old. He was neither proud of it nor ashamed. It was what he did, period. Whenever his mother gave him a hard time about getting an honest job, Bud Schwartz reminded her that he was the only one of her three children who was not in psychoanalysis. His sister was a lawyer and his brother was a stockbroker, and both of them were miserably fucked up. Bud Schwartz was a crook, sure, but at least he was at peace with himself. (81)

And in Danny Hiaasen builds both a childish innocence and a childlike sense of wonder that has him first entranced by nature shows on the Discovery Channel and then beginning a new life as a game warden in the Serengeti National Park in Tanzania. In *Strip Tease* there is Shad, the bouncer at the Eager Beaver. Almost as physically menacing as Chemo in *Skin Tight*, Shad is a very different kind of character. First, there are his comic attempts to defraud yogurt manufacturers. There is also his concern for the club's strippers, especially Erin. But the most striking thing about Shad lies in the fact that Hiaasen gives him a bit of an inner life:

> Shad gripped him by the soft meat of the shoulders. "I'm suffocating," he said, "in this world."
>
> "Get serious," said Orly, pulling free. "Wall-to-wall pussy, and you're suffocating? 'Scuse me if I break down and cry."
>
> "It's not your fault, Mr. Orly. I seen too much."
>
> Orly suggested a vacation. He told Shad to take a week off, fly to the islands, get laid repeatedly. Shad shook his head. "A week won't do it," he said.
>
> "Then make it ten days."
>
> "You don't understand Mr. Orly. I gotta get out completely. I've lost my sense of wonderment."
>
> "Oh, for Chrissakes," Orly said. He led Shad to a quiet corner . . . "When you were a little boy, what'd you want to be when you grew up? . . ."
>
> Shad said, "I wanted to play for the Forty-niners."
>
> "Right? And what happened?"
>
> "I got fucking busted in the ninth grade."
>
> Orly rolled his eyes. "Point is, almost nobody gets where they want in this life. Everybody's dream takes a beating. Me, I wanted to be an obstetrician . . . This is as close as I got. You follow? It's called facing reality."
>
> . . .
>
> "There's different kinds of reality," he told Orly. "I want the mystery back in mine." (299)

And finally there is the cast of religious entrepreneurs in *Lucky You*: Demencio and Trish with their weeping Madonna, Marva with her road-stain Jesus, Dominick Amador with his Black and Decker stigmata, and Sinclair with his apostolic turtles. Larcenous, sure. But they are also forthright, hard-working, neighborly, and, in the case of Sinclair turned Turtle-boy, appealingly innocent.

Alongside these innocent minor characters, Hiaasen has increasingly turned to women characters rather than ecoterrorists or traditional action heroes. In *Stormy Weather*, Skink states the politically correct view of men versus women in an exchange with Edie Marsh: "Edie, your opinion of men—it's not good. That much we share. Christ, imagine what Florida would look like today if women had been in charge of the program! Imagine a beach or two with no ugly high-rises. Imagine a lake without golf courses" (309). To which Edie replies, "You're wrong." Nevertheless, in Erin Grant and JoLayne Lucks Hiaasen creates characters who differ significantly from his other characters. Granted, they do possess the qualities Hiaasen shows as admirable in all of his characters—they are minimalists, they are forthright, they work hard, they are loners, etc. These women differ, though, in being innocent victims, one of a perverse legal system and the other of redneck racism. They are also in charge. In *Strip Tease* Garcia and Shad play decidedly minor roles and Erin directs the action without their help or advice. And although Hiaasen develops a love interest in *Lucky You*, he makes it clear that JoLayne calls the shots both in the relationship with Tom Krome and in the action. The two women characters differ, too, in having limited and attainable ends. Erin directs all of her actions solely to regain custody of her daughter, and JoLayne wants only to save Simmons Woods, not the Everglades, and not the world.

Hiaasen has been writing detective stories about Florida for more than a decade and has been writing columns in the Miami *Herald* even longer. There hasn't been a mass exodus from Florida. Developers haven't joined the Sierra Club. The Everglades hasn't been saved. People haven't stopped wearing white belts or gold chains or knit shirts with fauna on the breast. Disney World is larger than ever. And I suppose that Hiaasen never expected anything else:

It is not a fragrant world, but it is the world you live in, and certain writers with tough minds and a cool spirit of detachment can make very interesting and even amusing patterns out of it. (Raymond Chandler, "The Simple Art of Murder")

EARL EMERSON

Earl Emerson has written eleven Thomas Black books: *The Rainy City* (1985), *Poverty Bay* (1985), *Nervous Laughter* (1986), *Fat Tuesday* (1987), *Deviant Behavior* (1988), *Yellow Dog Party* (1991), *The Portland Laugher* (1994), *The Vanishing Smile* (1995), *The Million-Dollar Tattoo* (1996), *Deception Pass* (1997), and *Catfish Cafe* (1998). Up until *Deception Pass*, each one begins with an epigraph from Chandler. With *The Rainy City,* I suspect that this was incidental. Fulfilling one of the criteria of the genre, Emerson set out to ground his books in local color and the local color he knew best was that of Seattle. So Chandler's "God help all men on rainy afternoons" worked both to start off the local color theme and to provide by association the imprimatur of the best of the original hard-boiled writers.

After *The Rainy City*, though, Emerson uses his Chandler references for other things: they provide mini-lectures on the basics of the hard-boiled story and the nature of the hard-boiled hero. Three of the later books (*Nervous Laughter, Deviant Behavior,* and *The Portland Laugher*) cite passages from Chandler's essay "The Simple Art of Murder." Two of these define murder by opposing it to the elegant crimes of Golden Age fiction and focusing on its suddenness and cruelty:

The boys with their feet on the desks know that the easiest murder case in the world to break is the one somebody tried to get very cute with; the one that bothers them is the murder somebody only thought of two minutes before he pulled it off. (cited in *Nervous Laughter*)

These are the flustered old ladies—of both sexes (or no sex) and almost all ages—who like their murders scented with magnolia blossoms and do not care to be reminded that murder is an act of infinite cruelty, even if the perpetrators sometimes look like playboys or college professors or nice motherly women with softly greying hair. (cited in *The Portland Laugher*)

The epigraph to *Deviant Behavior* recapitulates Chandler's classic description of the hard-boiled detective, the one everybody quotes that begins with "He is a relatively poor man" and ends with "He is a lonely man." In the remainder of the epigraphs, however, Emerson draws passages from a miscellany of Chandler's works. These sometimes convey the bitter-sweet melancholy of the hard-boiled world, as in the epigraph to *Fat Tuesday* from "The King in Yellow": " 'So long guy,' he said gently. 'You were a louse—but you sure had music in you.' " And they sometimes embody Chandler's emulsification of stoicism and despair, as in the passage from his letter to Carl Brandt that serves as epigraph to *The Million-Dollar Tattoo*: "The best way to find out if you have any friends is to go broke. The ones that hang on longest are your friends. I don't mean the ones that hang on forever. There aren't any of those." When greeted with introductions like these, we're all ready for reheated Chandlerian fare: the corrupt world, the decayed city, the cancer of wealth, the ubiquitous betrayals, the pyrrhic victories, the relatively poor and lonely hero, and the prose as tough and evocative as Los Angeles in the Depression. But Emerson surprises us.

Start off with the local color. Emerson really likes Seattle. There's not much of the city gone to seed here. Of course he puts in passages about the weather. It's Seattle, after all. That's why Emerson or somebody entitled his first book *The Rainy City*. But he doesn't whine about the weather; he just occasionally describes it in passing. As Eskimos supposedly have a bunch of words to describe what most of us call snow, Emerson describes the range of wetness in the air in a number of ways—fog, mist, spray, rain, etc. Even though oppressive weather has long been a standard technique for creating what is aptly termed "atmosphere," Emerson doesn't describe Seattle's vulnerability to every front coming off the Pacific as odious or even bothersome. The most inconvenience the weather causes Thomas Black, Emerson's hero, is that his friend Kathy Birchfield insists on putting his umbrella in the gun-rack of his pick-up. Portland and Tacoma also serve as inconveniences. Emerson does describe them as squalid and undesirable places and Black never wants to inch down I-5 in order to do business in either place. But he surely loves Seattle: the Bay, the Space Needle, the underground city, the arboretum, the King Dome, the U. District, and all the rest of the city. Thus the euphoria in *Nervous Laughter*: "The residences were uphill and thus higher than the street, but even from the roadway I could see the entire Olympic Mountain Range, the hump that was West Seattle, Harbor Island, and most of downtown Seattle, including the Space Needle and the bustling water-front. To the east, the Cascade range was clouded over. It was enough to suck the blood right out of your heart" (3). In its best aspect, Emerson describes Seattle in many ways as a university town on steroids. *Fat Tuesday*, for example, revels in the exuberance and wacky fun that is uniquely Seattle's. And the only thing bad about the place is all the people. Significantly, both Hiaasen and Emerson use highways as a measure of inhospitality, and it's a toss up whether driving on I-95 or I-5 is a better argument for the abolition of the automobile—or the abolition of drivers. The mechanized madness on I-5, the inevitable break-downs and interminable delays on Seattle's floating bridge, periodically provoke outrage from Emerson's hero and especially from his friend Kathy Birchfield. She, in fact, is a card-carrying member of the actual group of Washingtonians who would seal the state's borders and require Californians to apply for green cards when they travel north. But Thomas Black can avoid all the traffic because he is a cyclist and, left to his own resources, he would rather bike.

Indeed, left to his own resources, Thomas Black has arranged a comfortable and satisfying life for himself. Like classical hard-boiled heroes, he has few possessions and those he has—other than his racing bicycle—are modest:

Mine was a modest frame house off Roosevelt in the University District: two bedrooms upstairs and a bachelor apartment in the basement which I rented to a student. My needs were few, my life tranquil except for an occasional messy divorce case. My truck was thirteen years old and squeaked in places I could not reach with a grease gun. I pedaled a bicycle when the Seattle rains abated. (*The Rainy City* 3)

Unlike other hard-boiled heroes, though, he does not, in effect, whine about his minimal possessions by calling attention to their age or shabbiness. In fact, Black calls attention to an attitude that approaches Thoreauvian, especially when one recalls that Henry occasionally loped over to the Emersons' for a hearty Sunday brunch: "I didn't work much, but then I didn't need to. I had a fifty percent LEOFF 1 pension, my requirements were simple, and I took pride in keeping them that way" (*Fat Tuesday* 9). Call him Thoreauvian or call him a hippie, compared to the other gumshoes worried about their bills and driven by the work ethic, at times Black simply lacks ambition:

"You really should wear a suit and tie. It's no wonder you don't get the big accounts. The firm has enough cases each year to keep three detectives scrambling and you slump in wearing jeans and a sport coat. Honestly, Thomas."

"I don't want any big accounts," I said. (*Poverty Bay* 14)

Mostly he wants, and in some measure has achieved, a life of contentment and fun:

In my spare time I grew roses and, along the south wall of the house where it was hot, tomatoes. I also maintained a vegetable garden in back where we had a mixture of sun and shade. A grand old crab apple tree grew in the yard, equipping us with ammunition each fall for apple wars with Kathy's nephews, the boys wearing thick ski hats, two pairs of pants, fencing masks, and bulky winter clothing. Kathy and I in wrap-around shatterproof sunglasses and parkas. *(Million-Dollar Tattoo* 30)

Kathy, whose semi-adult moments alternate with those of Black, calls him "the Peter Pan of private eyes" (98) in *The Portland Laugher*.

And there is a measure of truth in the "the Peter Pan of private eyes" label. Emerson emphasizes the fun of Black's vocation relatively early in the first book: "Besides, I had come to like snooping on people. It was fun. Sure, I was a voyeur. So was anyone who ever watched Doris Day mug with Rock Hudson, or gawked at Bill Holden kissing Kim Novak" *(The Rainy City* 51). And in recounting some of Black's past cases, as opposed to those narrated in the novels, Emerson chooses to focus on the hilarity of the absurd. Thus Black gives the following rundown on one of his cases to Buzz Steeb in *Deviant Behavior*:

Last Christmas a woman came in and claimed her husband's dog wouldn't stay out of taverns. Lived in a small town north of here. Every drunk in town fed the mutt in these taverns. So fat he could hardly walk. They were constantly getting calls at two in the morning to come and pry him out of some doorway. She finally had him put to sleep. The husband retaliated by having her cat gassed. She asked me to sink her husband's Seville in the Snohomish River. (25)

Then, too, Emerson inserts the vignette into *Yellow Dog Party* about the client who was selling autographed pictures of Jesus Christ and his turning to Black for assistance with the body shipped to him by one of his "clients":

He pushed a letter across the desk. It was from Rolanda Horton in Waterloo, Iowa, and she wrote that since Bumpus seemed to be on such good terms with the Savior, she would take three autographed photos and could he please ask the Son of God to raise up her Alvin, who'd only been gone a few days from the date UPS took him in hand. (76)

Black takes the five-thousand-dollar fee and stores the coffin in Kathy's law firm's back room. There's also the bizarre anecdote Black relates in *Deception Pass*: "I was called in after a stranger routinely began paddling past her property in an aluminum canoe and standing to shout slogans from the Korean War and various long-gone political campaigns. He was usually sans trousers when he did this" (4). And in *Catfish Cafe*,

Luther, as a hearse driver, constantly picks Black up in vehicles, including his car, containing corpses destined for the funeral parlor. Hardly the stuff of the usual hard-boiled case.

Along with occasionally recounting these comic episodes, Emerson creates several continuing characters who play comic roles. This starts with Black's grumpy neighbor Horace, who lives in a house full of canaries and views Black as a worthless hippie who manages a white-slavery operation from his basement. After Horace, Emerson introduces Desiree Nash in *Fat Tuesday*:

Built along the lines of a goblet, pipestem legs and an overly developed upper torso, Desiree looked at me . . . out of eyes that were deceptively gentle blue. Her face was comely in a rugged, boyish way; four earrings in one ear and a heavy coin on a hook dangling from the other. Her black hair fell in wet-looking ringlets and though she smelled like a biker in Walla Walla, she smelled like Arpege now. About fifteen ounces of it. Probably had shoplifted a bottle at Pay'n Save on her way over and baptized herself. (103-4)

Throughout the novel Desiree pursues Black in person and on his answering machine with ostentatious and embarrassingly rambunctious carnality. Emerson introduces his other main comic character, eventually to be paired up with Desiree, Elmer "Snake" Slezak, in *Yellow Dog Party* and goes on to base the plot of *The Million-Dollar Tattoo* on Snake's belief that he has been called upon to fertilize a race of space aliens. Snake

was a bandy-legged man who wore cowboy boots and almost always had a Stetson close by. In the headband of the hat you could generally find a two-shot derringer with rosewood stocks. His gray-brown hair was shaggy in back, and his grizzled beard would have been termed mere overgrowth on some. His piercing movie-star-blue eyes were always bloodshot, and you didn't have to get too close to smell beer. He was maybe five foot six, 125 pounds, and looked like what he was, a spent ex-bull rider. I'd once heard a woman say he looked like a guy waiting for the right time to kill himself. When he wasn't laughing outrageously, a morose view of life radiated from his face. *(Yellow Dog Party* 106)

Aberrant, weird, marginal outcasts, Snake and Desiree intrude into the well-ordered and usually sedate routines of Black's life—just as he occasionally intentionally and unintentionally intrudes into that of his neighbor Horace. Neither Desiree nor Snake has much in the way of social or sexual inhibitions and their actions occasionally put Black into comic predicaments. But each of them also saves the hero's life (Desiree in *Fat*

Tuesday and Snake in *The Portland Laugher*) and each also represents Black's sympathy with and for the free-spirited and spontaneous.

Free spirit and spontaneous, of course, reside most fully in Emerson's drawing of Kathy Birchfield. For all of the books she's the detective's best friend. Although it has been there the whole time, the romantic connection between the two of them does not become manifest until *Yellow Dog Party*. Up until that book, Emerson portrays their relationship as consisting of sharing important time. Significantly, that important time is made up of homey quiet—their ritualized Sundays spent with newspapers and comfort-food breakfasts—and hijinx, mostly organized by Kathy. The rowdy celebrations of the northwest's Mardi Gras in *Fat Tuesday* are as good an example as any. And then there is the bastinado by breast that Black experiences in the date Kathy arranges for him in *Yellow Dog Party*. Emerson makes a point of Kathy's extensive thrift-shop collection of diverse apparel and that she can dress outlandishly and retain her essential elegance and magnetic attractiveness. He also makes a point of her predilection for dressing up as a clown—white face, baggy pants, top hat, horn, paper flowers, juggling balls and all. In spite of his abhorrence of formal dress, Kathy's clown get-up and performance provide both a counterpoint and a challenge to the hero's assumptions about his own laid-back unpretentiousness. So does her habit of walking in and conducting conversations with Black when he is bathing. Given that Black is pretty much satisfied with his comfortable routines—has, if you will, Ambition Deficit Disorder—the impetus that involves him in the tortured lives of others comes from Birchfield. First to help an old friend in *The Rainy City*, and then in most of the other books as an attorney, Kathy brings the cases to Black. They form the substance of all the books. But the dynamic of the Black-Birchfield relationship runs through all of them as well. For the first half of the series, Emerson develops their relationship as a playful and platonic one. As Parker does in his Susan trilogy, however, Emerson creates a crisis in their relationship in three books: *Yellow Dog Party*, *The Portland Laugher*, and *The Vanishing Smile*. Except in Emerson it's not as tortured and artificial. Or it's more tortured and less artificial. Unlike the Svengali-Trilby bit that Susan falls into in *A Catskill Eagle*, Emerson has Kathy either finally accede to Black's misbegotten notion that sex would ruin their friendship or begin a serious relationship in order to shove Black into commitment. It works, but the fissure created by Black's accidental shooting of her inept new boyfriend and the grief thrust upon both of them lasts from the beginning of *The Portland Laugher* until the early parts of *The Vanishing Smile,* where Birchfield and Black discover that friendship and sex can coexist.

In addition to Horace, Snake, Desiree, Kathy, Smithers (Black's cop buddy who's wild about fat women), and Bruno, and the comic absurdity of a few of the incidentally related incidents in Black's career, Emerson includes other material that has comic potential. *Fat Tuesday*, for instance, opens with "I was trapped in a house with a lawyer, a bare-breasted woman, and a dead man. The rattlesnake in the paper sack only complicated matters" (1). But it's not comic. Indeed, alongside the hero's contented life and balanced disposition lurk occasional dark passages. The guy's name is Black, after all. First comes the recurrent mention of the shooting incident that moved Black to leave the Seattle police department. Black recounts the shooting of the fifteen-year-old car thief for the first time in *The Rainy City*:

Had he died instantly, I might not have felt it so keenly. But he didn't die instantly. He talked to me before he died. He said he was sorry. While the medic unit wailed in the distance, he wept through the blood and the glass and bits of face and told me to apologize to his mother for him: a promise I never kept, was incapable of keeping. And then he had the audacity to linger on through a seven-hour operation at Harborview, passing on only when the entire family had gathered in the hallway to confront me with their big brown, matching brother-sister-father-mother eyes. (49-50)

And this incident comes back to life throughout the books whenever events seem to call for firearms. In fact, violence in general precipitates depression in Emerson's books. This comes up after the knife-fight in *Nervous Laughter*:

I felt woozy. I wondered whether I was going to be depressed over this one. I wasn't a killer. I knew it. Whether it was compassion or a moral sense or what—I really couldn't say—I had not been bothered enough to dissect it. I had slain only one person in my life and I was determined to keep it that way. Maybe I had been around when a few others died, but I only counted the one. But every once in a while I got crazy and mauled or got mauled by some goon. Usually we deserved what we dished out to each other, or worse. But that didn't alleviate the personal misery I felt afterward. (196)

Dark thoughts, however, come from more than Black's flash-backs to the shooting or responses to violence. From the very beginning, pessimism and the defenses he has built against it punctuate Black's view of the world. Thus this passage early in *The Rainy City*: "I'm not easily frightened, but she was seeing something in conjunction with this family that didn't belong, something ugly, and I didn't know if I wanted to find out what it was. Years ago, I had wanted to know everything. Needed to know. Now, I realized there were some things you were better off not discovering" (34). And sometimes there are no defenses. Late in the series, in *The Vanishing Smile*, Black tells Kathy that he helped bag cadavers during what one can assume was the Vietnam War. Thoughts about interment become a minor thread in Black's consciousness. In *Poverty Bay*, in fact, Emerson runs a motif on graves. First, walking on the beach, Black observes, "The tide line . . . speckled with pools a foot or two across with mounds of sand, rocks and broken shells where people had been clamming and neglected to police the holes afterwards. The pools looked like dozens of miniature graves awaiting miniature burial parties" (30). And then one hundred pages later the image comes back in a dream: "In the morning I remembered only one dream. It was about miniature caskets on the beach, miniature corpses and miniature gravestones. A giant booted foot was crushing all the miniature shrieking pallbearers. I was wearing the boot, and cackling" (130). And graves continue into the next book as well, where Emerson moves from metaphor to meaning. After discussing the first case in *Nervous Laughter* with police detective Bill Crum, out of nowhere Black asks:

> "You ever get the feeling that all people are good for is filling up graves?"
> Dunking a piece of doughnut into his coffee and shoving it between his thick lips, Crum said, "Why, yes. I get that feeling quite often. How 'bout yourself?"
> "Once in a while." (*Nervous Laughter* 35)

But in spite of views like this that Black voices at times in the books, they hardly fall into the pessimistic category. The comedic stuff helps, but the thing that sets the Thomas Black stories apart from the bleak view that is the logical result of apprenticeship to Raymond Chandler is Emerson's insistence on compassion. He comes right out and says this in *Deviant Behavior* when Black answers the question "what do you admire in a man?" with "Try compassion for a start" (97).

Throughout all of the books Black has or comes to have sympathy for the dispossessed as individuals and as groups. Snake and Desiree certainly show this from a comic point of view, but Emerson fills the books with serious examples as well. In fact, he builds most of his books around this kind of people: *The Rainy City* has Burton and Melissa Nadisky; *Poverty Bay* has Lance Tyner; *Fat Tuesday* has Eric Castle; *Deviant Behavior* has Todd Steeb; *Yellow Dog Party* has Jo Schwantz; *The Portland Laugher* has Billy Battle; and *The Million-Dollar Tattoo* has Meade Barber. Each lives a marginal life, mired in despair and teetering on the edge of disaster. Castle has been accused of child pornography and Battle of murder. Jo Schwantz is an abused wife. Barber is homeless. Todd Steeb lives with echoes of his uncle's suicide. And the Nadiskys—he is ineffectual and she is an unwilling prostitute. Add to them the more peripheral characters: the teenage runaways in *Nervous Laughter*, the AIDS victims in *The Vanishing Smile*, the homeless in *Poverty Bay*. They form a considerable tally. Part of Emerson's point, too, is that these characters are both individuals and stand for many, many others lined up behind them. And Black's attitudes and acts take note of this. In *Fat Tuesday* while everyone else in the novel despises Eric Castle, Black finds, a bit grudgingly, that he actually likes him. That compassion thing that Black talks about to Buzz Steeb comes out both in his intuitive reading of individuals and in his growing understanding of the plight of his fellows. Emerson shows this most emphatically in this interchange in *Poverty Bay*:

"Man, don't you know nothin'? Down on his luck. We're in a fucking depression. I ain't worked in six months. Lance couldn't find work. He tried everything there was. Finally he got so down and dirty and hungry nobody would have taken him anyway. Where you been? I'm talking depression here."

He was right. I'd been secure on my pension so long I had forgotten what was going on in the rest of the world. Once in a while I'd drive past a food bank, or see an article in the paper highlighting the New Poor. But I didn't really understand it, was still shocked to hear somebody I knew was down and out. (128-29)

The issue of homelessness dominates this novel and plays a significant role in *The Million-Dollar Tattoo*. AIDS provides a central focus for *The Vanishing Smile*. And in *Catfish Cafe* Emerson involves Black with the dilemmas of an African-American family: "Everybody but me was black. As conscious as I was of the color of my skin, it occurred to me that this was only one evening for me in a very small neighborhood in a rather large city, while Luther was conscious of the color of his skin every minute of every day of his life, no matter where he went" (57).

When it comes to the dispossessed, the suffering of children paints the most graphic picture of all. Emerson fills the books with kids: Angel Nadisky in *The Rainy City*; the twins P. W. and D. W. in *Poverty Bay*; the adolescent Buzz Steeb in *Deviant Behavior*; Schuyler, Lucy, and Tad Castle in *Fat Tuesday*; Echo Boyd, Morgana and Amber Schwantz in *Yellow Dog Party*, Chester in *The Vanishing Smile*, and Meade Barber's sons in *The Million-Dollar Tattoo*. All have burdens placed upon them. Most are abandoned by one or both parents. Schuyler, and P. W. and

D. W. are developmentally disabled. Chaos, uncertainty, and privation fill their lives. In one sense or another their childhoods have been impoverished. Yet each of them possesses the potential for joy. Of course, Black has intuitive and immediate sympathy for them, and in several cases his unraveling of the novels' central dilemmas promises to give them fuller lives, fuller childhoods. The surrogate father theme holds strong attraction for a lot of hard-boiled writers—Burke, Parker, Mosley, and even Crumley. But Emerson doesn't make Black so much into a substitute father for the kids in his novels as maybe into something approaching a young and savvy uncle. He fixes the bikes of Meade Barber's boys, he mops up the milk Angel Nadisky has spilled so that her grandmother won't find out, he goes through a couple of series of juvenile jokes with P. W. and D. W., he goes roller skating with the girls in *Yellow Dog Party*, and he talks to and listens to Buzz Steeb as an equal. Most of these resemble the crab apple fights in his backyard with Kathy's nephews. Black doesn't take these kids' lives over as a parent. They get their families back, whether one parent or two, because of his unraveling of the crime in the novel. What Black directly brings to these kids is joy. The reason he can accomplish this lies in the fact that the child in him has never left or maybe he has found the essence of childhood in his adult world. He is, after all, the Peter Pan of private eyes.

By means of all of this, by means of his portrayals of children and the dispossessed, Emerson gets to the central theme in all of his books. They're all about manipulation, about power and control. Manipulation certainly descends to him as one of the standard motifs of the hard-boiled story. In the classics, somehow either the detective's clients or the bad guys or both always manipulate the hero, and this certainly happens to Thomas Black, too. But Emerson not only attaches manipulation to the detection, he also makes it the principal motive for the villains in his novels. In *The Rainy City* the novel turns on Angus Crowell's need to suppress evidence that two decades ago he accidentally killed his partner. Emerson returns to the motif of crime to cover up a crime again and again. Rev. Sam Wheeler commits several murders to camouflage his first mistake in *Nervous Laughter*. Fred and Margaret Pugsley die because Ashley Phillips doesn't want to be exposed as a child molester in *Fat Tuesday*. In *Deviant Behavior* Delores James commits a couple of murders to cover up her previous crimes. Floyd Boyd in *Yellow Dog Party* needs to clean up his past in preparation for achieving public office and turns to crime. Randolph Vanderhoef, in *The Vanishing Smile*, wants to keep secret that he is HIV positive. In each case the criminal possesses power, position, and wealth which make manipulation easier and, perhaps, more natural for them. Crowell is a wealthy, philanthropic industrialist, Wheeler is a well-known minister who volunteers as a counselor of runaway teens, Ashley Phillips is successful and public spirited, Floyd Boyd seems to be a shoo-in for congress, and Vanderhoef has a sporting goods empire. The only weird one is Delores James, but even this aging, hypochondriacal starlet is attached to the wealth and fame of legendary novelist and director Clayton James. And she, too, in her megalomania may have a connection with a couple of later villains, Jerome Johnson and Judson Bonneville. Opposed to all this wealth, power, and position, their victims have none. Thomas Black has neither wealth or position either—and doesn't want it. And in each case, for these people, covering up an old crime means creating new victims. Of course the most obvious victims are those characters who are murdered in the novels. But there are those, too, whose lives they consciously destroy without killing them. Thomas Black encounters a lot of them.

One such case is Eric Castle in *Fat Tuesday*. Cuckolded and framed for child molestation by Ashley Phillips, Castle becomes despised by his former associates, and loses his position, family, and possessions. He can't hold a steady job and is hounded by anonymous calls to employers. He lives isolated in embittered squalor, rejecting even Black's offers of help and friendship. Ashley Phillips engineered it all. But even at his death, Phillips believes in his own righteousness: "Okay, I played with a few kids. So what? What am I supposed to do? Kill myself? I didn't hurt anybody. And Fred? That was self-defense. He wanted to ruin my life. After all we meant to each other, he couldn't just forget what he found. I had to kill him. What did it matter if I put the blame on Eric? His life was wrecked anyway" (264). More disturbingly perverse is what happens in *The Rainy City*, in which Angus Crowell has spent his daughter's entire lifetime in a deliberate attempt to establish her as—indeed, to make her—mentally ill so as to protect himself from possible exposure of the crime that Melissa witnessed as a toddler:

Daddy deliberately played games with me, trying to destroy my credibility. And he did. Oh, how he did. Even I used to wonder about myself. He was always forcing me into situations where I had to lie or take the consequences. I remember when I was about six, he used to leave candy lying around the house, tell me not to take it, and then watch from the other room. Sometimes he'd let me take it and sometimes he'd catch me. If he caught me, he always did it when we had company. It was only when I grew more mature that I realized he did it all purposely. (232)

Emerson puts both the megalomaniac and the pathetic victim together in *The Portland Laugher*. In this novel everybody despises Billy Battle—

juvenile delinquent, arsonist, murderer, sadist, deviant. Everybody believes this and Kathy's pea-brained fiancé, Philip, even plans to assassinate him for the good of society. To complicate matters, Emerson draws Battle as something of a mixed character, not a virtuous, idiosyncratic, and suffering martyr like Castle. Except Battle never did any of the really bad things. Jerome Johnson did and always shifted the blame to Billy. Consequently, Billy's adult life mostly goes down the tubes. All this happens because Jerome is loopy. And control lies at the basis of his loopiness:

You'd be surprised how much control a god can exert. A snobby girl won't give a kid the time of day. Somebody steals her homework. Somebody makes a few dirty phone calls. Somebody puts her dog on a stick by her window. Pretty soon she's not quite so snobby. Pretty soon, she's having a nervous breakdown and the family is moving out of town. You may call it a god complex. You may call me a god. But remember the old saying, just because you're paranoid doesn't mean people aren't after you? Just because you have a god complex doesn't mean you aren't divine. (330)

As perverse as this seems, Emerson examines another and perhaps an even more disturbing kind of control in *The Million-Dollar Tattoo*. Here he creates Judson Bonneville as a Northern-Pacific version of Howard Hughes—unspeakably wealthy and equally mysterious. He buys whatever things and almost whatever people he wants. Bonneville decides that he does not like the man one of his daughters has married and so proceeds systematically to destroy him by dismantling his life:

Judson was never happy with my choice of a husband, but he decided there was nothing he could do about it. At least at first. I believe he gave Meade that first job with the intention of making it work, but then Meade got a little too familiar with him—something Judson hates. Meade thought they were close enough buddies that he could joke around with him. That was when my father pulled a few strings and made things go wrong with Meade's work. I went to Judson and blamed him. He denied it and then, just to prove he'd been right about Meade, he somehow tricked Meade into an affair with that woman. Later he tricked him into stealing money, which I *always* thought was a set-up. (262)

In *The Million-Dollar Tattoo*, however, Emerson plots what amounts to poetic justice with an ending in which the victim kills his tormentor and them himself.

It, however, may be something other than poetic justice. It may be just the way that Emerson's villains' deranged minds work. In some cases, if the bad guys had simply left things alone, their original crimes might have gone undetected. Without the elaborate shenanigans of the Yellow Dog Party, for instance, Floyd Boyd's past would have remained unexamined. She may have had to forego the loot, but the original murder would have remained on the record as a suicide if Delores James in *Deviant Behavior* had just let things alone. Then, too, the megalomania of Emerson's villains plays a part as well. Angus Crowell thinks that his wealth and position place him above the law: "They'll never pin Harry's death on me. I have too many friends. The absolute worst that could happen would be that I'd have to jump bail and leave the country. But I know plenty of places a man can live with my kind of money. Plenty of places where they can't extradite me" (*The Rainy City* 267). Tied to wealth and position, villains like Crowell have absolute faith in their own credibility. Thus in *Fat Tuesday*, even when he is chasing Black around the grounds and up the stairs of the Space Needle trying to nail him with a crossbow, Ashley Phillips continues to assume that no one will believe that he is a villain. In *Nervous Laughter*, Sam Wheeler's rhetorical power, in fact, almost moves Black to doubt his own reading of the evidence and accept the fiction Wheeler's twisted reality creates. In a number of instances, however, the bad guys just can't help bragging about their cleverness. "But this way is better because I get to talk to you. Tell you about it. The trouble with being a genius at this stuff is only dead people know about it. Even a genius needs applause" (*The Portland Laugher* 328). While, of course, this kind of braggadocio serves the author's purposes when it comes to unraveling the plot, it also serves as a kind of "murder will out" theme. Most of Emerson's bad guys participate in their own undoing by arrogantly assuming that they can control people and manage events. Probably this has something to do with brain chemistry—to which Emerson does allude. Somewhat typical of the genre, moreover, Emerson's detective can't be managed or controlled. Like almost every other gumshoe in the canon, his clients usually either fire or try to fire Black during the course of his investigations. Just as it is in the nature of evil to be self-destructive, the nature of private eyes insists that once they start looking for answers, they don't stop.

But in a couple of instances, Emerson adds something else to the wrap up of the cases. The hero becomes as much an observer as an investigator. In *The Rainy City*, for instance, to some extent Black goes along for the ride: Melissa's need to put her life together requires a confrontation with her father, and this prompts all of the revelations and the resolution at the end of the book. It's a villain's cupidity that brings about the exposure at the end of *Deception Pass*. In *The Million-Dollar Tattoo*, in fact, Black acts as a bystander to the resolution of evil. While

Black does eventually figure things out, the evil of the book is resolved when the victim, Meade Barber, kills his tormentor and then clears the slate of justice by killing himself. In the books after *The Vanishing Smile,* Black's contact with those associated with the crimes increasingly provokes his moral indignation. Thus his response to Vanderhoef, Bonneville, and Lainie Smith, the center of attention in *Deception Pass.* Perhaps significantly, while Black does play a role in tracking the villain down, Emerson ends *The Vanishing Smile* by giving Vanderhoef a redemptive death. Then in *The Million-Dollar Tattoo* Black does not play an active role in the resolution to Bonneville's evil, and in *Deception Pass* he impotently witnesses an ending that leaves the principal moral issues of the plot unresolved.

All of the nastiness in Emerson comes from people who think too much of themselves and who inflict misery on those who typically think too little of themselves and become victims. His challenge, then, is to place his hero somewhere in the middle of the continuum. Black possesses the kind of self-deprecation that has been typical of the American hero since Cooper. As opposed to self-inflation, he inclines toward the opposite. Take his description of the complexity of finding Lance Tyner in *Poverty Bay*: "It was almost a joke, a fiasco, a regular debacle. Martin Tyner could have unearthed his son in an hour. A one-eyed taxi driver with a wooden leg and no sense of humor could have cracked the case" (17). At the conclusion of the same book, Black reviews his experience with confronting a group of suspects: "An evening of exposing murderers in front of an audience was not something I had believed in, or been particularly adept at. The one time I had tried it, it had resulted in a choreographed routine of undiluted slapstick" (292). And when it comes to derring-do, Black consistently ascribes his success in fights to luck and a swell sucker-punch. Thus, in *Deception Pass*: "The only reason he didn't unscrew my head and talk directly to my brain was because I startled him" (31). Success doesn't go to Black's head. Even though once he begins a case he has the same kind of semi-obsessive tenacity as anyone in the private detective's guild, Emerson does remind readers that detecting is, after all, a job and Thomas Black has made a comfortable private life for himself and has a relationship that can provide him with all he can handle. This becomes even more important in the later books when troubling moral issues stand at the heart of the plots. Black's relationship with Kathy Birchfield perhaps delineates best why the hero differs from the villains. Black's life does not intersect with many people. There are anonymous cycling acquaintances and later on Snake and maybe even Bruno. But there is especially Kathy Birchfield. The chemistry is there and Emerson teases readers for six books with the ultimate nature of their relationship. For a number of years Kathy lives in Black's basement apartment, wanders upstairs uninvited, shares news of her dates, drags Black on outings, and involves him in cases. Throughout all of the books, Emerson describes Kathy as the spontaneous and essentially uninhibited person, in her dress and in her actions. All the books also show not so much Black's disinclination but his lack of capacity to manipulate or control his best friend. And in that he is fundamentally different from those who create the chaos that occurs in the novels.

A fair amount of what Thomas Black is all about as well as Emerson's view of the hard-boiled novel shows up in the language of his books. Thus far I have spent some time discussing the conventions of hard-boiled style and the apprenticeship that most writers of the seventies and eighties have served with Raymond Chandler. Emerson is no exception. All the epigraphs from Chandler are there for more than decoration. It doesn't take long to find all of the hallmarks of hard-boiled style in any of Emerson's books—hyperbole, action verbs, wisecracks, the whole palette. But he's particularly fond of similes. There are not only a lot of them in the books but he also gets a kick out of making them. Here's the clue. In *Yellow Dog Party* when Black and Kathy discuss the prospect of looking for the thugs, the exchange goes like this:

> "What do you think those goons are going to do when you show up?"
> "Help me color-coordinate my wardrobe?"
> "They're going to take that neck-brace and spin it like a duck's butt on a frozen pond."
> "Not bad. I'll give you a nine-point-one for that." (60)

And I suspect that Emerson would like his readers likewise to pause occasionally to hold up cards rating the ingenuity of his similes with 9.5s and maybe even 10s on them. Here's an Emerson simile sampler:

Burton looked like a man in a Chinese restaurant who'd just been informed that his bill was six thousand dollars, no charge for the fortune cookies. (*The Rainy City* 26)

She struggled with her reply, grasping the small purse in her hands tighter and tighter, like a nervous starling fixing itself on a sun-hot wire. (*Poverty Bay* 48)

I wondered why my stomach suddenly felt as if I had swallowed a quart of warm grease. (*Poverty Bay* 87)

The air felt like the air in a cramped, unventilated bathroom five minutes after someone had drawn a hot tub. (*Poverty Bay* 201)

He was living like fungus on the bottom of last year's pumpkin. (*Fat Tuesday* 37)

The slacks were a pinch too long like those of a schoolboy whose mother bought everything for him to grow into. (*Fat Tuesday* 76)

You look like the cat dragged you through a hundred miles of backyards. (*Yellow Dog Party* 139)

My lawn looked like a battalion of tiny green bayonets poking through the white. (*The Vanishing Smile* 136)

For a moment I was as giddy as a librarian with a brand-new tea bag. (*The Vanishing Smile* 9)

My chest felt as if it had been collapsed and reinflated with air from a dusty old basement. (*The Million-Dollar Tattoo* 166)

It was almost five-thirty and my eyeballs felt as if they'd been rolled in sand and dropped into a wool pocket. (*The Million-Dollar Tattoo* 27)

The solid musculature of his back began rolling around under me so that it felt like I was holding down a snake with a plastic fork. (*Deception Pass* 144)

a set of atrophied legs that protruded awkwardly to one side from hips as thin as a folding chair. (*Catfish Cafe* 33)

A couple here touch on the senses (warm grease, humidity-laden air, basement air, and the combination of grit and wool), one turns a cliché (the cat dragged in), two reference the behavior of fauna (starling and snake), two the nature of flora (grass and pumpkins), one uses satire (the librarian and her tea-bag), one cites a bizarre nightmare (the Chinese restaurant), and one summons up a recollection of youth. They are concrete and surprising, just what hard-boiled similes are supposed to be. Additionally, even in these few examples, Emerson displays a fairly extensive range in his choice of the second element in the simile.

The sampler, to be sure, represents only a very small fraction of the similes in Emerson's books. He uses a lot of them. By my count, Emerson averages right around one hundred and forty similes per book, with

Fat Tuesday taking first place with one hundred and eighty-one similes in the two hundred and seventy-five pages of the Ballantine paperback edition. While Emerson's similes display a considerable variety in length and function, his most characteristic similes occupy more space than most. In *Nervous Laughter*, for example, fifty-six similes have five or more words. In fact *Nervous Laughter* contains Emerson's longest simile: "The four chaps abetting him looked like farmers from the Mekong Delta, recently emigrated with enough English to get them a basket of Bok Choy at Safeway and a tank of unleaded at the local service station" (49). The length equals richness of description. Check out the descriptors in the example I just cited: farmers, Mekong Delta, recently emigrated, enough English, Bok Choy at Safeway, tank of unleaded at the service station. It even uses four proper nouns. This is where the epigraphs from Raymond Chandler mean the most. While neither he nor any contemporary writer can match Chandler, Emerson understands some of what Chandler did stylistically and strives to incorporate it into his own works. And this doesn't mean simply attempting to measure up to the verbal surprise and aptness of Chandler's similes, it also means striving to touch the common world of readers through the subject matter of the simile.

Similes are meant to expand readers' insight by comparing something unknown or indefinite to something with which readers are familiar. Reconstructing that common ground, the world that authors presume will put them in contact with their readers' understanding and sympathy, ought to say something about their intent, or at least about the consistency of their vision. If we take a look at Emerson's similes, this seems to be the case.

Taking all of the books together, there are some subjects with which Emerson doesn't bother with very much: art, history, literature, music—none of them appears often in the similes. There aren't even the stream of references to other detectives or detective writers that has been a convention of the detective story since the twenties. Even though Black and Birchfield call each other Ward and June, Cisco and Pancho, Emerson's similes rarely use television as their point of common reference. Admittedly, he does summon up *Dragnet* in *The Million-Dollar Tattoo* (15), but that's it. In fact, Thomas and Kathy mostly watch PBS. He does occasionally bring films into his similes. There's citation of Robert Altman's films in *Deviant Behavior* (106), but most of Emerson's scattered allusions to films in his similes look back to older flicks: *The Wizard of Oz, Giant, Snow White*, and even D. W. Griffith's movies. But it's really Estleman's territory.

Emerson does bring into his similes those areas that one would expect to find in fiction originally intended for guys as well as the areas that have become conventional in hard-boiled similes since Chandler. Sports come into all of the novels, with boxing ("You went down like a white boxer," *Fat Tuesday* 203), football ("She swiveled around and pawed through a stack of notes on her desk, looking as if she'd birthed the entire Green Bay Packers front line," *Deception Pass* 134), and bowling ("They carried a stuffed pig that wore a lei and sunglasses, and we could see right away that all three of them were about as sharp as the leading edge of a bowling ball," *Fat Tuesday* 151) leading the way. Along with sports, Emerson's similes make reference to mechanical things: "like he dropped an engine block on you" (*The Vanishing Smile* 191); "like an outboard motor with a bad plug" (*Yellow Dog Party* 234); "like a cylinder was starting to miss" (*Deviant Behavior* 82). Coming more directly from the conventions of simile-making in hard-boiled writing, Emerson's books contain a lot of references to facts of common domestic life. Hence these: "like something left over from dinner" (*The Rainy City* 104); "like somebody slapping a rug with a broom handle" (*The Portland Laugher* 298); "as a line of laundry after a June rain" (*Deviant Behavior* 95); "like a dirty dishrag steeped in hot water" (*Deviant Behavior* 28). All of the cat and dog references in Emerson's similes probably belong in this category as well. Just as with domestic references, connections to rural life have long been a standard feature of hard-boiled style. Take this sample from Emerson: "like a nervous chicken after the hound has been shooed out of the coop" (*The Rainy City* 40); "like a farmer conniving a calf into a slaughtering pen" (*Poverty Bay* 79); "like a terrified heifer that had fallen out of a truck" (*Poverty Bay* 212); "like some people yodeled hogs out of a wallow" (*Poverty Bay* 265); "like a pig trough at feeding time" (*Deviant Behavior* 22). Typically, though, rural references in hard-boiled similes also connect to wry country humor. In *The Portland Laugher*, for example, Emerson uses both "like a pig on roller skates" (29) and "like the back end of a dizzy pig in trousers" (142). By returning again and again to similes that use domestic and rural images, hard-boiled writers assume that they relate the experience in the narrative with something essential about their audience, that they make connections because they embody the experience of the common person whose existence centers on the domestic. Additionally, they assume that the common person's experience is rural—even though it hasn't been for a long time. And Emerson does the same thing.

Emerson's similes, however, also reflect on another area of common experience. In examining the books, one can find an awful lot of similes that refer to children and childhood:

like a child concealing a pocketful of snitched cookies. (*The Rainy City* 15) like the sixth grade bully extorting baseball cards from a third grader. (*Poverty Bay* 169)

like a nerd in his first self-defense class. (*Nervous Laughter* 48)

like a little boy his mother had just put into his Sunday best. (*Fat Tuesday* 169)

as a raw egg on a school bus. (*Deviant Behavior* 165)

as if I were a child caught playing with a cigarette lighter. (*Yellow Dog Party* 53)

like a couple of sixth-grade girls who'd found a dirty book. (*The Portland Laugher* 141)

like a couple of twelve-year-olds who had only just discovered the telephone. (*The Vanishing Smile* 57)

like a mischievous ninth-grader who'd just successfully phoned his first dirty nine-hundred number. (*The Million-Dollar Tattoo* 205)

as if some monster child had mixed all of the day's watercolors together until there was no real hue at all. (*Deception Pass* 58)

like a boy who had to pee after a long car trip. (*Catfish Cafe* 202)

In fact, Emerson uses childhood in his similes more frequently than any other subject—even food. And most of these references dwell on the nastiness of children or the agony of childhood: thus in addition to those cited above we find actions and reactions like those of "unregenerate kids" (*Poverty Bay* 61), "eerie children" (*Poverty Bay* 157), "scared students" (*Poverty Bay* 276), a "sadistic kid" (*Nervous Laughter* 195), an "angry child" (*Nervous Laughter* 203), an "oversexed adolescent pervert" (*Nervous Laughter* 240), a "nervous kid" (*Yellow Dog Party* 4), "drymouthed high school boys" (*Yellow Dog Party* 23), a "high school nobody" (*Yellow Dog Party* 174), a "naughty child" (*Vanishing Smile* 3), a "kid lying" (*Vanishing Smile* 35), a "panicky kid" (*Vanishing Smile* 197), and an "idiot schoolkid" (*Portland Laugher* 167). In these instances, children and looking back at childhood are no picnic.

But then again, the Emerson similes that draw upon adult professions and roles don't offer much in the way of an alternative. In them he refers to pimps and whores, executioners, down-on-their-luck salesmen, grease monkeys, drunks, bikers, carnival barkers, pickpockets, and debt collectors—not an ophthalmologist or entomologist in the canon and no references to responsibility or duty. On the level of similes at least, adulthood seems a depressing place to be. Emerson, for example, compares Burton Nadisky to "a last-place marathon runner" (*Rainy City* 51) and cites a report that Elmer Slezak "looked like a guy waiting for the right time to kill himself" (*Yellow Dog Party* 106).

With all of this in mind, the question remains, how does Emerson's figurative language, the similes in particular, serve the purposes of his books? We can take as a given that it puts them squarely in the camp of hard-boiled fiction and the school of Chandler. But that could simply mean they're there as wallpaper, for in too many writers the stylistic elements simply decorate an empty room. The case seems different with Emerson, especially in the tension between the images that portray childhood as an awkward and difficult time and those that portray adulthood as seedy and sordid. It's borne out in the novels. Children live blighted and damaged lives and most of the adults do too. Obviously the bad guys do. The incidental characters in Emerson, however, mostly live vapid, pre-packaged lives—the TV watchers in *The Rainy City*, and the Steebs with their carpet empire in *Nervous Laughter*, for example. Not a lot of good choices here. But Emerson provides Black and Birchfield with a third alternative, the alternative of creating, insofar as they can, the spontaneity and joy that should belong to childhood in the midst of and around the edges of their adult lives and adult burdens. And in their success they demonstrate that youth is wasted on the young.

ROBERT CRAIS

Robert Parker's hero only has one name, a name taken from a sixteenth-century English poet. Robert Crais' hero has two, the first one taken from the King of Rock and Roll. To date, Crais has written seven novels about that hero, Elvis Cole: *The Monkey's Raincoat* (1987), *Stalking the Angel* (1989), *Lullaby Town* (1992), *Free Fall* (1993), *Voodoo River* (1995), *Sunset Express* (1996), and *Indigo Slam* (1997). Each one of the books participates wholeheartedly in the traditions of the hard-boiled story. In the first one, almost as we have come to expect, Crais quotes (actually misquotes) Chandler: "Ah, Hollywood. *Down these mean streets, a man must walk who is himself not mean. How mean ARE they???? So mean . . . well, just ask Morton Lang*" (*Monkey's Raincoat* 83, author's italics). Unlike some of his peers who have little good to say about Spenser or his creator, Crais adopts and adapts some of the things that Robert B. Parker gathered around about the hard-boiled hero when he gave the form new life and new readership in the 1970s. But he does more than this.

So what is it about Parker that Crais finds appealing enough to build upon? First of all, it's the yuppification of the form. After the first couple of books, Parker decided that minimalism by and large has little to recommend it. As we have seen, he dresses Spenser and his associates in expensive, brand-name clothes and gives them a style of living that is the aspiration and the envy of his readers. No more two room, cold water flats, threadbare suits, wheezing cars spurned by Rent-A-Wreck, or Spam washed down with store-brand beer. Who knows what a cold water flat is or wears suits, anyway? To some extent, we can see the same thing in Crais. Elvis' ride is pretty classy: he drives a "Jamaica-yellow" 1966 Corvette. While his own dress emphasizes casual nonchalance—white Levis and a Hawaiian shirt the first time he appears in the books—Elvis notices, and identifies, the expensive clothes and accessories other characters wear: Wesley Barron, Versace, Giorgio Armani, Rolex, etc. He, after all, is the Hollywood Detective. He doesn't even quote a daily rate to his clients, but works for a lump-sum of two thousand dollars per case. Even though it's secluded, Elvis' A-frame off Woodrow Wilson Drive is in Hollywood. He takes pride in his office, and, like Spenser, has a woman in a neighboring office to ogle. While Crais doesn't rise to Parker's level of epicurianism, Elvis hardly survives on McDonald's or Froot Loops—both of which he derides. From the beginning, though, Elvis drinks Falstaff rather than Anchor Steam beer.

Along with the Falstaff, Crais does do a number of things to miti-gate the yuppiness of his hero. First of all, we learn that Elvis did most of the work on his A-frame himself—instead of having to go off to build a cabin in the wilderness to demonstrate his competence and work-ethic. In fact, unlike Parker, Crais lets his hero's archetypal small town origins show through in a number of places. First of all, Elvis muses on the alienness of Southern California weather in *The Monkey's Raincoat*: "Where I grew up, there was much rain of the beating, pounding, falling-in-sheets variety that Southern California almost never enjoys" (146). In *Lullaby Town* there's nostalgia about nature: "The cold air and the winter woods smell made me think of when I was a boy, hunting in the autumn for squirrel and whitetail deer, and I felt the peace that comes from being alone in a wild place" (97). *Free Fall* has both nostalgia for the other place that is not Los Angeles: "It was a clean, healthy smell, and made me think, as it always does, of open country and little boys and girls climbing trees and chasing fireflies . . . There are no fireflies in Los Angeles" (108) and reflections on places like Dayton, or Pleasantville, or the dreamland of sixties television:

San Vincente was nicer, with interesting shops and elegant cafes and palatial homes that somehow seemed attainable, as if the people within them got there by working hard, and were still the type of folks who would give you a smile if you passed them on the sidewalk. Sort of like the Cleavers or the Ricardos. (29)

But these things alone do not by themselves entirely undercut the strata of yearning for affluence one finds in Parker. Crais does this also by his drawing of the details of his hero's inner life, upon which I will com-ment later, by describing Elvis' cat, and by introducing his partner, Joe Pike.

Somebody must have already done a Sunday supplement fluff piece on detectives and their pets going all the way back to Sherlock Holmes and his pooch. How many Schnauzers—or terriers of any variety for that matter—have been named "Asta"? How many hard-boiled detectives have pets? Well, as we've seen, Vic Warshawski shares a dog with her downstairs neighbor. Andrew Vachss' Burke has Pansy, a 140-pound Neapolitan Mastiff. And Spenser and Susan have Pearl the Wonder Dog. It's hard to look tough walking down the mean streets toting a pooper-scooper, but then again, maybe Boston's sanitation laws aren't very strict. Pet people just don't fit very well into the hard-boiled milieu—except perhaps for people with whom cats choose to associate. Elvis

Cole is one of them. Crais describes the cat who lives in Elvis' house in every book. Here's the passage from *Stalking the Angel*:

There was a black cat crouched under a Weber charcoal grill I keep out there. He's big, and he's mean, and he's black all over except for the white scars that lace his fur like spider-webs. He keeps one ear up and one ear sort of cocked to the side because someone once shot him. Head shot. He hasn't been right since.
. . .
The cat crept out from beneath the Weber, walked over, and sniffed at my beer. I poured a little out onto the deck for him and touched his back as he drank. It was soft.
Sometimes he bites, but not always. (25-26)

The cat tolerates Elvis, but displays uniform hostility toward almost everyone else who visits the A-frame. Indeed, Elvis sometimes projects speculation about the human condition on to the cat. Alone, tough, damaged, surviving, unpredictable, but soft: the cat isn't such a bad metaphor for the classic hard-boiled hero. He likes beer, too. The cat also tolerates Joe Pike, with whom he shares some characteristics.

Pike owes some things to Parker's depiction of Hawk in the Spenser books. It used to be that the hard-boiled hero traveled alone. When he defined the genre in "The Simple Art of Murder," Chandler insisted on the hero's essential aloneness. When he introduced Hawk, however, Parker changed the formula. The hero now has a sidekick, a buddy. Of course this says a lot about the way in which the hero's character gets defined. No matter how limited it is, the hero now belongs to a group and is no longer quite an outsider. As I have already shown, with Hawk Parker also set the pattern of focusing expertise in violence and violence based on simplistic and often hyper-moral principles in the character of the partner. This, in turn, gave rise to subsequent partner characters like Burke's Clete Purcell and Mosley's Raymond "Mouse" Alexander. Strangely enough, drawing one-dimensional characters like these creates the opportunity for writers to make their heroes both simpler and more complex. On one hand, they do not really have to come to terms with inclinations toward simplistic judgments and spontaneous violence in themselves because these reside in another character. On the other hand, the characters of their partners along with their acts often force the heroes to consider the human implications of violence, vigilante justice, self-reliance, and friendship.

Anyway, Joe Pike is not so much a one-dimensional character as he is one who in 1975 chose to simplify everything about his life:

"People change."

"You haven't changed since 1975."

"Other people." (*The Monkey's Raincoat* 131)

Although he owns the detective agency with Elvis, he stays at his gun shop and never goes to his office, which is always vacant. He invariably wears the same thing: faded jeans, a gray sweat-shirt with the sleeves cut off, and blue Nikes. Day and night he wears "government issue pilot's sunglasses." "He never smiles. He never laughs" (*The Monkey's Raincoat* 80). In conversation he asks no questions and makes no comments. When he speaks, Pike uses the fewest words possible. The greeting on his answering machine, for example, is "Speak." Throughout the books, Crais connects Pike with atavistic, natural, and mechanical forces. In *The Monkey's Raincoat* he's a force from the past: "Pike moving like something from another age, like part of a medieval mist, slewing down over the ground and between the trees without apparent effort. The jaberwock" (179). Pike is the panther in *Free Fall*: "When he moved, he seemed to glide, as if he were flowing over the surface of the earth, moving as a panther might move. To move was to stalk. I'd never seen him move any other way" (99). And in *Stalking the Angel* there is Pike the machine: "Pike moved without hesitation or doubt, as precise and controlled as a well-made machine" (61). In the first few books Crais uses martial arts to form part of both Elvis' and Pike's characters, but with Pike they also help to delineate who he is: "Think of a samurai. I said. A warrior who requires order. That's Pike" *(The Monkey's Raincoat* 153). "No one will see him and no one will hear him. You ever see a ninja movie? That's Pike" (*Lullaby Town* 147). Mixed in with this is Pike the mercenary: "But sometimes he goes to places like El Salvador or Botswana or the Sudan. So I guess that makes him a part-time professional soldier" (*The Monkey's Raincoat* 152). And then there's violence: as he says to Elvis in *Lullaby Town*, "I have the capacity for great violence" (310). A lot of this follows the same pattern Parker used for Hawk. So does the gratification Pike derives from mortal challenges—"If it were easy, it wouldn't be fun" (*Free Fall* 175)—and his occasional jocular self-confidence ("I'm too good even for me" [*Stalking the Angel* 93]) does, too.

So, like Hawk, Pike exudes purposefulness, awe, and danger. There's more than a bit of adolescent male wish-fulfillment here. But Crais does more with Pike. First he creates a question about his past that he does not answer. Although he repeatedly tells readers that Pike resigned from his job as a police officer and often includes the antipathy the cops feel toward him, Crais also repeatedly declines to explain why any of this happened. More importantly, he includes in Pike's character both adherence to consummate order and occasional insights into the losses that this state brings with it. Hence the arrows on Pike's deltoids: "The arrows point forward and are not a fashion statement. They are a statement of being" (*Sunset Express* 85). Acting as opposed to just believing is important to Pike. Thus his reply to Elvis' assertion in *The Monkey's Raincoat* that Morton Lang "gave himself up": "No. He gave nothing. He lost himself. The distinction is important" (82). Especially in the later books, though, Crais—insofar as it is possible with a character as tight-lipped as Pike—brings out a sensitive side to Pike. Thus in *Sunset Express* we get this passage: "Joe Pike stepped to the gate and murmured something I couldn't hear. Pike didn't seem threatening now. He seemed gentle and calming" (213). Later in the same book he expresses concern for the state of Elvis' relationship with Lucy Chenier:

> "Is it going any better with Lucy?"
> "Not yet, but soon. I'm about to turn on the charm."
> "Why don't you try working it out instead?" (267)

But this acknowledgment of a humane side to Pike's character is not simply a late addition. From the first book Pike recognizes the existence and the value of approaches to life other than the one to which he adheres. This comes out in a conversation between Elvis and Ellen Lang:

> "The arrows."
> "Yeah. The arrows allow him to impose order on chaos. A professional soldier needs that."
> She thought about it. "And that's what you are?"
> "Not me. I'm just a private cop. I am the antithesis of order."
> "He said you were a better soldier than he." (*The Monkey's Raincoat* 153)

This statement shows both the similarities between Pike and Elvis and their differences, differences that make Elvis the detective and Pike the silent partner and minor participant in the intellectual and even in the physical action of the books.

In all of the novels, during his idle moments, Elvis makes up titles for himself: thus it's Elvis Cole, "the World's Greatest Detective"; "the Perfect Detective"; "the Bumpkin Detective"; "Master Detective"; "Smooth Detective"; "detective for the nineties"; "Happy Detective"; "Family Detective"; "Master of Instant Rapport"; and "Professional Thug." He's all of them and, of course, none of them, because Elvis creates most of these titles as he reflects on his own failures. Elvis also could be the Ironic Detective—but even this captures little of what Crais' hero is all about. Maybe the toys in his office capture a bit more. In every book Crais mentions the Pinocchio clock with eyes that move from side to side, the Mickey Mouse phone, and the figurines of Jiminy Cricket lined up on the desk. First of all, these things are toys, but they are also mementos and links to the fantasy world of childhood. They're like the kids' television shows Elvis watches: he mentions, for instance, *Sesame Street, Rocky and Bullwinkle, 3-2-1 Contact.* Crais includes all of this because childhood holds special importance for his hero. In *Lullaby Town* and *Free Fall* Crais includes passages of sentiment in which Elvis identifies with children and childhood:

Sometimes when I practice in the early evening, the two little boys who live in the cantilevered house down the street come over and watch and we talk about things that are important to small boys. I find that they are important to me, too. (*Lullaby Town* 55)

Mesquite smoke: It was a clean, healthy smell, and made me think, as it always does, of open country and little boys and girls climbing trees and chasing fire-flies. Maybe I was one of the little boys. Maybe I still am. (*Free Fall* 108)

But there's more to it than this. In the first book in his conversations with Ellen Lang Elvis provides the fundamental logic for his attachment to childhood:

I learned [in Vietnam] that I could survive. I learned what I would do to keep breathing, and what I wouldn't do, and what was important to me, and what wasn't. (*The Monkey's Raincoat* 39)

There were some real disadvantages to being there [Vietnam], yes . . . But adversity has a way of strengthening. If it doesn't kill you, you learn things. For instance, that's when I learned I wanted to be Peter Pan. (38)

You're eighteen years old. You're sitting in a rice paddy. Most guys give it up. I decided that eighteen was too young to be old. I work at maintaining myself. (57)

Here Elvis is not talking about childhood yearnings for surfing or video games or first dates or hooking school or any of the things children actu-ally do.

Part of childhood resides in the freedom of playful fantasy. That's what he's talking about. And since Crais makes it easy to find things about Elvis, it's easy to find this in his hero. When not written to include dialogue, Crais' usual practice is to end paragraphs of Elvis' narration with a summary sentence. He provides, in effect, Elvis' personal comment about people, places, and acts in these locations. An awful lot of these terminal sentences begin with "maybe." Check out this passage from *Lullaby Town*:

Karen Nelson had no phone in either name, but I had sort of expected that. After ten years, the odds were large that she had remarried. The credit cards were another matter. If she had a credit card under Nelson or Shipley listed as a former name, she should've turned up. That was odd, but there were explanations. *Maybe* she had joined a cult and no longer had a name. *Maybe* she had given over all earthly traits and artifacts to a higher being named Klaatu, and in return Klaatu had blessed her with eternal bliss and escape from snoopy private cops. Or *maybe* she didn't like credit cards.

I had run through all of my leads and had come up with nothing and it made me feel small. I needed another line. *Maybe I should ask Klaatu.* (56-57, my emphasis)

That's how he works. Sometimes he makes up zany scenarios for his experiences with mundane people and events. Here's a selected list of some more of Elvis' "maybes" from the first four books:

Maybe I'd spoken Russian without realizing it and confused her. (*The Monkey's Raincoat* 54)

Maybe severe public reprimands. (*The Monkey's Raincoat* 158)

Maybe I could put a one and write zeroes until my arm fell off, and endorse it Elvis Cole, Yachtsman. (*Stalking the Angel* 9)

Maybe with the white jacket and the convertible and the blank check in my pocket, someone would think I was Donald Trump. (*Stalking the Angel* 9)

Maybe Bradley Warren had bought the place from the Munsters. (*Stalking the Angel* 11)

Maybe I would wake up and find myself in a 7-Eleven parking lot and think, *Oh Elvis, ha ha, you really dreamed up some zingo clients this time.* (*Stalking the Angel* 50)

Maybe if you got too near the wall, thugs in chain mail poured boiling oil on you from the parapets. (*Lullaby Town* 4)

Maybe, like Pinocchio, she was a wooden puppet he had brought to life. (*Lullaby Town* 27)

Maybe he knew who to call to find out where the action was, and upon making the call, he and his buddy were going to whatever it was I didn't know about. Maybe I could go with them. (*Lullaby Town* 36-37)

Maybe Pike could see through walls. (*Lullaby Town* 243)

Maybe if I went down to the bank and had the forty changed to ones, it would feel like more. (*Free Fall* 9)

Maybe they thought we were the CBS version of the Universal stunt show. (*Free Fall* 98)

Teleportation, maybe. (*Free Fall* 105)

If the neighbors saw us sitting there, maybe they would think we were scouting for the NBA. (*Free Fall* 138)

Every one comes from the end of a paragraph, and every one only has Elvis himself as its audience. Every one adds fancy to the reality—often intransigent or confusing reality—Elvis has just experienced. This is one of the parts of childhood to which Elvis clings most tightly. But other aspects of childhood also play a significant role in Elvis' character.

Crais specifically connects childhood with fundamental values. Thus "All good things are in childhood. Innocence. Loyalty. Truth" precedes the passage "You're eighteen years old. You're sitting in a rice paddy" cited above. That's why Crais includes Pinocchio references: they're moral. He quotes part of the code of childhood to Janet Simon in *The Monkey's Raincoat*: "Prove yourself brave, truthful, and unselfish, and someday you will be a real boy. The Blue Fairy said that in Pinocchio" (58). And he quotes again from Pinocchio in *Stalking the Angel* when he says to the teenaged Mimi Warren,

"Because I am the Lord High Keeper of the Knowledge of Right and Wrong, and I am trying to figure out what to do."

She blinked at me.

"Jiminy Cricket said that," I said. "He was also Counselor in Moments of Temptation, and Guide Along the Straight and Narrow Path. You need that." (180)

On top of the biblical reference in the last part, this probably has some connection with Pike's arrows. It also has a lot to do with the role Elvis takes on in all Crais' novels.

When Elvis observes that "All good things are in childhood. Innocence. Loyalty. Truth," what he probably means is that children believe that adults revere, uphold, and act according to these ideals. Children believe that adults are responsible, that they behave responsibly and accept as a matter of faith their obligation to be responsible for themselves and, especially, for their children. In every novel this becomes an issue, not only with respect to children but also with respect to adults as well. And Elvis acts as the adult who is responsible both to truth and for the welfare of those around him. First the welfare of innocents. In *Lullaby Town*, for example, a number of problems beset Karen Lloyd, chiefly her famous, arrogant ex-husband and the Mafia. When events reach a crisis in the novel, she has the following exchange with Elvis:

"I have a B.A. in finance. I am Toby Lloyd's mother. I will not lose those things."
"No. You won't."
"I will not lose who I am."
"I won't let you." (238)

And Elvis and Pike make sure that she comes out of the chaos that people and circumstances have thrust upon her without losing herself. They act as the protective parents. In the most recent book, *Indigo Slam*, Crais again shows Elvis' nurturing side. During the course of his search for the Hewitt children's father, he has this exchange with fifteen-year-old Teri, the eldest:

She looked at the floor. "I'm all they have. If I fall apart, who will take care of Winona and Charles?"
I stared at her. "What about you? Who do you have?"
She pursed her lips. When she spoke, her voice was small and soft. "I don't have anyone."
I shook my head. "No, that's not true. You have me." (145)

But committed friendship and surrogate parenthood can only do so much in a world predicated upon self-indulgence, weakness, and confusion. There's also the business about truth, in which children are supposed to believe. In terms of the novels, truth means doing what is right, and what is moral. It also means doing what is just, and Lucy Chenier defines justice for Elvis in *Sunset Express*: "The law is an adversarial contest that defines justice as staying within the rules and seeing the game to its conclusion. Justice is reaching a conclusion. . . . The law gives us order. Only men and women give us what you want to call justice" (371). And Elvis makes it his responsibility to make conclusions happen. Indeed, he quite literally forces people to acknowledge and fulfill their duties to others. It happens first with respect to children. Thus in *Stalking the Angel* he confronts Bradley Warren with his daughter's accusations of sexual abuse:

I stared at Bradley Wilson past the Dan Wesson [Elvis' handgun], and then I moved a half step closer. I said, "I'm told that what has happened here is complex and that you are not what we less sophisticated types call a bad man. That may be. I don't give a rat's ass if you are helped in this process or not. I don't care if you have to fake every moment of therapy for the next ten years. You will see to it that everything that can be done to help your daughter will be done. *If you do not, I will kill you, Bradley.*" (201; my emphasis)

But in later books Elvis concentrates the same kind of ardor in forcing characters to live up to their obligations both to themselves and the law. In *Free Fall* there is this confrontation with police officer Mark Thurman:

"He had a brother named James Edward and a mother and a grandfather." The muscles across the back and the tops of my shoulders felt tight and knotted. I dug my fingers into his face and neck and pressed. "You have been a part of something bad. It's unfair, and it's ugly, and you didn't know what you were supposed to do, but now you do, and you have to be man enough to stand up. If you don't Ida Leigh Washington will have lost two sons for nothing and *I will not allow that.*" (226, my emphasis)

Elvis does quite the same thing—uses the same words, in fact—in *Voodoo River* when he discovers the complexities and grief brought about by a miasma of prejudice and denial. This time it's with Sheriff Jo-el Boudreaux. "Your choices are limited, Jo-el. The one choice you do not have is inaction. Inaction has led to this and *I will not allow it to continue*" (298, my emphasis). In these instances Elvis reenacts the childhood fantasy that pain can be healed, loneliness banished, justice enacted, and innocence restored if only one (again in the words of the Blue Fairy) can "prove yourself brave, truthful, and unselfish." Some of it seems like Parker.

One doesn't have to read many of the Spenser books to realize that for Parker most troubles grow from the difficulties characters have with defining their roles in male-female relationships and with nurturing children. In most of the novels Spenser acts as much as a psychiatric social worker as he does a private detective. Well, he does beat people up, but mostly he helps women characters toward personhood and he helps neglected children toward healthy maturity. Thus Susan pinpoints his motivation in the following exchange in *Looking for Rachel Wallace*:

"You were brought up with a fierce sense of family. But you haven't got a family, and so you transfer that great sea of protective impulse to clients, and me."

"Maybe not you, but usually clients need protection."

"Yes. That's probably why you're in business. You need people who need protection. Otherwise what would you do with the impulse?" (92-93)

Reviewing the sections from Crais I've quoted above, Elvis looks a lot like Spenser for the nineties. In the first novel, as in Parker's *Promised Land*, Elvis helps a woman who draws all of her self-esteem from her role as wife and mother realize a larger extent of her personhood and the value of independence. The same issue lies at the center of the plot in *Lullaby Town*, and, to a lesser extent, in *Sunset Express. Stalking the Angel* involves Elvis with the issues of child neglect among the affluent and child sexual abuse, just as *Indigo Slam* brings in the dilemma of abandoned children. *Voodoo River* begins with the agony of finding birth parents of an adopted child. Seems like they could be supplementary readings in a social work course on the family. While Parker's books could be used as readings to make such a course zippier, however, Crais' books wouldn't work out too well. Sure, in *The Monkey's Raincoat* Elvis talks to Ellen Lang about her self-image and getting out of her subservient rut, but after that, even though personal and family problems appear in Crais' novels, the dynamic of human situations becomes more complex. Though most of them end happily, many of the books acknowledge that some problems defy old formulas, have no simple solutions, and the human heart can be twisted beyond recognition. Therapy isn't the answer. And some of them, *Stalking the Angel* and *Sunset Express* in particular, do not end happily.

Actually the erosion of certainty starts off in the first book. In part, *The Monkey's Raincoat* rests on the assumption of Morton Lang's worthlessness: he fails in business, runs off with a bimbo, and gets mixed up with dopers and mobsters. For most of the novel, on the character level, Elvis focuses on helping Ellen Lang rebuild her life and the assumption persists that Mort was a loser without redeeming qualities. But then, at the very end of the novel, Elvis, in effect, partly resuscitates Morton

Lang's reputation when, almost out of the blue, he tells Ellen that "Mort wasn't kidnapped and Mort wasn't dealing with these people. Duran's goons took the boy and Mort went after them. That's where the .32 was. Mort wasn't there for you any more, but he tried to be there for Perry. He died trying to save his boy" (200). This kind of reevaluation becomes one of the central character issues in the second book, *Stalking the Angel*. The ambiguity of good and evil strikes Elvis at the beginning of the novel when he has to extort information from Malcolm Denning, a likable dealer in Asian artifacts with a history of criminal associations:

I watched the sad eyes. He was a nice man. Maybe even a good man. Sometimes, in this job, you wonder how someone managed to take the wrong turn. You wonder where it happened and when and why. But you really don't want to know. If you knew, it would break your heart. (24)

And Crais includes more profound and more personal reevaluations at the end. First, there is the death of Eddie Tang, a yakuza gangster and seemingly one of the chief bad guys in the novel. In *Stalking the Angel* the Samurai tradition plays a significant role, and Pike refers to it when he transforms Eddie's death from mindless savagery into a meaningful act. The most significant reassessment in *Stalking the Angel*, however, comes with the character of Mimi Warren, the teenager whose salvation becomes the central focus of the novel. What becomes apparent at the end of the book, however, is that Mimi may have fabricated the traumas from which Elvis seeks to save her: her father may not have sexually abused her and she definitely staged her own kidnapping. Thus, the end of the novel finds the hero without certainty about what has happened and about himself: "'I assumed a lot of things that were wrong. I needed her to be a victim, so that's the way I saw her.' I looked at Joe. 'Maybe she wasn't'" (254). In *Lullaby Town*, Crais largely takes a break from the problematic issues of certainty about human motives. Elvis and Pike solve problems and make characters better people. They straighten out Karen Lloyd's life and in the process deflate the arrogance of Peter Alan Nelson. But in this pollyannaish fiction, Crais inserts Elvis' admiration for consistent behavior even among gangsters ("Sal knew how a man acts. You behaved like a man behaves," 312) and the universal qualities of human nature possessed even by the wicked ("Sal and Karen Lloyd. Each worried about their children," 281). *Free Fall*, however, returns, once again, to examine the painful human dilemmas associated with crime. Here police officer Mark Thurman must confront his role as an accessory to a murder by one of his fellow officers. In the novel Crais has Elvis fabricate a plan that will allow Thurman to survive the debacle created by his fellow officers but then dashes it to pieces when the video-taped evidence is destroyed. Even though his past acts deny Thurman the opportunity to fulfill his ambition to continue as a police officer, however, Crais does allow him to build a new life for himself, one possible because of Jennifer's love for him. And Crais continues the love theme in *Voodoo River*, with Elvis and Lucy falling in love with each other. Here, however, Crais does make the complications of motive an ancillary issue, illustrated by Elvis' reflections about the death of Jimmie Ray Rebenack: "He was a goof and an extortionist, but somewhere near his final moment a young woman had called and said that she loved him" (137) and by two other brief ruminations on the human condition:

I thought I had known why I was coming back, but now I didn't. Maybe I was expecting to find some great evil, but instead there was only a frightened woman and the greedy men around her. (170)

The cat crept out onto the deck and sat downwind, barely visible in the dark. Watching. I often consider, *Does he wonder at the human heart?* (183)

Elvis returns to the enigma of the human heart in *Sunset Express*, a novel in which injustice goes unpunished and unavenged, after hearing of Lucy's abusive ex-husband: "There are those times when intellect fails us. There are those moments when the modern man fades to a shadow and something from the brain stem reasserts itself, and in that moment the joking is gone and we frighten ourselves with our dark potential" (271-72). And while *Sunset Express* provides a clear-cut example of good and evil, in his most recent book Crais returns to blurring distinctions. In *Indigo Slam*, Clark Hewitt abandons his children for prolonged periods, and returns to his trade as a counterfeiter. Rather than being irresponsible, however, Hewitt's actions are the only way in which he can provide security for his children after his imminent death from cancer. Indeed, in the middle of the action Elvis and Pike, in effect, change sides and become his allies. Nothing, then, in the world Elvis inhabits is simple.

The hero's diction, in fact, echoes the problematic human situations he encounters in the books. That Elvis begins a number of the paragraph summary sentences I've described above with "maybe" and "probably" connects, as we have seen, to the childlike attitude he wishes to cultivate for himself as a refuge from chaos. But probably it's more than that. Take *Free Fall*, for example. Crais begins twenty-three final paragraph sentences in the novel with "maybe" and four with "probably." That's a lot. And they're not all playful. Eleven of them, in fact, express doubt about people or events. Take these, for instance:

He didn't answer. He stood there, staring, like he didn't know what to say. Maybe he didn't. (16)

No one shot at me on the way, but maybe they were saving that for later. (129)

If Pike was here, he might be able to see them, but Pike was probably on the other side of the park, still watching the cops. But maybe not. (145-46)

Here Elvis expresses uncertainty both about people's motives and about events. While Crais' novels surely run on the notion that the detective uncovers evil both because of his moral authority and his intuitive understanding of human affairs, understanding why people behave as they do is a chancy business. So is predicting what's going to happen. Too often, one just doesn't know. Too often plans just don't work right. Because this is the case, Crais puts emphasis on the importance of process. This lies at the base of the Tai Chi Elvis practices at some juncture in every book, just as the manner in which one behaves forms the center of Joe Pike's character. If one cannot always understand others' motives or manage the way things will turn out, one cannot control one's own behavior. And fulfillment comes from working on it, from appreciating the process itself rather than just the results. Elvis explains some of the importance of process when he talks about his home and his office in *The Monkey's Raincoat*: "There were books on the shelves that I liked to read and reread, and prints and originals on the walls that I liked to look at. Like the office, I was proud of it. Like the office, it was the result of a process and the process was ongoing. The house lived, as did the person within it" (118). Later, in *Voodoo River*, as he watches surfers, Elvis gives the idea of process a universal application:

They did it again and again, and the waves were always small, but maybe each time they paddled out they were thinking that the next wave would be the big wave, the one that would make all the effort have meaning. Most people are like that, and, like most people, the surfers probably hadn't yet realized that the process was the payoff, not the waves. (10)

Here Elvis elevates process into a general statement about the proper relationship between people and events. And it applies to the books, too. Crime will always be—that's one of the reasons that every book (except *Sunset Express*) introduces organized crime in its background—and individuals will continue to be weak and confused, so the detective validates himself not only by what he accomplishes but also by the way he does it and by his demeanor—both of which, ultimately, may be even more important than what he does.

Indeed, one of the principal features of hard-boiled fiction resides in the process through which first person narrators reveal themselves. They create themselves for their readers as they go along. Crais, like most other hard-boiled writers, establishes Elvis' demeanor through the characteristics of what he says and the way he says it. Hammett and Chandler, of course, established the major features of hard-boiled, first-person narration back in the thirties and made it look easier than it really is. And some of those stylistic features have to form part of any hard-boiled narrator's style—features like terse expression, irony, wisecracks, etc. Enough flexibility exists within this framework, however, to allow writers to put their own stamp on the voices, and, therefore, the characters, of their own hard-boiled heroes.

Crais uses a number of elements to give Elvis his distinctive tone. And as I've mentioned a couple of times, he locates most of them in the final sentences of paragraphs of Elvis' narration. First of all, their form fits the standard: a lot of these final comments come either in short sentences or fragments or even one word. So they're tied to the economy and terseness of hard-boiled style. It's in the content of these utterances that Crais develops his hero's character. Above I've dealt with the "maybe" sentences that link to the hero's light-hearted sense of fantasy as well as his tentative approach to motives and actions. Elvis, however, does other things in these places. He uses the final sentences to make summary comments about other characters: "Great legs, though" (*Monkey's Raincoat* 1), "Nice legs" (*Stalking the Angel* 115), "Vegetarian" (*Lullaby Town* 143) "Marshall Dillon" (*Lullaby Town* 52), "Boris Badinov" (*Free Fall* 12), and "Asshole" (*Monkey's Raincoat* 76), for instance. And what these mean is that he is both observant and hip. Sometimes Crais gives readers one-word editorial interjections such as "Inspired" (*Monkey's Raincoat* 44), "Outstanding" (*Lullaby Town* 65), "Classy" (*Monkey's Raincoat* 73 and *Free Fall* 54), "Cosmic" (*Stalking the Angel* 61), "Style" (*Lullaby Town* 5 and 136), "Nice" (*Lullaby Town* 196), "Cool" (*Free Fall* 134), and "Wow" (*Stalking the Angel* 52 and 61). Once again, comments like these communicate Elvis' hip nature, but they also add to it an almost youthful enthusiasm. Sometimes Elvis expresses immediate reactions to people and events that are more restrained: "Hmmmm" (*Stalking the Angel* 111, *Lullaby Town* 57, *Free Fall* 129), "My, my" (*Stalking the Angel* 165 and *Free Fall* 96), and "Sonofagun" (*Free Fall* 128). With these kinds of casual interjections, Crais bolsters the illusion of the intimate relationship between the hero and the reader. Then, too, Elvis occasionally opts for encapsulated wisdom in longer sentences:

Everything always goes wrong when the camera's turned away. (*Monkey's Raincoat* 23)

But good news, like magic, is sometimes in short supply. (*Monkey's Raincoat* 19)

Sometimes there is no smart move. (*Free Fall* 178)

It hadn't been necessary, but then, most things aren't. (*Monkey's Raincoat* 166)

There are always options. (*Free Fall* 219)

You do what you can, but you can't do everything. (*Lullaby Town* 239)

With this kind of comment, what Elvis says links to the overall sober theme of the books, to the wistful, world-weary knowledge typical of the hard-boiled hero. But Crais also balances this kind of comment by having Elvis round off narration by consciously slipping in clichés like these:

Service with a smile. (*Monkey's Raincoat* 26)

Time equals money. (*Stalking the Angel* 4)

My country right or wrong. (*Stalking the Angel* 88)

Just another story in the naked city. (*Lullaby Town* 165)

A Kodak moment. (*Free Fall* 104)

A man with friends is the wealthiest man in the world. (*Free Fall* 261)

Here, of course, he's back to sarcasm, one of the hallmarks of the hard-boiled narrator. And along with the sarcasm, Elvis employs the more traditional form of the wisecrack, like these from *Stalking the Angel*: "Did Banana Republic sell shoulder holsters?" (129), "They could call it Banal-land" (28), "Nancy Reagan would have been proud" (90), "He wouldn't notice the Circus Vargus troupe rumbling past" (170), "There are some things even the great and wonderful Oz does not know" (147). So, like all of his predecessors, he's Elvis Cole, Wiseass Detective. But interspersed with all of the above, Crais includes remarks in which his hero takes ironic pot-shots at himself:

I think of the damnedest things. (*Monkey's Raincoat* 164)

I was taking stupid into unexplored realms. (*Free Fall* 85)

There are women who will tell you that not thinking is one of my best things. (*Stalking the Angel* 156)

There was more driving and more stops and more phone calls and not once did I see anyone dressed like a ninja or carrying a sword. (*Stalking the Angel* 160)

Did Mike Hammer use a 7-Eleven as an office? (*Lullaby Town* 34)

Scared hell out of that yorkie. (*Monkey's Raincoat* 134)

And in directing irony and sarcasm at himself, Elvis connects himself with what is perhaps the most defining element of the hard-boiled narrator. That heroes describe the world they experience with irony and sarcasm is one of the givens of hard-boiled fiction: theirs is a world gone to seed, and irony and sarcasm are two of the ways in which narrators convey this and their position in the world to their readers. Unrelieved irony and sarcasm, however, suggest moral certainty, dogma, superiority, and pretense—the characteristics of most of the evil people in the books. So by directing irony at themselves, hard-boiled heroes both portray themselves as fallible, likable, and human, and separate themselves from those who set themselves up as infallible and who impose their judgments on others.

A lot of this has to do with the traditions of hard boiled heroes, the way in which they relate to their worlds, and the casually intimate connection Crais wants to establish with his readers. The point of the ranks of quotations above also lies in Crais' portrayal of his hero as a person who responds flexibly to the variety of people and events he confronts during the course of the books. Sometimes he dishes out both moral censure and sometimes sympathetic understanding. He's ironic and sarcastic as well as serious and stoic. Elvis calls himself Mr. Nonchalance, Mr. Charm, Mr. Convinced, Mr. Seduction, Mr. Confidence, Mr. Kick Back and Mr. Threat. And, as Crais develops his first person narration, Elvis is all of these things. So while Parker makes his hero act according to the credo of autonomy by which Spenser defines himself, and the red arrows on his deltoids dictate the way in which Joe Pike approaches everything, Crais develops Elvis in a different manner. Although sympathy and humanity remain at the core of his character, he bases his acts and attitudes on the principle of flexibility. Crais defines this in one of Elvis' passages in *Indigo Slam*: "The world had changed. It often does, I've found, yet the changes are still surprising and, more often than not, frightening. You have to adjust" (92). This, of course, hardly counts as a unique approach to life. That one needs to adapt, in fact, falls pretty securely into the category of no-brainers. But in a world in which dogma—about gender, about justice, about race, etc.—plays such a large role, it's sometimes the best way to be.

JAMES LEE BURKE

It's no coincidence that when Conan Doyle wrote the Sherlock Holmes stories he was also busy writing stories about the Middle Ages and about knightly virtue. Maybe that's even where Chandler got the notion of attaching the metaphor of the knight to Marlowe in *The Big Sleep* and then expounding on it in his essay "The Simple Art of Murder." Out of this tradition comes the notion that the heroes of detective stories are not only supposed to represent their cultures but also to embody and put into practice the ideals of those cultures. As Chandler would have it in "The Simple Art of Murder," the detective hero "must be the best man in his world and a good enough man for any world."

In a number of ways Burke grounds his hero, Dave Robicheaux, in the culture of the last half of the twentieth century. Burke builds many of Dave's childhood images out of recollections of playing American Legion baseball, hunting and fishing with his father, making out with pretty girls in convertibles, and vibrating with the energy and enthusiasm of early New Orleans rock and roll. Dave grows up in the idyllic place, New Iberia, Louisiana: a place that combines small town virtues, a rich historical past, a closeness to nature, and a profound cultural identity with the mores and folkways of the Cajun population of southern Louisiana. And as part of that culture, Dave is a religious person. One of the places Burke locates Dave's past is in Catholic school, and he portrays him as a practicing Catholic: as an adult Dave regularly makes confession, attends mass, and both the writings of Church Fathers and passages from the Scriptures stay with him. So, too, does the literature he learned as an English major in college (there are four allusions to Shakespeare; two each to Hemingway and Yeats; and one each to e. e. cummings, Malory, Walter Scott, Kerouac, Crane, Milton, Frost, Goethe, Conrad, Forester, and Tolstoy scattered throughout the books). Indeed Dave more often relies on metaphors from Blake to portray his experience than he does metaphors from the Bible. After college Robicheaux goes to Vietnam and serves as a lieutenant, and while the war remains as one of the central traumas of his life, Dave returns untainted by the cruelty and personal dishonor that characterizes the memories of other veterans. Upon his return from the war, Robicheaux serves as a police officer (first on patrol and then as a homicide detective) in the First District of New Orleans and then, on and off, as a detective for the New

159

Iberia Sheriff's Office. And as a police officer, Burke gives Robicheaux some ideal qualities. Thus, Dave's most telling criticism of the corrupt Nate Baxter in *Dixie City Jam* is "You're bad not because you're on the pad; you're bad because you don't understand that we're supposed to protect the weak" (196). Indeed, the role is part of Dave's identity, as witnessed by his reply to the question "Why do you give a fuck?" in *A Morning for Flamingos*: "Because I'm a police officer" (306). From *Heaven's Prisoners* onward Burke makes fatherhood a principal component of his hero's character and continues Dave's dedication to caring for his adopted daughter, Alafair. Just as persistently, Burke portrays his hero as a thoughtful individual who does not accept superficial or simple answers to the questions raised by social injustice, crime, politics, and other conundrums of the human condition.

It all sounds pretty good. Growing up during the idyll of the fifties, steeled by the crises of the sixties and seventies, and stalwart enough to confront the dilemmas of the eighties and nineties, it all sounds like Dave Robicheaux is truly a paragon who embodies the ideals of the last half of the twentieth century. Maybe he does. But he is also messed up in a major way. And that, too, may be one of the realities of the last quarter of the twentieth century.

Sometimes it's clear from the start and sometimes Burke makes it up as the novels progress, but he always means to show Dave Robicheaux as a tormented soul who is holding things together, but only tenuously. To be sure, there is Dave's alcoholism, around which Burke built the first novel, *Neon Rain*. But this is effect rather than cause, and Burke's real success does not come until he begins to examine the causes of his hero's troubles. So in many of the subsequent books, Burke spends a great deal of time creating a detailed and twisted past for his hero which accounts for the personal troubles he experiences in later life. In *Heaven's Prisoners,* Burke presents us with a glowing portrait of the hero's childhood:

If, as a child, I had been asked to describe the world I lived in, I'm sure my response would have been in terms of images that in general left me with a sense of well-being about myself and my family. Because even though my mother had died when I was young, and we were poor and my father sometimes brawled in bars and got locked up in the parish jail, he and my little brother and I had a home—actually a world—on the bayou that was always safe, warm in the winter from the woodstove, cool in the summer from the shade of the pecan trees, a place that was our own and had belonged to our people and way of life since the Acadians came to Louisiana in 1755 . . . and most of all my father—a big, dark, laughing Cajun who could break boards into kindling with his bare hands, throw a wash tub full of bricks over a fence, or pull a six-foot 'gator out of the water by its tail. (45-46)

But as the books continue, Burke largely forgets about brother Jimmy, who had been a major actor in *Neon Rain,* and concentrates on undermining key ingredients in Dave's idyllic past.

Most importantly, whether by design or by accident, as the books proceed, the phrase "even though my mother died when I was young" acquires layer after layer of new meaning. So, in the next book, *Black Cherry Blues,* Burke tells us that Dave's mother, in fact, did not really die when he was young. Here Dave recounts his mother's last visit to their home. While her lover waits impatiently to take her away,

My mother leaned over me and pressed me against her body. Her voice was low, as though the two of us were under a glass bell.

"I ain't bad, Davy," she said. "If somebody tell you that, it ain't true. I'll come see you again. We'll go somewheres together, just us two. Eat fried chicken, maybe. You gonna see, you." (241)

She, however, never does come to see him again. Instead, several paragraphs later Dave describes his last encounter with his mother:

Then when I was sixteen years old and I went for the first time to the Boundary Club on the Breaux Bridge highway, a rough, ramshackle roadhouse where they fought with knives and bottles in the shale parking lot, I saw her drawing draft beer behind the bar. Her body was thicker now, her hair blacker than it should have been, and she wore a black skirt that showed a thick scar above one knee. She brought a beer tray to a table full of oil-field workers, then sat down with them. They all knew her and lit her cigarettes, and when she danced with one of them she pressed her stomach against his loins. I stood by the jukebox and waved at her, and she smiled back at me over the man's shoulder, but there was no recognition in her face. (242)

There is more to come. In the sixth Robicheaux book, *In the Electric Mist with Confederate Dead,* Dave recalls returning home one day early from school:

I looked from the hallway through the bedroom door and saw a man's candy-striped shirt, suspenders, and sharkskin zoot slacks and Panama hat hung on the bedpost, his socks sticking out of his two-tone shoes on the floor. My mother was naked, on all fours, on top of the bedspread, and the man, whose name was Mack, was about to mount her. A cyprus plank creaked under my foot, Mack twisted his head and looked at me, his pencil-thin mustache like a bird's wing above his lip. Then he entered my mother.

For months I had dreams about a white wolf who lived in a skeletal black tree on an infinite white landscape. At the base of the tree was a nest of pups. In the dream the wolf would drop to the ground, her teats sagging with milk, and eat her young one by one. (288)

After this trauma, though, the child displaces the dream of the white wolf by recalling a happy incident when he watched two nuns dancing "with their flushed faces inside their wimples and the laughter they tried to hide behind their hands when it became too loud" (289).

As if all of this is not bad enough, in the next book, *Dixie City Jam,* Burke gives an expanded version of the same incident, using, as is his practice, some of the same phrases as in the original. This time, however, Mack confronts Dave about witnessing his mother's adultery:

"What you t'ink you seen?" he said.
I looked at my shoes.
"I ax you a question. Don't pretend you ain't heard me," he said.
"I didn't see anything."
"You was where you didn't have no bidness. What we gonna do 'bout that?" He held out his right hand. I thought he was going to place it on my shoulder. Instead he put the backs of his fingers under my nose. "You smell that? Me and yo' momma been fuckin', boy. It ain't the first time either."
My eyes began to water, my face hot and small under his stare.
"You can tell yo' daddy 'bout this if you want, but you gotta tell on her, too." (157)

Before he revives this memory, though, Dave makes it clear to readers that "I had simply made my wife and her lover pay for events that had occurred many years earlier." In the manner of psychoanalysis, then, Burke peels away layer after layer to arrive at the cause for states of mind and behavior that lie at the core of his hero's behavior.

Burke presents the earliest manifestation of Dave's emotional problems in *Black Cherry Blues.* Here Dave recalls his earliest encounter with despair:

I could never explain these moments, and neither could a psychologist. It happened first when I was ten years old, after my father had been locked up a second time in the parish jail for fighting in Provost's Pool Room. I was at home by myself, looking at a religious book that contained a plate depicting the souls in hell. Suddenly I felt myself drawn into the illustration, caught forever in their lake of remorse and despair. I was filled with terror and guilt, and no amount of reassurance from the parish priest would relieve me of it. (120-21)

According to Burke's somewhat casual chronology, Dave would have been ten in about 1949 when this incident took place—he says he is forty-nine in *Heaven's Prisoners* in 1988. And in *Black Cherry Blues,* Burke clearly dates Dave's discovery of his mother's adultery in 1945. Maybe neither psychologist or priest could explain what was happening to Dave in 1949, but even the most inept psychologist and innocent priest could explain it in 1988 or 1998: Dave is clinically depressed.

In many ways depression becomes one of the most important subjects of Burke's early Robicheaux books. Burke pays particular attention to attempting to portray the perverse mood into which depressed persons descend, and his books contain one of the most extensive attempts to describe the interior landscape of depression in popular literature. The first instance comes in *Heaven's Prisoners* when Dave embodies his feeling in the form of a tiger:

I could almost hear his thick, leathery paws scudding against the wire mesh, see his hot, orange eyes in the darkness, smell his dung and the fetid odor of rotted meat on his breath. I never had an explanation for these moments that would come upon me. A psychologist would call it depression. A nihilist would call it philosophical insight. But regardless, it seemed there was nothing for it except the acceptance of another sleepless night. Baptist, Alafair, and I took the pickup truck to the drive-in movie in Lafayette, set out deck chairs on the oyster shells, and ate hot dogs and drank lemonade and watched a Walt Disney double feature, but I couldn't rid myself of the dark well I felt my soul descending into. (186)

Later in the same novel, when Dave stakes out Romero's apartment he muses that

I was never good at surveillance, in part because I didn't have the patience for it. But more important was the fact that my own mind always became my worst enemy during any period of passivity or inactivity in life, no matter how short the duration. Old grievances, fears, and unrelieved feelings of guilt and black depression would surface from the unconscious without cause and nibble on the soul's edges like iron teeth. If I didn't do something, if I didn't take my focus outside myself, those emotions would control me as quickly and completely as whiskey did when it raced through my blood and into my heart like a dark electrical current. (230-31)

With Dave carrying the additional burden of Annie's death, in *Black Cherry Blues* he experiences repeated episodes of hopeless feelings. They begin early in the novel with

I should have been bursting with the spring morning, but I felt listless and spent, traveling on the outer edge of my envelope, and it wasn't simply because of bad dreams and insomnia the previous night. These moments would descend on me at peculiar times, as though my heart's blood were fouled, and suddenly my mind would light with images and ring with sounds I wasn't ready to deal with. (10)

Later Dave tells readers that "It was a mood that I knew well, and it always descended upon me immediately before I began a two day bender. I felt a sense of failure, moral lassitude, defeat, and fear that craved only one release" (87). And then that "I felt as though I had been sent to a dark and airless space on the earth where memory became selective and flayed the skin an inch at a time. I can't tell you why" (120). Finally, there is the descent into unwarranted guilt:

I was tired of pursuing a course that seemed to have no resolution, of walking about in what seemed to be a waking nightmare, of feeling that I deserved all this, that somehow I had asked for it, that it was inevitable that I ride in a wood cart like a condemned seventeenth century criminal creaking over the cobbled streets through the mob toward the elevated platform where a hooded man waited with wheel and iron bar. (179)

In the next novel, *A Morning for Flamingos,* Burke puts much of this together in his comments about the failure of the early relationship between Dave and Bootsie:

It should never have ended. But it did, and for no reason that I could explain to her. Nor could I explain it to my father, a priest in whom I trusted, or myself. Even though I was only twenty years old I began to experience bone-grinding periods of depression and guilt that seemed to have no legitimate cause or origin. When they came upon me it was as though the sun had suddenly become a black cinder, and had gone over the rim of the earth for the last time . . . Even today I'm hard put to explain my behavior. But I felt somehow that I was intrinsically bad, that anyone who could love me didn't know who I really was, and that eventually I would make that person bad, too. It was not a rational state of mind. A psychologist would probably say that my problem was related to my mother's running off with a bourre dealer from Morgan City when I was a child, or the fact that my father sometimes brawled in bars and got locked up in the parish jail. I don't know if theories like that are correct or not. But at the time there was no way I could think myself out of my own dark thoughts. (78-79)

Having identified his mother's adultery and desertion in *A Morning for Flamingos,* as noted above, Burke turns from the portrait of depressed mood to its cause in several of the later novels.

But *A Morning for Flamingos* also signals another change in Burke's depiction of Dave's emotional condition. Here he describes the manic swing that so often accompanies depression:

And you cannot explain why one night you will sleep until morning without dreaming while the next you will sit alone in a square of moonlight, your palms damp on your thighs, your breath loud in your chest. No more than you can explain why one day you're anointed with magic. You get high on the weather, you have a lock on the perfecta in the ninth race; then the next morning you're on a dry drunk that fills the day with monstrous shapes prized out of your memory with a dung fork. (105-6)

"Anger beyond irritability" is one of the diagnostic criteria for manic states. In *Black Cherry Blues,* the therapist treating Dave in the aftermath of Annie's death tells him that "I don't think there's anything complex about depression. It's a matter of anger turned inward" (51). That being the case, Dave's manic behavior often becomes anger turned outward and manifested in intensely violent acts.

Burke includes a good deal of discussion in his books about violence and what it means. Thus, in *Heaven's Prisoners* Dave notes that "Most people think of violence as an abstraction. It never is. It's always ugly, it always demeans and dehumanizes, it always shocks and repels and leaves the witnesses to it sick and shaken" (108). In *Dixie City Jam,* Dave ironically acknowledges the ultimate futility of violence after the sheriff makes him a furtive gift of an assault rifle: "No application of force or firepower so far had been successful. Since we've concluded that we don't understand what we're dealing with, use more force and firepower" (202). As is his wont, Dave also apprehends the theological implications of violence on those who use it. First comes the "inflated self-esteem or grandiosity" characteristic of manic behavior. Thus in *Heaven's Prisoners:* "But I had killed people before, in war and as a member of the New Orleans police department, and I know what it does to you. Like the hunter, you feel an adrenaline surge of pleasure at having usurped the province of God. The person who says otherwise is lying" (240). And in *A Stained White Radiance,* Lyle Sonnier describes his state of mind as a tunnel rat during the Vietnam War: "You didn't send me down there. I liked it down there. It was my own underground horror show. I made those zips think the scourge of God had crawled into the bowels of the earth. It wasn't a good way to be, son" (25). The ultimate result of this perversion of self is that "One day a curious light dies in the eyes. The unblemished place where God once grasped our souls becomes permanently stained. A bird lifts its span of wings and flies forever out of the heart" (*Heaven's Prisoners* 240).

In spite of the fact that he knows all of this, Dave Robicheaux is subject to fits of extreme violence. Even his friend Clete Purcel, whom Burke creates as a locus for violence in the books, acknowledges that "There's a secret that everybody seems to know except my old podjo from the First. You're one of the most violent people I've ever known" (*Dixie City Jam* 265). And he is. Dave commits graphically violent acts in most of the books. In *Neon Rain* he beats three men with a canvas bag filled with bolts, nuts, and ball bearings; in *Heaven's Prisoners* he pushes Jerry's face into a fan; in *Black Cherry Blues* he whips two men with a chain; he beats Julie Balboni with baseball bat in *In the Electric Mist with Confederate Dead;* and he pistol whips Tommy Lonighan and attacks Max Calucci with a shovel in *Dixie City Jam.*

While some of Dave's violence serves other thematic purposes, Burke usually connects it with his hero's abnormal emotional state. When he commits violent acts, Dave quite literally loses control. He understands what has happened only in retrospect, and then only vaguely and through the use of figurative language. From these episodes Dave recalls colors. In *A Morning for Flamingos:* "a rush of color in my mind, like amorphous red and black clouds turning in dark water" remains in Dave's memory (275); in *Dixie City Jam* it is "Pieces of torn color floated behind my eyes, like tongues of orange flame you see inside the smoke of an oil fire" (275); and in both *In the Electric Mist with Confederate Dead* and *Burning Angel* Dave describes feeling "a balloon of red-black color" rise in his head (*In the Electric* 90; *Burning* 240). Along with recalling color, Burke has his hero remember sound. In *Heaven's Prisoners, In the Electric Mist with Confederate Dead,* and *Burning Angel* Dave notes hearing the sound of wet newspaper being ripped. In *A Morning for Flamingos* and *Dixie City Jam* it is like hearing a Popsicle stick snapping.

During these episodes, Dave quite literally blacks out. He says so in *In the Electric Mist with Confederate Dead*: "I heard glass crunch under the sole of my shoe in the stunned silence, and looked down numbly at my own broken sunglasses on the floor like a man emerging from a blackout" (90-91). He uses the same term in *Dixie City Jam,* but this time comparing the condition to an alcoholic blackout: "I always wanted to believe that those moments of rage, which affected me almost like an alcoholic blackout, were due to a legitimate cause, that I or someone close to me had been seriously wronged, that the object of my anger and adrenaline had not swum coincidentally into my ken" (72).

But it is difficult to separate Dave's depression from his alcoholism. In fact, Burke's hero uses some of the same metaphors to describe both depression and alcoholism. Thus in *Heaven's Prisoners* one of the first times Dave attempts to paint an interior impression of what depression feels like, he uses the metaphor of the tiger: "I could almost hear his thick, leathery paws scudding against the wire mesh, see his hot, orange eyes in the darkness, smell his dung and the fetid odor of rotted meat on his breath." Then, three books later, in *A Stained White Radiance,* Burke uses almost the same words and images. This time, however, he uses them to describe Dave's alcoholism:

I could hear the tiger pacing in his cage, his paws softly scudding on the wire mesh. His eyes were yellow in the darkness, his breath as fetid as meat that had rotted in the sun. Sometimes I imagined him prowling through trees in William Blake's dark moral forest, his striped body electrified with a hungry light. But I knew that he was not the poet's creation; he was conceived and fed by my own self-destructive alcoholic energies and fears, chiefly my fear of mortality and my inability to affect the destiny of those whom I could not afford to lose. (75)

Burke's fusion of depression, violence, and alcoholism, moreover, is a natural one, one which Terrence Real describes in *I Don't Want to Talk about It: Overcoming the Secret Legacy of Male Depression.* Here Real notes that both alcoholism and violence (along with workaholism and avoidance of intimacy) are ways in which depression manifests itself in men. But whether it is a symptom of depression or a separate illness, in Burke not only the metaphors for both but also the feelings and actions attributed to depression and alcoholism are essentially the same. The difference comes in the way in which Dave approaches them.

In a number of places throughout the books, Burke describes his characters as having had experience with therapy. In several of these cases, therapy receives sympathetic treatment, as in the comment about depression being anger turned inward cited above and in the wisdom about his life that Dave alludes to in *In the Electric Mist with Confederate Dead*: "A therapist told me that I would never have any peace until I learned to forgive not only myself for her death but the human race as well for producing the men who killed her" (288). But these two examples from Dave are exceptions. Through his other characters' experience with therapy, Burke paints an altogether different picture. Thus he gives his readers Clete Purcel's experience with therapy in *A Stained White Radiance:*

When I started drinking my breakfast there for a while, I got sent by the captain to this shrink who was on lend-lease from the psychology department at Tulane. So I told him a few stories, stuff that I thought was pretty ordinary . . . and I thought the guy was going to throw up in his wastebasket. I always heard these guys could take it. I felt like a freak. I ain't kidding you, the guy was trembling. (66)

This incident simply repeats one described in *A Morning for Flamingos.* And it is a precursor to Dave's reminiscence in *In the Electric Mist with Confederate Dead*:

I once knew a young psychiatrist from Tulane who wanted to do volunteer counseling in the women's prison at St. Gabriel. He lasted a month. The inkblot tests he gave his first subjects not only drove him into clinical depression but eventually caused him to drop his membership in the ACLU and join the National Rifle Association. (192)

Other than being particularly hard on the psychiatry department at Tulane, Burke's characters repeatedly condemn psychiatric therapy. Dave is willing to admit that it does hold a certain fascination, as in this passage from *Dixie City Jam*: "if you have ever been in psychoanalysis or analytically oriented therapy, you're aware that the exploration of one's own unconscious can be an intriguing pursuit. It is also self-inflating, grandiose, and endless, and often has the same practical value as meditating upon one's genitalia" (251). However the books repeatedly reject psychotherapy because its practitioners have no experience in the perverse and violent world of their patients and because it does not work. Thus in *Black Cherry Blues* Dave poses the question

have you ever known anyone whose marriage was saved by a marriage counselor, whose drinking was cured by a psychiatrist, whose son was kept out of reform school by a social worker? In a badass, beer-glass brawl, would you rather have an academic liberal covering your back or a hobnailed redneck? (178)

Finally, and most essentially, Burke's hero views his own actions caused by alcoholism or by depression as being "morally insane," a view not held in high esteem by the psychological or psychiatric communities.

But it is a view that fits in pretty well at Alcoholics Anonymous. Everything that AA does rests on their system of 12 Steps, a system that relies heavily upon personal responsibility and religious faith. Since Burke refers to most of them, it may be helpful to look at all twelve of the AA Steps:

1. We admitted we were powerless over alcohol that our lives had become unmanageable.
2. Came to believe that a Power greater than ourselves could restore us to sanity.
3. Made a decision to turn our will and our lives over to the care of God as we understood him.
4. Made a searching and fearless moral inventory of ourselves.
5. Admitted to God, to ourselves, and to another human being the exact nature of our wrongs.
6. Were entirely ready to have God remove all these defects of character.
7. Humbly asked Him to remove our shortcomings.
8. Made a list of all persons we had harmed, and became willing to make amends to them all.
9. Made direct amends to such people wherever possible, except when to do so would injure them or others.
10. Continued to take personal inventory and when we were wrong promptly admitted it.
11. Sought through prayer and meditation to improve our conscious contact with God as we understood Him, praying only for knowledge of His will for us and the power to carry that out.
12. Having had a spiritual awakening as the result of these steps, we tried to carry this message to alcoholics, and to practice these principles in all our affairs. (*Alcoholics Anonymous* 58)

No one can read very far in Burke's books without knowing that Dave Robicheaux belongs to AA, believes in its teachings, and tries to live according to their precepts. Dave's references to the redemptive mechanics of AA—to meetings, to working the steps, to his "Higher Power," and to AA's "Serenity Prayer"—appear in every book.

As Dave views it, psychiatric therapy does little to help him because it is static, academic, theoretical, and does not actively grapple with the horrors of experience. AA works for him because it's confessional (thereby tying in with his Catholicism and his Cajun Catholic culture); it's moral (hence tied to Dave's belief in the existence of "moral insanity" and, by extension, moral sanity); it's prescriptive (as opposed to analysis which is descriptive); it's active (thereby appealing to a man used to action); it's ritualistic (tying, once more, to Dave's Catholicism); it's communal (appropriate to Dave's commitment to small town mores as well as his Cajun heritage); it's rooted in outreach (appropriate to Dave's need to help others); and it's perpetual (acknowledging the need for continual vigilance—once a drunk always a drunk).

Set against Dave's descriptions of depression, AA offers, and occasionally brings about, a different emotional state. Thus this passage from *A Stained White Radiance:*

It was a wonderful day. I had been to Mass and communion the previous evening. I had done a fifth step on my lapse of faith in my Higher Power, and I had determined once again to stop keeping score in my ongoing contention with the world, time, and mortality, and to simply thank providence for all the good things that had come to me through no plan of my own. (166)

Just as AA provides Dave with ritualized succor for the black mood of depression—along with guilt, isolation, terror, and self-abasement, its fellow-travelers—it also enhances and enables his deep-seated humanity and obligation to protect and serve others. This extends from his efforts on behalf of Dixie Lee in *Black Cherry Blues* to *A Stained White Radiance,* where Dave persists in his efforts to help Weldon Sonnier because "if other people had had the same attitude toward me, I had to remind myself, I would be dead, in a mental institution, or putting together enough change and crumpled one-dollar bills in a sunrise bar to buy a double shot of Beam" (16). Burke's books, then, are about his hero's confrontation with the problems inflicted on him by depression and alcoholism and the ways in which they affect him as a person and as a police officer. But they are not the only problems that Dave faces. There are plenty more. The others, however, don't altogether come from inside Burke's hero. Some come from outside.

The most prominent of these problems is that Dave grew up and lives in Louisiana. A large part of the allure of Burke's Robicheaux books lies in the fact that they take place in Louisiana. Burke devotes large passages of lush prose to describing the flora and fauna of southern Louisiana—the bayous, the pecan trees, the Gulf of Mexico. The books, too, dwell on Louisiana food: Dave and his family seem forever to be eating boudin, crayfish, dirty rice, shrimp, and enough Cajun delicacies to make Justin Wilson loosen his suspenders another notch. And Burke seasons his books with dialogue characters, like Aldous Robicheaux and Baptist, whose English is shaded with the Cajun French that was once the exclusive patois of the region. Along with this there are frequent reminders—the tomb of Evangeline and her lover, for instance—of the Cajun heritage of southern Louisiana, and of the non-Cajun portion of the state, the Kingfish's part, as well. Then, too, Burke includes excursions into the history of New Orleans and southern Louisiana—the anti-Italian riots of 1890 following the murder of Police Chief David Hennessey, the succession of loony characters to serve as the state's governor, and, of course, the Civil War—Generals John Bell Hood and Nathaniel Banks, the occupation of New Iberia, and the conquest of Teche by Federal troops. Good, exotic local color stuff. The living is easy, and life is one crayfish boil after another.

Except, going back to Hammett and Chandler, grim reality accompanies the exotic allure of local color in the hard-boiled story. Things look lush and beautiful, but corruption and decay lurk beneath the surface. Burke talks about the Cajun heritage of his state—Evangeline, zydeco, crayfish pie, and fillet gumbo—but also acknowledges that

Many people are currently enamored with Cajun culture, but they know little about its darker side: organized dogfights and cockfights, the casual attitude toward the sexual exploitation of Negro women, the environmental ignorance that has allowed the draining and poisoning of the wetlands. And, few outsiders understand the violent feelings that Cajun people have about the nature of fidelity and human possession. (227)

For Burke, too, New Orleans is more than Mardi Gras, beignets at a sidewalk cafe, and the French Quarter:

Then there is the edge of the Quarter, where, if you're drunk or only unlucky, you can wander out of a controlled and cosmetic libertine environment into a piece of moral moonscape—Louis Armstrong Park or the St. Louis cemeteries will do just fine—where kids will shoot a woman through the face at point-blank range for amounts of money you could pry out of a parking meter with a screwdriver. (*Morning for Flamingos* 235)

And Louisiana is more than Cajuns and New Orleans. It's also Metairie, "the only town in the United States to elect a Ku Klux Klansman and American Nazi as its state representative. What a depressing shithole. This place makes you think maybe the white race ought to be picking the cotton" (*Burning Angel* 252). Then there is the whole other part of the state, chronically economically depressed, and culturally different from the south:

Their cars came from Bogalusa, Denham Springs, Plaquemine, Bunkie, Port Allen, Vidalia, and mosquito-infested, dirt road communities out in the Atchafalaya basin. But these were not ordinary small-town, blue-collar people. This was the permanent underclass, the ones who tried to hold on daily to their shrinking bit of redneck geography with a pickup truck and gun rack and Jones on the jukebox and a cold Coors in the hand. They were never sure of who they were unless someone was afraid of them. They jealously guarded their jobs from blacks and Vietnamese refugees, whom they saw as a vast and hungry army about to descend on their women, their neighborhoods, their schools, even their clapboard church houses, where they were assured every Sunday and Wednesday night that the bitterness and fear that characterized their lives had nothing to do with what they had been born to, or what they had chosen for themselves. (*A Stained White Radiance* 291)

But the most meretricious aspect of the landscape, of the way things seem to be, is that it is different from the way it used to be. This is a constant lament of the middle-aged heroes of hard-boiled fiction. And it is particularly acute in Burke. Most apparently, Dave laments the loss of Cajun culture and a heritage that he can trace back to the Acadians' arrival in Louisiana in the eighteenth century. As a double whammy, Dave also associates this with his father and the loss of his father:

He couldn't read or write and never traveled outside Louisiana, but his heart possessed an intuitive understanding of our lives, our Cajun vision of the world, that no philosophy book could convey. He drank too much and he'd fistfight two or three men in a bar at the same time, with the enthusiasm of a boy hitting baseballs; but inside he had a gentle heart, a strong sense of right and wrong, and a tragic sense about the cruelty and violence that the world sometimes imposes on the innocent. (*Heaven's Prisoners* 216)

Indeed, Burke associates the loss of Cajun culture with the departure of a congenial world-view: "But something else was gone, too: the soft pagan ambiance that existed right in the middle of a French Catholic culture" (*Heaven's Prisoners* 160). And all of this coexists with Dave's memories of his childhood after World War II, of American Legion baseball games and of Bootsie, his first love.

Dave, however, is rarely willing to write off the loss of the past to the shifting perspectives of age. He attributes its loss to some very real causes. Most prominently, Dave places the blame for the loss of his Louisiana and his past on the greed and indifference of corporations and their camp-followers. Mostly it's because of the arrival of the oil companies:

The inside of the poolroom was like a partial return into the New Iberia of my youth, when people spoke French more often than English, where there were slot and race-horse machines in every bar, and the cribs on Railroad Avenue stayed open twenty four hours a day and the rest of the world was as foreign to us as the Texans who arrived after World War II with their oil rigs and pipeline companies. (*Heaven's Prisoners* 82)

But there are others as well:

Over the years I had seen all the dark players get to southern Louisiana in one form or another: the oil and chemical companies who drained and polluted the wetlands; the developers who could turn sugar cane acreage and pecan orchards into miles of tract homes and shopping malls that had the aesthetic qualities of a sewer works; and the Mafia, who operated out of New Orleans and brought us prostitution, slot machines, control of at least two big labor unions, and finally narcotics.

They hunted on the game preserve. They came into an area where large numbers of people were poor and illiterate, where many were unable to speak English and the politicians were traditionally inept or corrupt, and they took everything that was best from the Cajun world in which I had grown up, treated it cynically and with contempt, and left us with oil sludge in the oyster beds, Levittown, and the abiding knowledge that we had done virtually nothing to stop them. (*A Stained White Radiance* 32)

While Dave never lets the oil and natural gas companies off the hook for what he views as the rape of Louisiana, in calmer moments he finds a different answer for the loss of the past he knew as a child: "I'd like to blame it on the boys at the Rotary and the Kiwanis. But that's not fair. We had just become a middle-class people, that's all" (*Heaven's Prisoners* 160). In addition to the way in which Dave responds to the disparity between the Louisiana of his childhood and the Louisiana of the present, being brought up in the state brings with it other problems than those of the twentieth century. In addition to everything else they are, Burke's books are southern novels, and one doesn't need to reread Faulkner to know about the ways in which being southern can make one miserable.

The most palpable of these is the heritage of race. For this, Dave does not have to go back to antebellum times. Recollections of the lives of African Americans during his own lifetime are affecting enough, as in Dave's reflections on the connections between the land and racism in *Burning Angel*:

The piece of land was our original sin, except we had found no baptismal rite to expunge it from our lives. That green-purple field of new cane was rooted in rib cage and eye socket. But what of the others whose lives had begun here and ended in other places? The ones who became prostitutes in cribs on Hopkins Street in New Iberia and Jane's Alley in New Orleans, sliced their hands open with oyster knives, laid bare their shin bones with the cane sickle, learned the twelve-string blues on the Red Hat gang and in the camps at Angola with Lead-belly and Hogman Matthew Maxey, were virtually cooked alive in the cast-iron sweatboxes of Camp A, and rode Jim Crow trains North, as in a biblical exodus, to southside Chicago and the magic of 1925 Harlem, where they filled the air with the music of the South and the smell of cornbread and greens and pork chops fixed with sweet potatoes, as though they were still willing to forgive if we would only acknowledge their capacity for forgiveness.

Tolstoy asked how much land did a man need.

Just enough to let him feel the pull of the earth on his ankles and the claim it lays on the quick as well as the dead. (215-16)

In a number of places, Burke makes his hero an unwitting and unwilling observer of racial injustice or violence: the dead black girl in the bayou in *Neon Rain,* the vigilante killing of a manacled black man recounted in *In the Electric Mist with Confederate Dead;* the Sheriff's account of the executed fourteen-year-old in *Cadillac Jukebox;* and Moleen Bertrand's eviction of black families from their land. Racial violence even haunts place names in Dave's South: "I could never hear the name of the Pearl River without remembering the lynchings that took place in Mississippi in the 1950s and 1960s and the bodies that had been dredged out of the Pearl with steel grappling hooks" (*Morning for Flamingos* 246). Rather than just being remnants of a shameful past, moreover, Dave discerns the persistence of racism even in the so-called New South:

Moleen didn't see it. His kind seldom did. They hanged Nat Turner and tanned his skin for wallets, and used their educations to feign a pragmatic cynicism and float above the hot toil of the poor whose fare they saw as unrelated to their own lives. The consequence was they passed down their conceit and arrogance like genetic heirlooms. (*Cadillac Jukebox* 48)

And Dave's shame for the past his region made and his outrage at its very real vestiges form yet another aspect for his character. At times, they threaten his ability to act effectively, as well as his emotional balance. In this, however, Dave's counselor is Baptist, who tells him:

You bothered by the way t'ings are, the way we got trouble with the colored people all the time, you bothered 'cause it ain't like it used to be. You want sout' Lou'sana to be like it was when you and me and yo' daddy went all day and went everywhere and never spoke one word of English. You walk away when you hear white people talking bad about them Negro, like that bad feeling ain't in their hearts. But you keep pretend it' like it used to be, Dave, that these bad t'ings ain't in white people's hearts, then you gonna be walking away the rest of yo life. (*A Stained White Radiance* 220)

But it's more than racism that forms part of the southerner's character.

While it may have lacked the drama of Vicksburg, Atlanta, or Richmond, opposing armies fought across the whole of Louisiana for almost the entire duration of the Civil War. In 1862 New Orleans fell to David Farragut's flotilla. A year later General Nathaniel Banks ventured out of New Orleans with 35,000 troops and brought Bayou Teche and the entire Atchafalaya basin under Federal control. Over the next two years Confederate Generals Richard Taylor, Nathan Bedford Forrest, and John Bell Hood led rag-tag troops across the state in their attempts to prevent the inevitable.

It may have been in the past, but the reminders of the Civil War are very much in the present for Dave. A short walk down the road from his home there is "A sugar planter's home [that] had been built in the 1830s, but the second story had been torched by General Banks's soldiers in 1863" (*Heaven's Prisoners* 172). Near it "my father, my brother, and I had dug out a bucket full of minie balls as well as canister and grapeshot, bits of chain, and chopped-up horseshoes fired by Union cannon into the Confederate rearguard" (*Heaven's Prisoners* 173). One does not have to look very hard in southern Louisiana for the archeological reminders of events that took place more than a century ago. But in the South, these artifacts have more value than simple antiquarian curiosity. So, as Dave tells readers in *A Stained White Radiance,*

No matter how educated a southerner is, or how liberal or intellectual he might consider himself to be, I don't believe you will meet many of my generation who do not still revere, although perhaps in a secret way, all the old southern myths that we've supposedly put aside as members of the New South. You cannot grow up in a place where the tractor's plow can crack mine balls and grapeshot loose from the soil, even rake across a cannon wheel, and remain impervious to the past. As a child I had access to few books, but I knew all the stories about General Banks's invasion . . . and Louisiana's boys in butternut brown who lived on dried peas and gave up ground a bloody foot at a time. (265)

In a world largely devoid of the concepts, all of this creates an ingrained belief in the importance of self-sacrifice and honor:

I wondered what it would be like to step through a window in time, into another age of belief, and march alongside Granny Lee's boys, most of them barefoot and emaciated as scarecrows, so devoted to their concept of honor and their bonnie blue flag they deliberately chose not to foresee the moment when their lives would be scattered by grapeshot like wildflowers blown from their stems. (*Burning Angel* 263)

Dave is particularly susceptible to all of this. With his commitment to living an upright life, to protecting the weak, and to preserving the values of his childhood and his culture, Burke's hero becomes quite literally a throw-back to an earlier time. This begins with Dave's musings at the end of *A Stained White Radiance* cited above and comes to full fruition in *In the Electric Mist with Confederate Dead*. Here the residual effects of being drugged with LSD take Dave back to 1865 and introduce him to John Bell Hood and his worn down troops fighting the last battles of the war in the swamps and bayous around Dave's home. Interspersed throughout the novel, General Hood offers Dave counsel on honorable conduct. And at the end, leafing through a book on the Civil War, Alafair finds her father's exact likeness in one of the soldiers photographed with John Bell Hood. All of this leads Dave to romantic notions about warfare which his experiences in Vietnam show are false. And his notions about personal honor mark him as an anomaly in a world where "It's all business today. The ethos of Robert E. Lee is as dead as the world we grew up in" (*Burning Angel* 232).

With all of his emphasis on the impact of the Civil War on his hero's consciousness, Burke occasionally alludes to the idea that all events, past and present, exist simultaneously. This briefly comes out in a passage in *Burning Angel*: "I've often subscribed to the notion that perhaps history is not sequential; that all people, from all of history, live out their lives simultaneously, in different dimensions perhaps, occupying the same pieces of geography, unseen by one another, as if we are all part of one spiritual conception" (38). It is, however, pretty difficult to build a narrative based on this concept. Instead Burke has Dave use the past as a refuge and a bulwark:

I wanted to go into yesterday. And I don't think that's always bad. Sometimes you simply have to walk through a door in your mind and lose thirty or forty years in order to remember who you are. Maybe it's a self-deception, a mental opiate that I use to escape my problems, but I don't care. We are the sum total of what we have done and where we have been, and in many ways I sincerely believe that in many ways the world in which I grew up was better than the one in which we live today. (*Black Cherry Blues* 188)

Dave's refusal to abandon this idea, that the past was better than the present and is responsible for much of what we are, has much to do with his character. Hence the following exchange with his wife: "'New Iberia is never going to be the same place we grew up in. That's just the way things are,' she said. 'That doesn't mean I have to like it'" (*In the Electric Mist* 94).

Likewise, Dave's stubborn adherence to the past has a great deal to do with his standards of behavior, and his commitment to traditional ideals such as responsibility, honor, and justice. And for Burke, this is not simply something he uses to form a discursive part of Dave's character. He also builds pieces of plot around his hero's commitment to his past. So the action of *Heaven's Prisoners* pivots on the life of Bubba Rocque, with whom Dave and his brother set bowling pins; *Black Cherry Blues* begins when Dave meets his old college roommate, Dixie Lee Pugh; Dave grew up with the Sonnier family, whose troubles motivate *A Stained White Radiance*; and Julie Balboni, who threatens the serenity of New Iberia in *In the Electric Mist with Confederate Dead,* was the catcher on Dave's high school baseball team. It's the same in every book after *Neon Rain.* Someone from Dave's past returns to New Iberia. But they return tainted by the world—by organized crime in the case of Bubba Rocque, Julie Balboni, and Tommy Lonighan from *Dixie City Jam.* Or political ambition has warped their perspective on life as in *A Stained White Radiance* and *Cadillac Jukebox.* In each case their incursion into Dave's world becomes a more important dilemma for Burke's hero than the crime problem upon which the novel runs. While each novel ends with these characters being taken off the board to leave Dave's world as it was in the beginning, their presence gives rise to the hero's moral outrage and contributes to the resigned sadness that affects the end of each book.

As if Burke's hero does not have enough to contend with, his job as a police officer brings him into contact with criminals. And Burke's treatment of criminals opens up yet more conflicts in Dave's consciousness. Starting at the top, Burke makes it clear that crime and criminals are not just those out on the streets. They are created by and exist because of larger forces:

any honest cop will tell you that no form of vice exists without societal sanction of some kind. Also, the big players would still be with us—the mob and the gambling interests who feed on economic recession and greed in politicians and local businessmen, the oil industry, which fouls the oyster beds and trenches saltwater channels into a freshwater marsh, the chemical and waste management companies that treat Louisiana as an enormous outdoor toilet and transform lakes and even aquifer into toxic soup. (*Burning Angel* 97)

Perhaps because of the magnitude of their crimes, politicians and businessmen never do jail time. It never crosses anyone's mind—except Dave's. While the surrogate wars in Central America and shadowy government agencies exert a seductive pull on Burke, there is little that his hero can do about the larger societal causes, and when he deals with them, they generally muddy his plots. Besides, police officers never come in contact with the people who profit from the macrocosm of crime and violence. The microcosm of crime—the rapists, the killers, the muggers, the pedophiles—keeps them busy enough.

From one point of view, the simplest way to deal with criminals is to exterminate them. That's Dave's old partner and friend, Clete Purcel's view of police work: "You see the handiwork and you hunt the bastards down. You bust 'em or grease 'em" (*Heaven's Prisoners* 141); "Bury your fist in their stomachs, leave them puking on their knees, click off their lights with a slapjack if they still want to play" *(Black Cherry Blues* 47); "make their puds shrivel up and hide" (*Burning Angel* 286); "weld it [the cell door] shut and burn their birth certificates" (*Heaven's Prisoners* 155); and "a three-day open season on people would solve a lot of our problems" (*In the Electric Mist* 95). This is an attitude from which Dave is not exempt. During his violent blackouts, it's the way he operates. And the same is true when, as happens in a number of books, a member of his real or extended family is threatened. Albeit immediately effective, it's a simplistic answer to the crime and criminals, and Dave knows it. That's the trouble.

So Burke has his hero face dilemma after dilemma trying to fathom the nature of criminals. From the first novel on Dave talks about "our dark fascination with man's iniquity" (*Neon Rain* 71). He repeatedly ponders the enigma of nature and nurture as applied to crime: "What produced them? Defective genes, growing up in a shithole, bad toilet training? Even after fourteen years with the New Orleans police department, I never had an adequate answer" (*Heaven's Prisoners* 27). On the side of nurture, Dave and his police colleagues come up with the concept of The Pool: "Members of The Pool leave behind warehouses of official paperwork as evidence that they have occupied the planet for a certain period of time. Their names are entered early in welfare case histories, child-abuse investigations, clinic admissions for rat bites and malnutrition" (*A Stained White Radiance* 76). Over the course of the novels, however, Dave encounters several significant characters whose humanity overcomes their backgrounds in poverty and abuse and their immersion in crime. There is Tony Cardo in *A Morning for Flamingos,* Tommy Lonighan in *Dixie City Jam,* and Sonny Boy Marsallus in *Burning Angel.* In each case they possess characteristics of compassion and sympathy which, for Dave, compensate for the criminal activity in which they have engaged. In each case, too, they perform actions near the end of the novels which demonstrate their kinship with Dave and the ideals he represents.

With others, however, it's different. Real criminals are different. For one thing, they are downright physically frightening: "they all seemed to contain a reservoir of rut and power and ruthless energy that made you shudder" (*A Morning for Flamingos* 212). Worse than the physical response they evoke, the quality of their eyes marks them off as dangerous. It's like there is nothing there:

Eddy Raintree's photo stared at me out of his file with a face that had the moral depth and complexity of freshly poured cement. (*A Stained White Radiance* 77)

He had the coarse, square hands of a bricklayer, the facial depth of a pie plate. I always suspected that if he was lobotomized you wouldn't know the difference. The psychiatrists at Mandeville diagnosed him as a sociopath and shot his head full of electricity. Evidently the treatment had as much effect as charging a car battery with three dead cells. (*In the Electric Mist* 29)

Or it's like what is behind their eyes is disturbingly alien:

Their eyes are dead. No, that's not quite correct. There's a light there, like a wet lucifer match flaring behind black glass, but no matter how hard you try to interpret the thought working behind it, you cannot be sure if the person is thinking about taking your life or having his car washed. (*Dixie City Jam* 203)

You knew they wanted something, but you weren't sure what it was, in the same way that you stare into a zoo animal's eyes and see an atavistic instinct that makes you step back involuntarily. (*A Morning for Flamingos* 292)

As with the term "atavistic" above, Burke sometimes tries to explain the character of criminals in terms of devolution. Thus in *Dixie City Jam* Dave describes Buchalter's acts as "something tribal and dark, far beyond the moral ken of a youthful law officer, a glimpse into a time before the creation of light in the world" (231). But coexisting with sociological or anthropological explanations for the nature of the criminal personality, early on Dave, as is his inclination, asks theological questions. Thus in *Heaven's Prisoners* he asks: "Was he made up of the same corpuscle, sinew, and marrow as I? Or was his brain taken hot from a furnace, his parts hammered together in a shower of sparks on a devil's anvil?" (197). Dave observes the same thing again about evil in the next book: "The men who did the work make you shudder. I've heard all kinds of explanations for their behavior and their perverse nature. My personal feeling is that they're simply evil" (*Black Cherry Blues* 214). And then in *Dixie City Jam* he extends it to: "I looked into his eyes, and if that man had a soul, I believe demons had already claimed it" (91). But in the end, Burke backs off from the Manichean view of criminals— that they are from some other species intent on pain and destruction— and holds that they simply represent a perverse exaggeration of the dark potential in all humanity.

They aren't fashioned from anvil and chain in a devil's forge, either. Judas Iscariot was us; there was no metaphysical mystery to Will Buchalter and his sister and the Calucci brothers. Their souls had the wingspan of moths; they functioned because we allowed them to and gave them sanction; they stopped functioning when that sanction was denied. (*Dixie City Jam* 366)

The crux of everything lies in being victims, and not being victims. For Burke, their environment along with epidemic institutional failure looses in criminals the dark potential inherent in all humanity. Their overwhelming need for any of the various permutations of power makes criminals single-minded, oblivious to values, indifferent to others, and cruel. More than anyone else, Dave can understand this. Painfully, he has come to understand the variety of forces—depression, alcoholism, violence, the heritage of being southern, the past—which have exerted control over his behavior and have made him a victim of the dark potential of all humanity. The first step to his recovery, and an essential part of his character, therefore, is his determination to stop being a victim himself and to prevent others from being victims as well.

Neither one is an easy job. For drunks like Dave, sobriety is always going to be a matter of one day at a time. So is relief from depression. These are difficult realities to accept. For Dave, the realities of crime and its victims are perhaps even more difficult to accept. And to make things even more complicated, Dave's views of crime, violence, and victims are tied up with his concepts of manliness.

A number of ingrained concepts of manliness come into Dave's examination of himself and his own conduct. Burke introduces this motif in *Heaven's Prisoners* when Dave describes his formative years:

I had learned most of my lessons for dealing with problems from hunting and fishing and competitive sports. No book could have taught me what I had learned from my father in the marsh, and as a boxer in high school I had discovered that it was as important to swallow your blood and hide your injury as it was to hurt your opponent. (84)

All of the lessons that form this part of Dave's character center on the basic importance of fortitude. Throughout the books he reminds Alafair of the importance of being what he calls "a stand-up" guy, as in his epitaph for Sonny Boy Marsallus in *Burning Angel*: " 'I've made my peace with Sonny,' I said. 'He was brave, he was stand-up, he never compromised his principles. That's not a bad recommendation to take into the next world' " (328). Being manly, however, means more than an unflinching commitment to principles. It means defining one's self with violence when necessary. This comes out in Burke's repeated allusions to baseball as a metaphor for how to approach life's dilemmas and vexations:

But maybe the most important lesson I learned about addressing complexity was from an elderly Negro janitor who had once pitched for the Kansas City Monarchs in the old Negro leagues . . . one day after I'd been shotgunned off the mound and was walking off the field . . . he walked along beside me and said, "Sliders and screwballs is cute, and spitters shows 'em you can be nasty. But if you want to make the batter's pecker shrivel up, you throw a forkball at his head." (*Heaven's Prisoners* 84-85)

Part of manliness is the capacity for violence in defense of principle: "But when they try to kill you, it gets personal. Then you play it only one way. You go into the lion's den and you spit in the lion's mouth" (*A Stained White Radiance* 64). Indeed, in *A Morning for Flamingos,* being involved with danger and violence is one of the ways in which the self is defined: "You got to go out there on the screaming edge. That's the only place to win. You don't know that, you don't know anything" (300). But General John Bell Hood gives what Dave finds to be the ultimate definition of manliness and violence in *In the Electric Mist with Confederate Dead* when he says, "That it's the innocent we need to worry about. And when it comes to their protection, we shouldn't hesitate to do it under a black flag" (236).

And Dave worries a great deal about protecting the innocent. Throughout the novels Burke focuses a portion of his hero's ardor in defense of the dispossessed: Robin in *Heaven's Prisoners,* Dixie Lee Pugh in *Black Cherry Blues,* Tee Beau Latiolais in *A Morning for Flamingos,* Elrod Sykes in *In the Electric Mist with Confederate Dead,* Bertha and Ruthie Jean Fontenot in *Burning Angel,* Lucinda and Zoot Bergeron in *Dixie City Jam,* and Aaron Crown and his daughter in *Cadillac Jukebox.* In fact, in *A Stained White Radiance,* Dave notes that

We all have an extended family, people whom we recognize as our own as soon as we see them. The people closest to me have always been marked by a peculiar difference in their makeup. They're the walking wounded, the ones to whom a psychological injury was done that they will never be able to define, the ones with the messianic glaze in their eyes, or the oblique glance, as though an M-1 tank is about to burst through their mental fortifications. (280)

Sometimes he can save these innocents from being made victims, and sometimes he cannot. His more difficult problems, however, come from trying to save those who have chosen to become the victims of affluence or power acquired in dishonest or dishonorable means. While Dave spends an inordinate amount of time on them, he has little discernible impact on the lives or actions of these people, beginning with Bubba Rocque and extending through Buford LaRose. In one way or another, tragedy attends these people at the end of the novels—in spite of Dave's insistent, almost obsessive concern.

Dave's most intense efforts, however, are directed at protecting his family. This is one of the essential changes Burke makes after *Neon Rain:* he gives Dave a home and a family. At the end of that first Robicheaux novel, Burke has Dave "buy a boat-rental and bait business in New Iberia" (281). In later books, though, he changes the place to the Robicheaux family homestead that Dave's father, Aldous, built himself. Here Burke assembles a family for Dave. First there is his daughter, Alafair, an orphan Dave saves from drowning in *Heaven's Prisoners* and whom Burke invests with motifs from his hero's own childhood: she bears the name of the hero's mother and her three-legged raccoon is the same one Burke describes as Dave's in *Heaven's Prisoners.* Starting with Annie, all of the women in Dave's life have been made been made victims in one way or another—Annie's unwanted pregnancy, Robin's drug addiction, and Bootsie's lupus. Much of the momentum of Burke's novels comes from Dave's need to protect his family, especially his daughter. Threats to Alafair come in *Heaven's Prisoners, Black Cherry Blues,* and in *In the Electric Mist with Confederate Dead. Dixie City Jam* brings in threats to Bootsie and Baptist.

Throughout the books Dave's compassion for all who suffer and his attempts to alleviate that suffering are key ingredients in his character. The magnitude of suffering in the past and in the present, however, he finds to be beyond measure. He comes to accept, as well, that evil will forever exist beyond human capacity to understand or control it. Thus the backwoods preacher in *Dixie City Jam* tells Dave that "You don't outwit evil. You don't outthink hit, you don't joke with hit, no more than you tease or control fire by sticking your hand in hit" (171). Dave himself brings up a broader theological answer to the problem of evil in the world: "When I was a child in Catholic school, we were taught that evil eventually consumes itself, like fire that must consume its own source" (*Dixie City Jam* 161). Trying to combat even a small measure of it, as Dave must, leads only to small victories associated with those closest to him, along with the temptations to lapse back into depression or alcoholism. Dave frequently finds the way out by repeating AA's "Serenity Prayer," the first two stanzas of which are:

> GOD, grant me the serenity
> to accept the things
> I cannot change,
>
> Courage to change the
> things I can, and the
> wisdom to know the difference.

Burke has Dave seek refuge or solace in this prayer a number of times throughout the novels. Additionally, in *Heaven's Prisoners* Dave turns to the Psalms (Psalm 69) when confronting the suffering of innocents, and in *Black Cherry Blues* Burke includes two occasions when Dave ties crime, suffering, and prayer together:

I don't have any answers for it, either. Sometimes cops can't do any good. That's why as I get older I believe more and more in prayer. At least I feel like I'm dealing with somebody who's got some real authority. (177)

I made a peculiar prayer. It's a prayer that sometimes I say, one that is perhaps self-serving, but because I believe that God is not limited by time or space as we are, I believe perhaps that He can influence the past even though it has already happened. So sometimes when I'm alone, especially at night, in the dark, and I begin to dwell on the unbearable suffering that people probably experienced before their deaths, I ask God to retroactively relieve their pain, to be with them in mind and body, to numb their senses, to cool whatever flame licked their eyes in their final moments. (195)

It's with the "wisdom to know the difference" from the "Serenity Prayer" that Dave has troubles, troubles that recur at the beginning of each successive novel. And in each successive novel the world presents Dave with mounting moral and ethical dilemmas, Pyrrhic victories over crime and suffering, and failed attempts to find the community his golden memories of his past have created. Except at the end, when Dave returns home. Thus at the end of each novel, Burke includes an epilogue which both wraps up loose ends of the plot and, more importantly, returns Dave to the house his father built on the bayou, shaded by pecan trees, near Civil War ruins, with Alafair's horse in the pasture and Tripod running on his leash, Bootsie weeding the flower beds, and Baptist ready to open up the bait shop in the morning. Just the way it should have been when he was a child. But wasn't.

WALTER MOSLEY

It all started before the war when Raymond Alexander talked his friend Ezekiel "Easy" Rawlins into going with him from Houston to Pariah, Texas, where he aimed to collect a pile of money from his stepfather. But not for us. It really all began for us after Easy left Houston, fought in World War II and moved to L.A. mostly to get away from the South and the life he led there. *Devil in a Blue Dress* (1990) takes off from there. And then comes *A Red Death* (1991), *White Butterfly* (1992), *Black Betty* (1994), and A *Little Yellow Dog* (1996). In the next year Black Classics Press finally published that first book, *Gone Fishin'*, which tells the story of Easy's travels to Pariah with Raymond Alexander. It's likely that we would have never known about that trip and that *Gone Fishin'* would never have been published had Walter Mosley not discovered Los Angeles and had his hero, Easy Rawlins, not discovered that acting as a detective provided a key ingredient to defining himself.

Gone Fishin' has mostly to do with a small, southern African American community with gothic undertow, as well as with the emerging maturity of Easy Rawlins. Mosley's other books, mind you, occasionally take nostalgic glances back at the ambiance of the place that his hero has chosen to leave behind. Thus early in *Devil in a Blue Dress* we get: "No matter where you live in a southern city (even in a wild and violent place like Fifth Ward, Houston) you see almost everybody you know just looking out your window. Every day is a parade of relatives and old friends and lovers you once had, and maybe you'd be lovers again one day" (49). And Mosley returns every now and again to the feeling of community that Easy abandoned when he left Houston—indeed, in a number of different ways, Mosley's hero tries to recreate or reestablish that "southern" sense of community in all of the subsequent books. Ostensibly Easy leaves Houston to free himself of the vestiges of Mouse Alexander's murder of his stepfather, to get away from the greed and violence that he saw as the basis for Mouse's character and the glimmering of the same within himself as well as from the unexamined hedonistic existence that was the sole resource of that segregated community: "All the people around me dancing, having a good time; they were just holding me back, wanting me to be the same old poor Easy—not a nickel in my pocket or a dream in my head" (*Gone Fishin'* 237). More importantly, Easy leaves Houston because he seeks a larger definition of himself:

Home is not a place to dream. At home you had to do like your father did and your mother. Home meant that everybody already knew what you could do and if you did the slightest little thing different they'd laugh you right down into a hole. After that you either accepted your hole or you got out of it.

There were all kinds of ways out. You could get married, get drunk, get next to somebody's wife. You could take a shotgun and eat it for a midnight snack. (*Black Betty* 31)

"Or," Easy tells us in the next sentence, "you could move to California."

California means a number of different things to Mosley's hero. For one thing, it lacks the amenities characteristic of southern life:

in L.A. people don't have time to stop; anywhere they have to go they go there in a car. The poorest man has a car in Los Angeles; he might not have a roof over his head but he has a car . . . The promise of getting rich pushed people to work two jobs in the week and do little plumbing on the weekend. There's no time to walk down the street or make a bar-b-q when somebody's going to pay you real money to haul refrigerators. (*Devil in a Blue Dress* 49)

But for Easy, Watts does possess some residual sense of southern community and has the advantage of being a cosmopolitan center for jazz and blues musicians: "They'd come in and listen to Coltrane, Monk, Holiday, and all the rest. . . . Sonny Terry, Brownie McGee, Lightnin' Hopkins, Soupspoon Wise, and a hundred others passed through the hotels and back-street dives that still cluttered Bone [Street]" (*White Butterfly* 62-63). Throughout all of the books the energy, power, and beauty of Los Angeles continue to enthrall Mosley's hero: "When I went out the front door L.A. was waiting for me. You could see as far as the mountains would let you. I didn't deserve it, but it was mine just the same" (*White Butterfly* 92). But beauty isn't the only advantage; California seems to offer security, anonymity, and freedom:

In California they wouldn't laugh at you, or anybody. In California the sun shone three hundred and more days a year. In California you could work until you dropped. And when you got up there was another job waiting for you. In California you could paint the slats of your house like a rainbow and put a smiling face on your front door. (*Black Betty* 31)

Racism, inhumanity, and power, however, too often dilute or destroy the promises of security, anonymity, and freedom.

Easy Rawlins's California, moreover, is not just a place, it is also a time, or rather a group of times, for Mosley conscientiously places his detective novels at specific times during a fifteen-year period: "I was used to white people by 1948" (*Devil in a Blue Dress* 1); "I heard Mofass drive up in his new '53 Pontiac" (*A Red Death* 11); "A black woman getting killed wasn't photograph material for the newspapers in 1956" (*White Butterfly* 14); "I tried to think of better things. About our new young Irish president and Martin Luther King" (*Black Betty* 11); and "Somewhere the only president I ever loved was lying dead" (*A Little Yellow Dog* 29). It's not just playful anachronism like Stuart Kaminsky's Hollywood novels. Each one of the dates carries with it implications of the larger world that affects the conditions of Easy Rawlins's community and his life. In *Devil in a Blue Dress* the post-war migration to California and the jitters of the Cold War take Easy to Los Angeles and give him a job at Champion Aircraft. McCarthyism reached its high-water mark in 1953 before the Army-McCarthy hearings, and Mosley reflects this in Chaim Wenzler and Easy's role as unwilling agent for the FBI in *A Red Death*. Easy develops the idea of the black-owned Freedom's Plaza the year the Montgomery bus boycott ended in *White Butterfly*. And the election and assassination of John F. Kennedy with his program of civil rights legislation bracket *Black Betty* and *A Little Yellow Dog*.

When Easy Rawlins decides to leave Houston, he does so in order to find a larger, freer existence. First he enlists in the Army and goes to Europe to fight in World War II. In the Army he finds systematic prejudice that makes all African American soldiers non-combatants, a system which Easy overcomes by volunteering for combat: "I got tired of all the white soldiers calling me a coward for working behind the lines. So when the call came up for any soldier, black or white, to volunteer for Patton's push I raised my hand" (*Gone Fishin'* 242). And out of his experience in Europe Easy both affirms his own selfhood and moves one step away from his segregated past: "There was always trouble between the races, especially when it came to the women, but we learned to respect each other out there too" (*Devil in a Blue Dress* 98). He goes to California with the assumption that there he will find respect for hard work, competence, and integrity as well as the opportunity to achieve selfhood that the limitations of his community had denied him. Instead, the first California book, *Devil in a Blue Dress*, begins with Easy being fired from Champion Aircraft by his racist boss. This provokes a number of responses. First comes the recognition of the gulf that history and the system has imposed between the races, here articulated in its most pessimistic form by Mouse: "That's just like you, Easy. You learn stuff and you be thinkin' like white men be thinkin'. You be thinkin' that what's right fo' them is right fo' you. She look like she white and you think you white. But brother you know that you both poor niggers. And a nigger ain't never gonna be happy 'less he accept what he is" (*Devil in a Blue Dress* 205). While it's racism and not community, it's the same thing that originally motivated Easy to leave Houston: "everybody already knew what you could do and if you did the slightest little thing different they'd laugh you right down into a hole. After that you either accepted your hole or you got out of it" (*Black Betty* 31). Except that bigots don't laugh and the hole is much, much deeper.

Mosley has his hero respond to racism in a variety of ways. There is subterfuge, playing the role expected by the white world:

I spoke in a dialect that they would expect. If I gave them what they expected then they wouldn't suspect me of being any kind of real threat. (*Black Betty* 72)

It was a habit I developed in Texas when I was a boy. Sometimes, when a white man of authority would catch me off guard, I'd empty my head of everything so I was unable to say anything. "The less you know, the less trouble you find," they used to say. I hated myself for it but I also hated white people, and colored people too, for making me that way. (*Devil in a Blue Dress* 13)

There is invisibility. First this appears as Easy's escapist fantasy at the police station in *Devil in a Blue Dress*: "I was awake but my thinking was like a dream. All I did was sit in darkness, trying to become the darkness and slip out between the eroded cracks of that cell. If it was nighttime nobody could find me; no one would even know I was missing" (74). But by the time of *A Little Yellow Dog* it has become real: "Somewhere on that lineup I had become invisible again. I'd taken on the shadows that kept me camouflaged, and dangerous" (154). "I used to live on the edge. I used to move in darkness" (184). There is also recognition of economic realities that compound racism: "I felt that I was just as good as any white man, but if I didn't even own my front door then people would look at me like just another poor beggar, with his hand outstretched" (*Devil in a Blue Dress* 9). Mosley's treatment of money, business, and work play a major role in his depiction of Easy as a man and as a black man. And we will come back to them later.

Perhaps more important than Easy's changing perspectives on economic issues comes his drive toward self-improvement, his need to educate himself. Briefly in *A Red Death* and consistently in the later books, Mosley makes his hero an obsessive reader:

"Lib'ary got its do' open, man. Ain't nobody tellin' you not to go."

There aren't too many moments in your life when you really learn something. Jackson taught me something that night in John's, something I'd never forget. (*A Red Death* 216)

From *White Butterfly* onward, we find Easy reading W. E. B. DuBois, Plato, the Brontë sisters, Marcus Aurelius, Zola, and even Ian Fleming: "I'm a book reader. There's always a book on my nightstand; sometimes more than one" (*A Little Yellow Dog* 105). And a fundamental part of his self-education is Easy's understanding and articulating pride in being African American. In the passage in *White Butterfly* about Stella Keaton, the librarian, Mosley makes this pretty clear:

We were on a first-name basis, Stella and I, but I was unhappy that she held that job. I was unhappy because even though Stella was nice, she was still a white woman. A white woman from a place where there were only white Christians. To her Shakespeare was a god. I didn't mind that, but what did she know about folk tales and riddles and stories colored folks had been telling for centuries? What did she know about the language we spoke?

I always heard her correcting children's speech, "Not 'I is,' she'd say, 'It's 'I am.'"

And of course she was right. It's just that little colored children listening to that proper white woman would never hear their own cadence in her words. They'd come to believe that they would have to abandon their own language and stories to become part of the educated world. They would have to forfeit Waller for Mozart and Remus for Puck. They would enter a world where only white people spoke. And no matter how articulate Dickens and Voltaire were, those children wouldn't have their own examples in the house of learning—the library.

I have argued with Stella about these things before. She was sensitive about them but when you told her that some man standing on a street corner telling bawdy tales was something like Chaucer she'd crinkle her nose and shake her head. (56)

Easy's burgeoning awareness of the richness of his race's worth and heritage coincides with the occurrence of social movements which increasingly liberate his ability to insist on recognition of his race and of himself as a person. This begins on an individual level at Champion Aircraft in the first book: "'I said you have got to treat me with respect. Now I call you Mr. Giacomo because that's your name. You're no friend to me and I got no reason to be disrespectful and call you by your first name.' I pointed at my chest. 'My name is Mr. Rawlins'" (*Devil in a Blue Dress* 66). That's 1948. In 1953 in *A Red Death*, Easy sees his first civilian example of racial equality in the police team of Reedy and Naylor: "And it made me proud. It was the first time I had ever seen civilian blacks and whites dealing with each other in an official capacity. I mean, the first time I'd seen them acting as equals. They were really working together" (82). By 1960, in *Black Betty*, Easy's experience along with societal change moves him to demand respect both for himself and for all African Americans. Hence this response to a bigot's calculated rudeness:

"I'm lookin for Alamo, cracker," I said. I had to say it. I wasn't marching or singing songs about freedom. I didn't pay dues in the Southern Christian Leadership Conference or the NAACP. I didn't have any kind of god on my side. But even though the cameras weren't on me and JFK never heard my name, I had to make my little stand for what's right. It was a little piece of history that happened right there in that room and that went unrecorded. (*Black Betty* 147)

And while the world of *Black Betty* is hardly one of racial harmony and mutual acceptance (Easy notes that "back then, any white person had to prove themselves to me before I could consider trusting them" [115]), there are Easy's neighbors, the Horns ("They were real people and so I rarely thought about them being white" [48]) and there is the white ex-convict Alamo Weir (successor to Chaim Wenzler from *A Red Death* in advocating socialist points) who reflect small changes in Easy's world and larger changes in his understanding of some of those realities of which racism is a symptom.

One of those realities is the law. And for Easy and his community the law means the police. Mosley depicts a number of incidents of police racism and brutality in the books. Take these from *Devil in a Blue Dress*: "You got a right to fall down and break your face, nigger. You got a right to die" (58). "Means we can take your black ass out behind the station and put a bullet in your head" (72). As the books proceed, Easy glimpses a glimmer of hope in the integration of the Los Angeles police department, reflected especially in his optimism connected with black detective Quentin Naylor, whom Mosley introduces in *A Red Death*. After that book, however, Mosley creates an antipathy between Easy and minority police officers, especially Naylor and Sergeant Sanchez from *A Little Yellow Dog*, an antipathy that has a number of bases. First of all, the ambition to ascend into the middle class has leached from them any sympathy for the poor. Hence Sanchez's self-righteous assault on Easy's integrity in *A Little Yellow Dog*: "And I'm not going to hold your hand and say how sorry I am that you were poor or that you think it's too hard to be as good as other people. That's why you're going to talk to me now—because I know what you are and I don't give a shit about you" (220). In the same book, Easy articulates a truth that he has known since the second book ("I remember thinking that those white people were just as afraid of the law as any colored man" [*A Red Death* 62]), that ultimately white or black, it makes no difference because "Cops is a race all its own. Its members have their own language and their own creed" (142). And part of that creed is power: "They had no idea of goodness or honesty. They had power and that's what they thought was good" (280). But that power, too, is illusory, and his gradual understanding of this lies under much of Easy's thoughts and actions throughout all of the books. In *Devil in a Blue Dress*, Mosley puts its first iteration into the mouth of the sinister DeWitt Albright: "The law . . . is made by the rich people so that the poor people can't get ahead" (20). And in *Black Betty*, detective Arno Lewis completes the syllogism as it applies to the police in his interview with Easy at the police station: "Criminals were just a bunch of thugs living off what honest people and rich people made. The cops were thugs too; paid by the owners of property to keep the other thugs down" (*Black Betty* 197). Mosley would have it, then, that the economic system comprises a major component in the perpetuation of racism.

Easy Rawlins consistently describes himself as poor. It's there in all the books. And even though after the first book he owns a substantial piece of L.A. real estate, the concept of poverty is intimately tied up with Easy's conception of himself and the ways in which he must navigate a world governed by economic imperatives. In some ways poverty looms larger than race. Almost as soon as readers meet him in *Devil in a Blue Dress*, Easy says, "I felt that I was just as good as any white man, but if I didn't even own my front door then people would look at me like just another poor beggar, with his hand outstretched" (9). And allied with this recognition comes what amounts to a philosophy of cruelty and pessimism. Here is a sample of Easy's thoughts on poverty:

Back in Texas, in Fifth Ward, Houston, men would kill over a dime wager or a rash word. And it was always the evil ones that would kill the good and the stupid. (*Devil in a Blue Dress* 34)

I had forgotten that a poor man is never safe.
When I first got the money I'd watched my friend Mouse murder a man. He shot him twice. It was a poor man who could almost taste that stolen loot. It got him killed and now it was going to put me in jail. (*A Red Death* 23)

There's no cure for living a life of poverty. There's nothing to say either. (*White Butterfly* 97)

The first thing a black man and a poor man learns is that trouble is all he's got so that's what he has to work with. (*Black Betty* 106)

Truth and Freedom: two great things for a poor man, a son of slaves and ex-slaves.

My arm ached. I could feel the deep reach of infection in my veins. One thing was certain—there was no escaping Fate. Fate hauls back and laughs his ass off at Truth and Freedom. Those are minor deities compared to Fate and Death. (*Black Betty* 219)

Poor men are always ready to die. We always expect that there's somebody out there who wants to kill us. That's why I never questioned that a white man would pull out his gun when he saw a Negro coming. That's just the way it is in America. (*Black Betty* 44)

It all leads to resignation, resignation to a life of privation, contempt, isolation, and death.

All of this shapes Easy Rawlins's character. Its impact on the way in which he views others is palpable:

Sometimes you're hoping that things will be different; that men and women will change over the years and become those good, if hard, folks that the preachers talk about. But it never changes. And if something does get good for a while you could be sure that it will turn sour before you have time to get any real pleasure. (*Black Betty* 106)

The logic of my childhood had never proven wrong.

If a man wore gold chains, somebody was going to hit him on the head. If he looked prosperous, women would pull him by his dick into the bed and then hit him with a paternity suit nine months later. If a woman had money, the man would just beat her until she got up off of it.

I always talk about down home like it really was home. Like everybody else who looked like me and talked like me really cared about me. I knew that life was hard, but I hoped that if someone stole from me it would be because they were hungry and needed it. But some people will tear you down just to see you fall. They'll do it even if your loss is their own. (*Black Betty* 109)

In examining his own past—his father's flight, his mother's early death, his hand-to-mouth existence as a child, the reality of the southern community of his childhood, and even his friendship with Mouse ("I wished that I had some kind of brother in arms to rely on. All I ever had was Mouse, and standing side by side with him was like pressing up against a porcupine" [*Black Betty* 190]) and Jackson Blue ("Scrawny, lying, and afraid of his own footsteps, Jackson was one of the many friends who would never abandon me—he had nowhere else to go" [*Black Betty* 27])—isolation looms as the only common element. And acting on the belief that cruelty, selfishness, and isolation are life's governing premises affects and warps Easy's character in ways which he gradually comes to understand and overcome.

Beginning with *Devil in a Blue Dress*, Easy comes to believe that money solves most of the problems that matter. At the beginning of the novel, he envies Joppy's shabby bar and throughout the book Mosley exposes Easy to Dewitt Albright's cynical view of the world, encapsulated in "When you owe out then you're in debt and when you're in debt you can't be your own man. That's capitalism" (101). Easy extends this to his own case: "I thought that there might be some justice for a black man if he had the money to grease it. Money isn't a sure bet but it's the closest to God that I've seen in this world. But I didn't have any money" (121). And he transfers this notion to those things closest to him. Most prominently, he associates his home with ownership:

When I was a poor man, and landless, all I worried about was a place for the night and food to eat; you really didn't need much for that. A friend would always stand me a meal, and there were plenty of women who would have let me sleep with them. But when I got that mortgage I found that I needed more than just friendship. Mr. Albright wasn't a friend but he had what I needed. (21)

And ownership overrides and extinguishes normal human contact: Easy tells us that "The bathroom didn't even have a shower and the back yard was no larger than a child's rubber pool. But that meant more to me than any woman I ever knew" (11). Indeed, throughout the novel, the idea of money continues to interfere with Easy's relationship with Daphne Monet. Thus after a Chinese meal: "Somewhere between the foo young and the check I decided to cut my losses. Daphne was too deep for me. Somehow I'd call Carter and tell him where she was. I'd wash my hands of the whole mess. I'm just in it for the money, I kept telling myself" (192). And the theme of money becomes a significant one in the next two books.

In *A Red Death* Mofass replaces Albright as the spokesman for the intractable demands of money. Thus when Poinsettia cannot pay the rent in one of Easy's apartments, Mofass tells him, "We in business, Mr. Rawlins. Business is the hardest thing they make. Harder than diamonds" (19). Later he defines right and wrong by saying "On'y right is what you get away wit', Mr. Rawlins" (21). Unlike Albright's menace, however, Mofass is a character deserving of some pity and he does warn Easy early on that "I'm a businessman and you cain't trust me" (56). Easy's troubles in the book, in fact, stem from Mofass' informing on him to the IRS to protect his own interests. The thoughts of being carried along with Mofass' cynical materialism and of Poinsettia's eviction and death—contrary to his own humane impulses—haunt Easy throughout *A Red Death*. And he exits the novel defeated and pathetic, unaware of the irony of his reference to his son, Jesus:

> "I ain't got no friends man. All I got is Jackson Blue, who'd give me up fo' a bottle 'a wine, and Mouse; you know him. And a Mexican boy who cain't speak English hardly an' if he did he cain't talk no ways."
> Sweat had appeared on Mofass' brow. I must have sounded pretty crazy.
> "I want you to keep workin' fo' me, William. I want you to be my friend." (283)

It doesn't seem that things can get much worse. But in *White Butterfly*, they do. Between books Easy has found and married Regina and she has given birth to the apple of Easy's eye, Baby Edna. Now, if anything, he has surpassed Mofass as a businessman: he realizes that "He was good in business day to day, but Mofass didn't know how to plan for the future" (25). Easy deals with the conglomerate of white businessmen adroitly, understands commercial value, and holds on to his property. He, however, does not, cannot tell Regina about his dealings or his secret wealth:

> All of what I had and all I had done was had and done in secret. Nobody knew the real me. Maybe Mouse and Mofass knew something but they weren't friends that you could kick back and jaw with.
> I thought that maybe Regina was right. But the thought of telling her all about me brought out a cold sweat; the kind of sweat you get when your life is in mortal danger. (169)

And as a consequence of his attitude toward money and property, Regina takes Edna and runs off with Easy's friend Dupree.

Simultaneously, however, Easy gradually comes to understand the hollowness of the illusion they hold out and the moral taint attached to money and business. One of the principal ways in which Mosley develops this is through Easy's attitudes toward his house and his property. In the early books, especially *Devil in a Blue Dress*, in many ways Easy defines himself by his house and it motivates many of his actions. After *White Butterfly*, however, this changes. In the beginning, Easy derives pleasure from both the most mundane aspects of being a homeowner

("Once I'd become a homeowner I got mail every day—and I loved it. I even loved junk mail" [*Devil in a Blue Dress* 44]) and from the more substantial beauty and bounty of his yard. Indeed, Easy's first real description of his house in *Devil in a Blue Dress* he emphasizes its yard:

I loved going home. Maybe it was that I was raised on a sharecropper's farm or that I never owned anything until I bought that house, but I loved my little home. There was an apple tree and an avocado in the front yard, surrounded by thick St. Augustine grass. At the side of the house I had a pomegranate tree that bore more than thirty fruit every season and a banana tree that never produced a thing. There were dahlias and wild roses in beds around the fence and African violets that I kept in a big jar on the front porch. (11)

When he notes that he has moved at the end of *White Butterfly*, however, the emphasis shifts: "We moved three months later. I bought a small house in an area near West Los Angeles called View Park. Middle-class black families had started colonizing that neighborhood" (271). This emphasis on the neighborhood parallels Easy's move away from obsession with his clandestine real estate holdings to his dreams of building Freedom Plaza. More than the simple, individual pride in possession demonstrated in the early books, houses come to represent order and racial pride: thus in *A Little Yellow Dog*, Easy despises Bartlett's slovenly house because of "the disrespect it showed for the neighborhood and for itself" (265).

As well as this shift in the attitude toward ownership, there is a change in Easy's views of nature. We can see it in the descriptions of California. Before *White Butterfly*, Easy's descriptions of the state emphasize opportunity, freedom, and power ("Just to look out on Los Angeles at night gave me a sense of power" [*Devil in a Blue Dress* 92]). But in *White Butterfly* the sweep of the city brings a sense of awe and humility: "When I went out the front door L.A. was waiting for me. You could see as far as the mountains would let you. I didn't deserve it, but it was mine just the same" (92). And in the next book the California landscape takes on an even larger significance:

The ocean and wind told me how small my problems were; how stupid I was to get involved with other people's troubles when there was so much beauty to be had. All I had to do was to look out and see the ocean, or go home and watch my children grow. I laughed and told myself to remember that the next time somebody comes pushing money at me. (*Black Betty* 113)

Then, too, while he retains his appreciation for beauty and residual pride in ownership, Easy's yard takes on a new significance in *Black Betty*:

"As tired as I was, I had to smile when I gazed out into my own yard. It was an open plot of grass surrounded by bushes that sported large mottled red-and-yellow roses. It was a picture-perfect yard in my opinion, but that's not what made me smile. Jesus and Feather were there" (49). Here Easy's children give his house and yard its worth.

While Easy's attitudes toward business, money, and property change during the course of the books, his attitudes toward work do not so much change as they come into focus. As the books progress, too, Mosley interweaves the issues of pride and independence with the issue of work. On one hand, work represents the legitimate and viable long-term response to necessity. Thus, in *Black Betty* Easy considers his own background:

> We [Easy and John] were men who came from poor stock. We had to be cooks and tailors and plumbers and electricians. We had to be our own cops and our own counsel because there wasn't anything for us down at City Hall.
>
> We worked until jobs was done or until we couldn't work anymore. (188)

But necessity brings nothing with it: the passage above ends with "It didn't mean a damn thing." Somewhat earlier in the same novel Easy sounds the same theme about the meaninglessness of work:

> I could have been a plumber, electrician, mechanic, or salesman. Gotten up every morning at six-thirty and dragged myself in to work by eight. I could have said "yessir" and "no sir" and taken home a paycheck. I could have been promoted because I was a good worker, spent every day for the next twenty-five years going into an office or workshop, and then one day they'd put me out and in a year there wouldn't be a soul to remember that I had ever been. (103)

On the other hand, from the very beginning, at Champion Aircraft Mosley also connects work with pride. Easy takes pride in competent, disciplined effort: "The men listened to me. I wasn't a team leader but Benny relied on me to set an example for others because I was such a good worker" (*Devil in a Blue Dress* 62). And in the same novel Mosley connects work with identity as well in Easy's description of his friend Ronald: "Ronald always wore his plumber's overalls no matter where he was. He said that a man's work clothes are the only real clothes he has" (156). In the world of *Devil in a Blue Dress*, however, racial bias will not permit Easy to maintain both his job at Champion Aircraft and his pride as a man. Thus the combination of pride, freedom, and work so characteristically part of the hard-boiled detective provides the exhilaration of independence and the worth Easy feels at the end of that book: "I had a feeling of great joy as I walked away from Ricardo's. I don't know how to say it, exactly. It was as if for the first time in my life I was doing something on my own terms. Nobody was telling me what to do. I was acting on my own" (124). Mosley restates this combination of independence and pride and work in the character of Martin, the aged and dying carpenter in *Black Betty*, and his advice to Easy:

"Always own your tools," he'd say. "Your tools and your house. That way they cain't take it away from ya. Don't live on no paycheck and don't never ask the man for a thing. You got what he want right here in yo' hands . . . That way you gonna be a man. A 'cause that's what a man is—it's what he could *do*." (151)

Between *Devil in a Blue Dress* and *A Little Yellow Dog* times change, things change, and Easy changes. In *A Little Yellow Dog* the uncertainty, chaos, and danger of being a detective are more destructive than fulfilling: "While convalescing I reflected on my life, wondering how it could be that I was in danger even from my friends. I had decided, upon coming home, to concentrate on getting honest work" (87). And Easy finds that his job as the supervising head custodian at Sojourner Truth Junior High provides some degree of pride and fulfillment and that in addition to being an end in itself, work serves as a means to what he has come to believe is a higher end: "There are moments in your life when you can tell what's right and wrong about yourself—your nature. I wanted my job and my everyday kind of life. I wanted to see Jesus get his track scholarship at UCLA and Feather to become the artist I knew she could be" (*A Little Yellow Dog* 73). And that higher end, of course, is his family.

As with money, and business, and work, the detective business undergoes real change as the books and time progress. Not in what Easy as a detective uncovers, mind you. That's always bad, evil, and sordid: the sorrow of mixed race relations and the pain of child abuse in *Devil in a Blue Dress*; blacklisting, more mixed race relations leading to murder, betrayal, and the arbitrary power of the government in *A Red Death*; murder and still more tragic mixed race relationships in *White Butterfly*; bloody revenge and yet again the tragedy and pathos of mixed race relationships in *Black Betty*; and finally drug dealing and murder in *A Little Yellow Dog*. What Easy finds out is always the same and is not a whole lot different from the world of Houston's Fifth Ward where he grew up. What changes is Easy's responses to himself as a detective.

At first Easy sees his role as a detective as both liberating ("I was doing something on my own terms" [*Devil* 124]) and as fulfilling a basic intellectual need. Thus, in *A Red Death* he tells Etta Mae "If a dog see sumpin' dead he just roll around on the corpse a few times an' move on, huntin'. But I find a dead man an' it's like he's alive, followin' me around an' pointin' his finger at me" (191). Easy even occasionally uses the language of intellectual analysis so frequently the staple of detectives in detective stories, as in this passage from *A Little Yellow Dog*: "The tiles began to fall together in my mind. The characters of my little play, living and dead, picked up their parts and rehearsed their lines. I started with a happy ending and then worked backwards from there" (212). He also sees his role as a detective as bringing some of the South and the humanity and sense of community he nostalgically associates with the South to the facelessness of Los Angeles:

On top of real estate I was in the business of favors. I'd do something for some-body, like find a missing husband or figure out who's been breaking into so-and so's store, and then maybe they could do me a good turn one day. It was a real country way of doing business. At that time almost everybody in my neighbor-hood had come from the country around southern Texas and Louisiana. (*A Red Death* 15)

He develops tradecraft from his sociability, his wide acquaintance in his community, his intelligence and knowledge, and from his capacity for subterfuge. Perhaps most importantly, being a detective is something Easy does naturally and well—he doesn't have the nickname for noth-ing—and for which he receives a wage and some approbation from his community as well as a measure of recognition from the police who come to him to help solve crimes in Watts. But playing a dual role—as a man and as a detective—becomes increasingly painful and distressing to Easy.

Indeed, in describing his first real experience as a detective in *Devil in a Blue Dress* Easy touches on several points that will continue to be morally disturbing to him in the upcoming novels:

It was those two days more than any other time that made me a detective.

I felt a secret glee when I went into a bar and ordered a beer with money someone else had paid me. I'd ask the bartender his name and talk about any-thing but, really, behind my friendly talk, I was working to find something. Nobody knew what I was up to and that made me sort of invisible; people thought that they saw me but what they really saw was an illusion of me, some-thing that wasn't real. (*Devil in a Blue Dress* 158)

First there is something very much like hubris in Easy's "secret glee" which Mosley counterpoints with his hero's repeated references to him-self as a "fool" in the later books. Next comes the dissimulation, pretending to be someone, something he is not. By the time of *A Red Death* Easy considers this part of the detective's role with revulsion:

Just the idea that I was there to fool those people, the same way I had fooled Poinsettia with my lies about being a helpless janitor, made my stomach turn. (149)

I was ashamed of what I'd done to Mouse and what I planned to do. Mofass shamed me because we were just alike. I made like I was friends with people and then I planned to do them dirt. (276)

Then taking and making money as a detective undercuts Easy's notion of his work as being an extension of the southern community. He thinks about this pretty seriously in *Black Betty*:

Taking that twenty-dollar bill was a changing point in my life. Up until that moment I used what talents I had to trade favors with my neighbors and friends. It was rare that I would take cash from one of my peers . . .

I felt myself becoming cut off from the human debt that had been my stock in trade. (191)

Finally there is the invisibility, the acceptance or wish for the same kind of non-identity which Easy uses as a ruse in his business dealings and which he occasionally as well experiences and associates with his blackness.

While he freely admits his age and his aging in the books, in some ways Easy associates his role as a detective with something both intimately connected to his nature and to his youth and to his past. In *White Butterfly* he describes his return to detecting as undergoing rebirth: "I hadn't hit the streets since my wedding. I tried to bury that part of my life. In one way, looking for this killer was like coming back from the dead for me" (53). But at the same time his role as a detective also loses his connection with those things which make him most human—it certainly loses him the friendship of Odell, his oldest friend, and forms part of the complex of isolation that drives his wife, Regina, from him. This loss becomes a constant source of pain.

One other constant contradiction and nagging source of pain for Easy as a man and as a detective is his friendship with Raymond Alexander, Mouse. As we know from *Gone Fishin'*, Easy's past is inextricably tied up with Mouse. In a number of ways, Mouse serves as a model for survival and success in a world governed by poverty. He possesses the love of Etta Mae, the woman to whom Easy is also magnetically attracted. He dresses stylishly and is given respect almost universally in his community. He acts consistently with his principles, and he is fiercely devoted to his son. Indeed, in a perverse way Mouse serves as a surrogate father for Easy: in *Devil in a Blue Dress,* when confronted with a difficult decision, Easy notes that "Without Mouse I didn't know what to do" (194) and he also connects leaving Mouse with the necessity of proving his own manhood ("I ran away from Mouse and Texas . . . I hated myself. I signed up to fight in the war to prove to myself that I was a man" [48]). From the very beginning, too, Mouse advocates the same aggressive capitalism that Easy sees, half fears and half admires in DeWitt Albright: "Mouse is a lot like Mr. Albright. He's smooth and a natty dresser and he's smilin' all the time. But he always got his business in the front of his mind, and if you get in the way you might come to no good" (*Devil in a Blue Dress* 10). Indeed, Mouse uses the same kind of hard logic that is Albright's stock in trade and he gives Easy advice based on the same kind of cruel realism. Here's an example from *Devil in a Blue Dress*:

Nigger can't pull his way out the swamp wit' out no help, Easy. You wanna hold on t' this house and git some money and have you some white girls callin' on the phone? Alright. That's alright. But, Easy, you gotta have somebody at yo' back, man. That's just a lie them white men give 'bout makin' it on they own. They always got they backs covered. (153)

And one from *A Red Death*: "You like some stupid cowboy, Easy. You wanna yell 'Draw!' 'fore you fire. That kinda shit gets ya killed" (274). It is an approach that saves Easy's life any number of times beginning when Mouse intervenes to save him from Frank Green and then from Albright in *Devil in a Blue Dress*. It is also an approach to life, a way of life from which Easy constantly recoils. His first thought of Mouse in *Devil in a Blue Dress* is "Just thinking about Mouse set my teeth on edge" (5). Again and again, up until *A Little Yellow Dog*, Easy comments on the repellent part of Mouse's make-up:

Mouse probably meant to keep his word to me; he could keep from killing if he tried. But if he got a whiff of that thirty thousand dollars I knew that nothing would hold him back. He would have killed me for that much money. (*Devil in a Blue Dress* 155-56)

Mouse was the truest friend I ever had. And if there is such a thing as true evil, he was that too. (*A Red Death* 73)

Most violent and desperate men have a kind of haunted look in their eyes. But never Mouse. He could smile in your face and shoot you dead. He didn't feel guilt or remorse. He was different from most men. (*A Red Death* 74)

But not Mouse. He was like an ancient pagan needing to celebrate and anoint his freedom with blood. (*Black Betty* 62)

He [Mouse] was the darkness on the other side of the moon. (*Black Betty* 64)

In spite of his knowledge of and aversion to Mouse's nature, Easy both accepts its inevitability and depends on it for his salvation in his dealing with others whose lives are predicated on violence. At first this is criminals like Frank Green, but by the time of *White Butterfly* Easy uses Mouse and the threat of violence to intimidate the white businessmen who seek to buy his properties.

In *Black Betty* and *A Little Yellow Dog*, however, Easy's connection with violence undergoes significant changes. First of all, in *Black Betty* Easy runs across Ortiz, the strong-arm man in Jackson Blue's numbers scheme. While Easy accepts violence as a natural part of Mouse's make-up, with Ortiz he understands it can and does have real causes and its debilitating effects: "I knew Ortiz and the dark anger inside him. He lived in a haze of rage; probably couldn't even make love because he was so mad. The anger was a deep hole of despair that he lived in. I'd lived next to that hole since I was a boy" (*Black Betty* 131). Additionally, in this novel Easy uses violence to achieve a noble purpose: he deflects Mouse's murderous intent from the man who put him in Chino for five years for manslaughter of his friend Martin, destroyed by cancer and wishing for the death that would not come. Finally, Easy's own acts take on a new motive. As the novel progresses the dream of Freedom's Plaza is destroyed by the connivance of entrepreneurs and politicians. This serves to confirm the lesson Easy's friend Alamo Weir learned way back in 1917: "He would have hated Negroes if it wasn't got World War One. He felt that all those white generals and politicians had set up the poor white trash the same way black folks were set up. He was right" (37). The problem doesn't come down to race, it comes down to power. And in the end, rather than acquiescing to the dictates of power, Easy turns to subversion:

They condemned Freedom's Plaza and bought up the property for the city. Then they found that the soil was unsuitable for a waste-processing plant. They sold the property to Save-Co with Mason LaMone as the managing agent.

I hired on to the construction crew that laid the foundation for the shopping center. No one ever suspected that it was me who put the extra sand in the cement that made it crumble only one year after the opening ceremonies. Nobody except maybe Mason LaMone. (255)

In *A Little Yellow Dog*, violence takes yet another turn. In this book Mouse and Easy exchange roles. In *A Little Yellow Dog*, Mouse, the gangster, the killer, the force of nature, changes. After shooting his friend Sweet William in a rage, Mouse feels contrite: "Raymond was crying. Not blubbering or shaking, but there were real tears in his eyes. I had never seen him even sad over anything he'd done" (31). And as a consequence of this Mouse gives up his gun: "I don't have a gun on me but that's just because I don't wanna kill anybody right now. I mean, if I had to do it I could get me a firearm. But right now I just wanna see what it's like to live wit' your family an' work a job. But I ain't scared. I'm lookin' for a new way—that's all" (252). Having given up his gun, Mouse literally assumes Easy's role, talking to solve problems. Thus when he and Easy meet with Puddin' and Tony, Mosley inserts the following exchange:

> "See that, Easy?" Mouse was jubilant.
> "What?"
> "Ain't no need to be all mad an' surly. All you got to do is talk. People will listen." (255)

But people don't always listen. When the new Mouse without his gun accompanies Easy to make the exchange to save Jackson Blue's life, Sallie Monroe shoots and mortally wounds him.

And Easy recognizes something about Mouse and what Mouse means in *A Little Yellow Dog*. Beginning in *Devil in a Blue Dress*, whenever Easy is in grave trouble he hears an internal voice that counsels him, urging manliness and bravery:

> The voice only comes to me at the worst times, when everything seems so bad that I want to take my car and drive it into a wall. Then this voice comes to me and gives me the best advice I ever get.
> The voice is hard. It never cares if I'm scared or in danger. It just looks at all the facts and tells me what I need to do. (97)

The voice also includes violence in its repertoire of ways to survive in a hostile world. Thus in *A Red Death*, it tells Easy, "'An' if that don't work,' a husky voice in my head said, 'kill the mothahfuckah'" (57). While in all of the previous books Easy has viewed the violence in Mouse's character as alien and repellent, in *A Little Yellow Dog* thoughts of Mouse take on the role formerly performed by Easy's inner voice: "Thinking about Mouse and his drive to survive flowed through me like molten steel. I stood straight up and yelled, 'What the fuck's goin' on here!'" (187). Or perhaps at last it becomes clear that the voice was Mouse's voice all along and that violence is a natural and essential part of Easy's make-up as well. Indeed, near the end of *A Little Yellow Dog* Easy views violence in that way: "For a moment the violence we both wanted seemed okay, like it was just an expression between men—rough humor, healthy competition, survival of the fittest" (272). But it is just for a moment.

Although the world visits violence upon Easy Rawlins with some regularity, he very rarely responds to it in kind. Rather, humaneness characterizes him far more completely, the same quixotic and stubbornly naive humaneness that characterizes all hard-boiled heroes. And the novels tell stories of his search for people and a society that justifies his adherence to that ideal. They also tell stories of the hero's attempts to escape those things, things Mosley calls "holes," that would strangle growth and change. Thus escape from Pariah, escape from Mouse, escape from racism, escape from poverty, and escape from ignorance dictate many of the things Easy does. And sometimes his drive to escape blinds him to the importance of those things in which he finds and will find the most satisfaction and fulfillment. This was the case with his marriage to Regina, but, fortunately, it is not the case with Jesus and Feather, his family. In the midst of all of the chaos in his life, Easy's greatest pleasure—ultimately his only pleasure—comes from his adopted children. Thus this reverie in *Black Betty*: "It was a rhythm more satisfying than good music. I could have spent a whole life watching my children grow. Even though we didn't share common blood I loved them so much that it hurt sometimes" (19). Easy's children enable him to contribute to something worthwhile—healthy lives for two souls who otherwise would have had no chance. They give him perspective on his life and the humility to see that perspective. Thus this recognition in *A Little Yellow Dog*: "All the times I'd come home bruised or bleeding came back to me; them and my deep blue moods he could never understand. Jesus loved me but he didn't trust that I could handle the hard world. He was my backup and I didn't even know it. He was more of a man than I" (159). And caring for them gives meaning to work and brings order and ritual to his life: "Preparing a meal for me was like going to church; there was a miracle and a deep satisfaction in my soul" (156). In spite of the very real meaning of his family, though, Easy does not exist in a world without trouble and danger, trouble that Mosley inserts in the form of Pharoah, the pestilential little yellow dog that Easy reluctantly allows to stay in his home: "As the days passsed I began to accept him [Pharoah] as a part of my life; the dark, dangerous part that always threatened. As long a[s] Pharoah was around snarling and cursing I'd remember the kind of trouble that a man like me could find" (299). But if trouble is a scrawny, evil-minded, nasty little dog, Easy Rawlins is a man. He proves it in every one of the books.

CONCLUSION

In the thirties, Marlowe worries about stopping the distribution of nudie pictures of Carmen Sternwood. In the eighties, Murdock and Leo Haggerty worry about stopping the production of snuff films, pornographic films in which a woman is gruesomely murdered after the male ejaculates. In the hard-boiled world, some things change and some stay the same.

The one thing that stays the same in the hard-boiled world is the literary style. The hard-boiled books of the last quarter of the century repeatedly and clearly pay homage to Raymond Chandler. Everybody, it seems, wants to write like him and they're not coy about it either. Timothy Harris, for example, uses one of Chandler's leftover titles for his *Good Night and Goodbye* (1979). And in addition to *Perchance to Dream* (1991), which features Marlowe, Robert B. Parker has undertaken to complete Chandler's unfinished novel in his (their) *Poodle Springs* (1989). On the stylistic level, all of the similes I have catalogued above—and all the ones I have not—come straight from Chandler. So does the use of hyperbole and the wisecrack. So does the first person narration and the naked, sometimes brutal declarative sentence. Chandler may not have been the first hard-boiled writer to use these devices—he just used them more artfully than his contemporaries—or anyone else for that matter. And recent hard-boiled writers know a good thing when they see it.

But style does not just consist of the manipulation of words. In Chandler, and in most hard-boiled writing, the words portray both the hero and the hero's world. In his entry on Chandler in the second edition of John M. Reilly's *Twentieth-Century Crime and Mystery Writers,* Robert B. Parker emphasizes the essential connection in Chandler between style and substance:

I learned to write from Raymond Chandler. I learned how to use the concrete phenomena of the story's setting to advance the story. I learned how to characterize the narrator protagonist by the way he reports these phenomena. I learned the place of wit in a serious story. I learned that a good story could be sentimental, and a good writer romantic. I learned also that the evocation of place lends resonance to the work. (153)

As much as Chandler's works serve as a stylistic template for much of the hard-boiled fiction of the last quarter of this century, the last few paragraphs of his essay "The Simple Art of Murder" have had an even greater impact. "But down these mean streets a man must go" resonates in one way or another in every hard-boiled hero—resonates in a way in which Chandler might not recognize or like very much.

Nowhere in "The Simple Art of Murder" does Chandler say anything about self-justification, or self-definition, or self-analysis. He says rather the reverse: "He must be, to use a rather weathered phrase, a man of honor—by instinct, by inevitability, without thought of it, and certainly without saying it." In an age burdened with analysis of everything, however, hard-boiled writers have made self-definition and self-justification regular features of the new hard-boiled hero. And here Parker led the way with Spenser mouthing passages about autonomy that sometimes sound like patches of his dissertation on Hammett and Chandler. After Parker, in fact, defining THE CODE becomes a regular feature of the genre.

One of the realities of new hard-boiled writing is that it's literary: the writers know both the original fiction and at least some of the analysis and criticism that has grown up around it. And the place this shows up most is in the elements they use to establish THE CODE for their heroes. A lot of them go for the archetype, so references, both direct and indirect, to the parallel between their hero and established cultural icons come into a number of the books. Probably because Chandler used it, a lot of writers turn first to the knight:

"I put an olive between my teeth and pulled a little pink sword out of it, like a plastic Excalibur." (Max Byrd, *California Thriller* 1)

"maybe because of my own need to feel like a knight in shining armor." (Les Roberts, *An Infinite Number of Monkeys* 19)

"Ezell Barnes, the Black Knight." (Richard Hilary, *Snake in the Grasses* 80)

"Sir Rafferty, one of these days you're going to annoy the wrong dragon and get your butt kicked all over the castle." (W. Glenn Duncan, *Rafferty's Rules* 49)

"Sir Lancelot asks you about a dragon, you don't figure they're working together."

"I'm Sir Lancelot?"

"You think you are." (Robert B. Parker, *Sudden Mischief* 39)

But there's more than one kind of knight. There's the kind with chaps, a ten-gallon hat, and a six gun. In Estleman, the code of the West that Amos Walker describes in connection with Bum Bassett (and himself) is just another permutation of the metaphor of the knight. And in a far more sophisticated way it's there in Crumley, too: Sughrue even knows parts of the script of *The Magnificent Seven*. Then there is the metamorphosis of the knight into samurai. Back when everybody was talking about the imminent domination of the world by Pacific Rim countries, the attendant Asian chic sometimes transformed the metaphor of the knight into that of the samurai. Since it is an alien concept, characters can get away with explaining what it means in connection with their characters without compromising their integrity. Crais, of course, uses the samurai metaphor to define Joe Pike. Stereotypes from Asian warfare also play a defining role for characters in Andrew Vachss's books, starting with *Flood* (1985). And Benjamin Schutz uses it as a way of explaining one of his characters in *A Tax in Blood* (1987):

When I say Arnie's a samurai, that's not quite true. He can't be. This isn't feudal Japan and he wasn't raised from the cradle to be a warrior. Underneath that shell there's still twenty years of corn-fed American dreamer. What he's added on is the Japanese idea of *giri* or debts of obligation. All relationships in Japan are based on them. They must be discharged to maintain your honor. (*A Tax in Blood* 4)

But writers also look for and find other stereotypes besides the eastern or western knight to explain their hard-boiled heroes. Max Byrd, in *California Thriller* (1981), and Les Roberts, in *An Infinite Number of Monkeys* (1987), both bring in New England Puritanism to explain why their characters act the way they do. Here's Byrd: "You're a cop of sorts, yes. But I've watched you for four years and four months, in action, at work. You have your own private code as well. Some inscrutable combination of New England Puritan and bleeding heart" (135). And sometimes writers just come out and have their heroes explain their actions in plain, elemental terms without recourse to metaphors or archetypes. Thus Robert Ray's hero, in *Bloody Murdock* (1986), tells readers that "It helps me to think I'm doing good for society. So motive number two, I told myself, was idealistic—cleaning up the world. At the same time there was a chance I could one-up the cops, and I'm not above a little professional competition" (26).

Writers, to be sure, try to have it both ways: to have heroes act instinctively and to have them define themselves. First off, beginning with Parker, writers make a point of saying that their heroes in particular and men in general have trouble talking, especially when it means talking about themselves. They just don't want to do it. They frequently say so. Thus Rob Kantner follows Parker's lead in *The Back-Door Man* (1986) when Ben Perkins says, "I'm not one of these whining, pampered, self-indulgent introspective kind of guys. I never give a second thought to what I'm like. I've never worried about 'finding myself'; I may not be an intellectual giant, but I know where I am: right here, see?" (9). And then, not three pages later, Perkins does, in fact, talk about why he is the way he is. And he also puts it in the context of his family and his past: "Daddy found his niche building caskets. I found mine in maintenance. Cleaning up. Fixing. Putting things back the way they were. Life in the gray zone between construction and destruction, including some of both" (12).

The other way in which writers surmount the problem of defining their heroes in words as well as actions is the introduction of partners and significant others in their books. This, quite clearly, presents a departure from the orthodoxy of hard-boiled fiction, but it's something that lots of recent writers do. I've already been through the list of partners—Hawk, Pike, Mouse, Clete Purcel, etc.—and touched on the ways their embodiment of radical hard-boiled approaches to life tells readers something about the hero as well: we know more about the heroes because we know about how they relate to their single-mindedly violent partners. But women play at least an equal role in helping the new heroes define themselves. After all, relationships—when they go right—provide for men one of the few times in life when self-definition isn't braggadocio or whining, but acceptable and even mandatory communication. Thus conversations with their partners often provoke self-defining passages from many of the heroes in contemporary hard-boiled books. Their partners' vocations, too, have something to do with defining and analyzing what motivates the heroes. Susan Silverman in Parker and Dinah Farrell in Max Byrd are both psychotherapists. And if shrinks don't bring up the topic of motive, who will? Significantly, too, more than a few lady lawyers inhabit recent hard-boiled fiction: there's Nancy Meagher in Jeremiah Healy, Kathy Birchfield in Emerson, and Lucy Chenier in Crais. And when the hard-boiled hero's acts almost inevitably involve a conflict between statute law and natural law, who is more likely to provoke an examination than an attorney?

Another way in which recent writers provide self-definition for their characters is in their often elaborate and detailed accounts of their heroes' childhoods. Part of this links to the nostalgia that appears almost universally in contemporary hard-boiled books. But most of this connects with the way the present has changed places for the worse. With people's pasts it's something different. Looking back, though, we know next to nothing about when, where, or how Spade or Marlowe grew up. Forget about his childhood, we don't even know the name of the Continental Op, Hammett's first hero. We, however, know a great deal about Dave Robicheaux's childhood—his mother's adultery and his father's brawling. Crumley puts together a grossly twisted past of alcoholism, adultery, revenge, and suicide for Milo Milodragovitch. In every book Grafton mentions the car crash that killed Kinsey's parents and over the course of them she develops background for Kinsey's Aunt Gin. V. I. recalls momma and poppa Warshawski in every book. And Mosley's first novel, *Gone Fishin'*, recounts the events that brought Easy's youth to a close. Part of this comes from the child is father (or mother) to the man (or woman) notion. Writers have their heroes tell us about their childhoods so that we can understand them not just by what they do but by what they were. That many have overcome adversity helps to define them as hard-boiled. Appropriately, too, in books that so often center on protecting or salvaging innocents and innocence, the heroes' own childhoods supply background, explanation, and motive for what they do once the action begins. "[I] Prayed to that god in the orphanage, in the foster homes, in reform school. Somebody would come. Be my family" (Andrew Vachss, *Hard Candy* [1989] 111).

In addition to inventing for their heroes childhoods relevant to the fables they create—childhoods, in some cases, that could or maybe even should disconnect their heroes from leading wholesome and fulfilling adult lives—many recent hard-boiled writers also insert accounts of traumatic adult experiences their heroes have undergone before they introduce themselves to the reader. Robicheaux and Milo and Healy's John Cuddy are alcoholics. Cuddy has also watched his wife die of cancer. Joe "Zank the Tank" Zanca in Frey's *The Long Way to Die*, Hiaasen's R. J. Decker in *Double Whammy*, and Morgan Hunt in Geoffrey Norman's *Blue Chipper* have all done jail time. Vachss, in fact, uses up considerable space explaining Burke's prison time (especially in *Blue Belle*) and the lessons he taught himself in the slammer about how to be hardboiled. Thomas Black lives on his Seattle Police disability pension occasioned by the emotional aftershocks of having killed a teenage car thief. As a reporter, Brian Keys in *Tourist Season* has come up against carnage and violent death once too often. Building on a convention that goes back to *The Red Harvest*, recent hard-boiled heroes rerun their characters' traumas in dreams, bad dreams. Worse than that, a theme of mental illness runs through a number of these books, especially Crumley's and Burke's. Even Kinsey Millhone talks about her serotonin levels in one of the later novels. Quite aside from the horrors they confront during the course of their adventures, the new detective has been, in effect, assaulted by—and has overcome or at least dealt with—some of the terrible things which life can inflict on an individual. And by depicting the chaos in their own lives from which their heroes have emerged, writers add yet another layer to their characters' definitions of themselves and their motives.

By common consent, though, the worst kind of thing with which life can assault a man in the last quarter of the twentieth century has been the Vietnam War. The First World War had about the same chronological relationship to the original generation of hard-boiled writers (some of whom, like Chandler were veterans) as Vietnam has to the writers of the eighties and nineties (few of whom, incidentally, are veterans). But their experience as soldiers and the ghastly, beastly carnage in the Great War in Europe never directly enter the fiction of the old writers. Not so with current writers: Crumley's Sughrue sums up what most recent writers depict in their heroes when, in *The Last Good Kiss*, he identifies the Vietnam War as "the central trauma of my adult life." Indeed, the recent hard-boiled novel presents its readers with a cross-section of images of the ways in which men in this country responded to the war in the jungles of Southeast Asia.

These begin with superficial and passing references to the military draft. Thus, "Without Lyndon Johnson's draft I might be there [Europe] still" (*California Thriller* 71). With the draft, some characters, like Roberts's Saxon, did tours stateside: "you served in the army during the Asian unpleasantness but the only action you saw was in the Signal Corps at Fort Gordon Georgia" (*An Infinite Number of Monkeys* 108). Even in cases in which men's numbers did not come up in the draft, Vietnam affects heroes like Allegretto's Jake Lomax, who gives this rationale for becoming a police officer:

> "What did you feel guilty about?" she asked, still smiling.
> "Would you believe not going to Vietnam?"
> "Now you *are* kidding."
> "Maybe I felt guilty about not fighting over there, so I decided to fight the bad guys over here." (*Blood Stone* 64)

As for experiences in-country, writers rarely depict the mundane, occasionally absurd nature of being in Vietnam. One exception, though, is Simmons's account of his tour in Crumley's *Dancing Bear*:

> Well, shit, man. I spent my sixteen weeks of the war riding an armored personnel carrier and firing fifty caliber rounds into the fucking bush. Man, I never

even saw Charlie. I was a fuck-up before the war—got into the Army because a judge in Denver gave me the choice of the slammer or Uncle Sam on a little pot bust—and I got my Purple Heart when a gook rocket hit the half-track parked in front while I was sitting on the side of the APC reading a Spiderman comic, took a piece of shrapnel no bigger than a pencil eraser. (130)

In terms of describing the Vietnam experience, writers often invent more graphic events, events like the jungle patrol. They do, however, use the jungle patrol for different purposes. In Geoffrey Norman's *The Blue Chipper*, for example, hunting in the Florida panhandle brings back not unhappy recollections of night patrols:

This time of night always reminds me of going out on night patrol. Laying in ambush and lying there with the mosquitoes and leeches sucking on you while you wait for something that never comes . . . [*sic*] almost never, anyway. It always did surprise me when Charlie did come easing down the trail, like ghosts or something.
    Pine and I had walked some of the same hills at different times. That was a long time ago and seemed longer, part of a past that neither of us could quite believe had actually happened. (*Blue Chipper* 18)

Sometimes, however, the jungle patrol becomes a means of demonstrating the heart of darkness, the unleashing of the savage potential in some men:

He lives for it. Ray was over in Vietnam for three tours of duty. Couldn't get enough of it. He was a LURP, you know what that is? Elite of the elite. Long-Range Reconnaissance Patrol, this special branch in the Green Berets. Go out into the bush solo for two months at a crack, wearing tiger suits and grease paint on their faces. Hide in the bushes and ice whatever comes by. I would think, you live like that, like an animal, you never get it out of your blood. (Hilary, *Snake in the Grasses* 89)

Most often, because James Lee Burke does it so often, the combat patrol serves as the occasion for demonstrating the reality of pain, mortality, and courage. Here's part of Burke's first lengthy description of a patrol gone bad from *A Morning for Flamingos*:

I can smell the sour odor of mud, stagnant water in the coulee, the foul reek of fear from my own armpits. An eighteen-year-old kid nicknamed Doo-Doo, from West Memphis, Arkansas, lies next to me, his bare chest strung with bandoleers, a green sweat-soaked towel draped from the back of his pot.

His ankle is broken, and he keeps looking back at it and the boot that he has worked half way off his foot. His sock looks like rotted cheesecloth. The whites of his eyes are filled with ruptured veins.

"They got Martinez's blooker. Don't go out there, lieutenant. They're waiting for you in the tree line," he says.

"They'll hang him up in a tree."

"He at the bottom of the ditch. You can't get him out. They waiting for you Lieutenant." (50)

Other recollections of the war center on its atrocities. Perhaps the earliest is Sughrue's memories in *The Last Good Kiss* of Plei Bao Three where "I grenaded a hooch and killed three generations of a Vietnamese family." Jeremiah Healy's *The Staked Goat* (1986) may as well be a Vietnam horror book. Cuddy recounts seeing a Vietnamese child blown up by a landmine, witnessing a torture/interrogation session of a suspected member of the Viet Cong, as well as his memories of the following horrors of Saigon during the Tet Offensive:

A mother lying face down in the street, her eyes open, snot and blood and broken teeth all around her. Her daughter, maybe four years old, howling and beating her fists bloody on the pavement while two National Policemen stripped and looted the Viet Cong bodies in the stairway.

Standing in the gutter, I look down and see an arm. A black left arm. With a faded gold high school ring on the fourth finger. A blue stone.

Two B-girls, still in their slit-sided hostess dresses crucified on a side wall of a Tu Fo Street bar for fraternizing with the enemy. (183–84)

And there is also the combination of the putrescence of death and black humor as in the following from Hilary's *Snake in the Grasses*:

My first year of residency, I got drafted. Put in charge of the Eighth Army Forensic Laboratory in Saigon. Worst job in the military services, I thought at the time. It meant I was in charge of shipping the corpses back stateside.

. . .

Some cadavers were so badly decomposed, we could never embalm them arterially. We'd just sprinkle powdered formaldehyde over them and pack them up in body bags. "Shake and bake," they call it in the trade. (69)

On top of these memories of death and suffering, some writers look at the political dimension of the war. One of these is that the impact of the war fell largely on those without power or privilege. In *The Staked Goat*, for example, Healy touches on this (albeit pretty innocuously) when he recounts the difference between what happened to Cuddy and his friend Al Sachs ("The Jew from CCNY and the Harp from Holy Cross") and officer recruits from Yale and Virginia: "Al . . . and I eventually found ourselves as street MP officers in Saigon. I heard that Yale and Virginia ended up guarding VIPs in some appropriately front-page battle sectors and conferences" (3). More forcefully, some characters in hard-boiled stories acknowledge the intimate way in which the failure of international policy affects those who suffer its consequences. Thus, Leo Haggerty's friend Arnie in Schutz's *A Tax in Blood* says: "Shit, man, we were beautiful. We could do it all. You name it. We had heart, let me tell you. We did every damn thing they asked us to. We never backed up. They just never let us win. Do you understand that?" (68). This, of course, posits that no matter how misguided they are, governments and their policies have a some kind of purpose or vision. More defeating still is the notion that Simmons expresses in *Dancing Bear*—that those in charge have no vision or understanding whatsoever: "'Just like over there, right, dad? Nobody fucking knew.' I didn't have to ask where *there* might be. 'Nobody knew, and you don't know shit from wild honey about it, dad, what it was like'" (40).

So one day back in the world, Simmons just pulls over the armored truck he drives for Haliburton Security and starts shooting at passing cars with his .38. Post-traumatic stress: more than anything else about Vietnam it affects the hard-boiled heroes of the eighties and nineties. Here are just three examples:

"Think about it. I came back with this chest," I said. "And a lifetime of bad dreams. Used to scare my radio-car partners half to death, when we'd snooze on night patrol and I'd wake up screaming." (*Snake in the Grasses* 173)

That didn't help, either. It was okay as long as I kept my eyes straight ahead, on the wet asphalt. But when I glanced out to sea, the waves turned into green jungle and in the center of the jungle was a mound of earth with a little white cross sticking up from it. It was a grave, and on the cross was a small shiny plate with my name on it. And some fat words, filled with hot air. Inside my head, the metal plate winked in the tropical sun. (*Bloody Murdock* 13)

It seems to me that the names of every Vietnam vet who kills himself ought to go on that wall. They may not have died "in country" but the country was still in them. (*A Tax in Blood* 68)

And, of course, I didn't even include anything about post-traumatic stress from James Lee Burke, the writer most absorbed with Vietnam. On top of his other afflictions, post-traumatic stress has a malarial hold of Robicheaux in all of the books. Burke even puts Dave's flashbacks to Vietnam in italic text. And living with the psychic repercussions of the war, in fact, provides the central focus for Burke's A Morning for Flamingos.

None of this, however, appears in first-generation hard-boiled writers. It's hardly that World War I was not a horrific, ghoulish, and senseless exercise in carnage, waste, and mass brutality. The war poets of the generation give vivid and startling glimpses into this. Perhaps what then carried the generic name of "shell-shock" had too great a stigma attached to it to be acceptable in mass-market fiction of the twenties and thirties; certainly inherited notions of self-possession and the nature of manliness had yet to begin to accept the value and virtue of emotional self-awareness and revelation; and it certainly was not in the best interests of those in power to broadcast the effects that modern warfare has on all who take part in it. Whatever the cause, however, the effect of making the recollections of Vietnam an integral part of so many contemporary hard-boiled heroes bears some similarity to the inclusion of heroes' other assorted explanations for and justifications of their acts. In both cases they reveal a double perspective about the heroes, making them at once tough and high-minded, sensitive and humane. In hearing the anecdotes and seeing the battle scars, we understand both what the heroes have gone through and that they have managed to overcome what has been done to them. And in first person fiction, if they do not tell us, we will never know about this dimension of their heroism.

Another thing about recent hard-boiled fiction has a tangential connection with Vietnam and is also radically different from the hard-boiled story of the first part of this century. It's guns. Although in first-generation works writers did occasionally introduce firearms, they aren't all that important. Marlowe, in fact, doesn't even regularly pack heat. Now, maybe just because they are there, hard-boiled stories regularly include firearms, awesomely powerful firearms at that. Every P.I. worth his or her condiments carries a handgun, a handgun with a brand name. While the women opt for the smaller .9 millimeter piece, the guys tend to go for magnums: "load one up with the water-filled hydroshock bullets, that gun will knock a Cadillac sideways" (Snake in the Grasses 175). Then, too, Vietnam era assault weapons make their debut:

"Ballistics says they were all shot with the same piece. Military hardware, probably an M-16, or one of those Russian jobs. High-speed ammo. Ballistics says the slugs were twenty-two caliber."

"They mean 5.56 millimeter. About the same thing."

. . .

"It's not an assassin's weapon. Doesn't have the shock power of a heavier slug. That high speed's a waste at such close range. The bullets fly so fast that they tumble around as soon as they hit something. That's why the girls were so torn up inside." (Andrew Vachss, *Blue Belle* 96-97)

But that's not all. Offspring of the Uzi, little submachine guns make an appearance: "He was holding one of those ugly little machine guns they all like to carry these days for lots of firepower at close range. An Ingram or a MAC-10. One of those" (*Blue Chipper* 212); "Although I had only seen them in movies and magazines, I recognized the small submachine gun at once. An Ingram M-11. Not much larger than a .45 automatic pistol. Eight hundred and fifty rounds a minute. So simple a child can operate it. I dug deeper, looking for clips and ammo" (*Dancing Bear* 84). In James Frey's *The Long Way to Die*, Zank debates a black-market purchase of a 9 gauge combat shotgun: "It looked strangely ominous. The gun had one purpose only. Not just killing, but dismembering" (176). And recall the passage in *The Mexican Tree Duck* in which Sughrue gets hold of a heavy machine gun. Forget (or remember) all of the Freudian implications; a number of the new heroes just plain like firepower:

Question: what toys would I need for Philo? Answer: .357 Magnum; 12 gauge pump loader. Humming now, ready to rescue, destroy, save, kill. One. Two.
   Simple rhythm, like a dance. (*Bloody Murdock* 192)

I reassembled the Colt [.45], dry fired it, reloaded it, put it down, and smiled at it. I always liked that big, ungainly cannon. The army has replaced it now with a wimpy little 9mm Beretta. Dumb. (*Rafferty's Rules* 117)

Right on top were three fragmentation grenades still in their cardboard tubes. Below them, two flat packages wrapped in heavy plastic. I opened the first one and nearly shouted with joy. Not that guns kept you from running . . . but if you're done with running, a gun feels better than a woman, more comforting than your mother's breast. (*Dancing Bear* 84)

All of this emphasis on firearms may simply be an extension of the gun-love introduced in the middle period of hard-boiled history by Mickey Spillane, or it may be the felt influence of movies like the Dirty Harry films. Certainly it says something about the availability to good and bad alike of diverse and powerful firearms. It also reflects something deeply imbedded in American culture about independence and power. Their attitude toward possessing and using guns, however, surely plays a part in defining how hard the new hard-boiled hero is.

Women, though, play a much larger part. Remember here that Chandler includes in his definition of the hero that "He is a lonely man." In first-generation hard-boiled stories detectives do not have genuine continuing relationships with anybody—especially women. Perhaps writers like Chandler took the knight analogy—the ideal of chastity—too seriously. Then also the popular stereotype of the vamp and a good deal of misogyny certainly shaped the fiction of the twenties and thirties. Back then, too, the hard-boiled novel had yet to go through its soft-porn phase of the fifties or the "sexual revolution" of the sixties and seventies. Therefore, while the contemporary hard-boiled scene is not without its throwbacks—see Paul Coggins's *The Lady Is the Tiger* (1987), for example—contemporary detective heroes have domestic situations radically different from those depicted by first-generation writers. This is true, oddly enough, except for women writers. Paretsky and Grafton's heroes do not have committed relationships with men—unless they are octogenarians—and V. I. Warshawski, at least, fears entering into relationships because of their potential to erode her independence. With men it's different. Read the shelves and you will find that most of the male heroes have paired up: Spenser and Silverman (Parker), Dinah Farrell and Mike Haller (Max Byrd), Nancy Meagher and John Cuddy (Jeremiah Healy), Kathy Birchfield and Thomas Black (Emerson), Nameless and Kerry Wade (Pronzini), Lucy Chenier and Elvis Cole (Crais), Hilda Gardner and Rafferty (W. Glenn Duncan), Jessie Boudreaux and Morgan Hunt (Geoffrey Norman), Samantha Clayton and Leo Haggerty (Benjamin Schutz), and Bootsie and Dave Robicheaux (Burke). Everybody in Hiaasen gets paired up at the end. Easy Rawlins has a wife in the middle books. In *Bordersnakes* Sughrue is married and, disregarding his multiple matrimonial, sexual, and romantic disasters, Milo may have found a partner at the conclusion of the action. Significantly, almost all of the women these writers depict hold responsible, independent, professional positions. The sole exception, occasioned by Burke's commitment to portraying victims, is Bootsie Robicheaux. While some of these couples are married, most at least begin their involvement with monogamous, committed relationships that do not include marriage. Most of them, too, build their relationships upon a combination of mutual respect and restraint, boisterous and fulfilling sexuality, and witty banter. But they do more than this. I've already discussed the role women play in helping to define the heroes' motives. In doing this they also demonstrate that the heroes are sensitive, liberated seventies or eighties or nineties kind of guys. Sensitive, though, doesn't mean wimpy. And the women in recent hard-boiled books don't want their partners to have nine-to-five jobs and lawns to mow. They accept that their professions involve violence and danger. Because so many of these women have committed themselves to "helping" professions, because their own jobs seek to provide or promote justice, sanity, and peace, and because they know the limitations of what they can do to achieve those ends, they accept and admire the heroes for what they, uniquely, can accomplish.

And adding women may have played a small part in something else. Chandler says, "He is a relatively poor man or he would not be a detective at all." When it has a place in first-generation hard-boiled writing, affluence is bad. Writers link affluence with authority and power: two other bad things. Thus the original hard-boiled heroes live modest lives. They have minimal lodgings, shabby offices, and threadbare wardrobes. They eat in greasy spoons and sleep on Murphy beds. Part of what they are comes from these heroes' attitude toward things which they neither possess nor wish to possess. It's one of the fundamental points of the *Maltese Falcon* with all of the folks running around after a dingus made of lead. While some of the writers like Crumley, Estleman, Mosley, Paretsky, Grafton, and Vachss make motions toward the attitudes we find in the stories of the twenties and thirties, the contemporary hard-boiled milieu usually either disregards the proletarian fundamentals of the early form or must do gymnastics to stay at least parallel to values of the original. Okay, introducing relationships has a bit to do with this change. Like it or not, women in professions have to demonstrate a certain level of affluence in their dress, their cars, and their accommodations. And most of the contemporary hard-boiled heroes have partnered up with women in professions. Food, too, plays a standard part of beginning and sustaining relationships and here affluence comes in as well. The shared restaurant meal has become a regular feature of the contemporary hard-boiled world and so has cooking—ostensibly together but usually with the guy at the stove. We're not talking about Taco Bell and Pepsi or microwaved delights and Old Milwaukee here. It's all very fancy, even snooty eating and drinking. Most of the heroes also live in places they own—even Amos Walker owns his place. Except in Crumley and Vachss, marginal lives are a thing of the past. But then, too, the world these heroes live and work in reflects the fact that the American standard of living has skyrocketed since the days of Hammett and Chandler—try to buy a new car without electric windows.

The need persists, however, to present the proletarian ideals of the original hard-boiled story in some form. Dynamite fishing though it may be, a number of writers define their heroes' proletarian virtues by saying that at least they are not yuppies. It's an underlying theme of Paretsky's *Guardian Angel* and Vachss sums up a number of hard-boiled characters' points of view when Burke watches joggers in *Strega*: "Yuppies working up an appetite for breakfast yogurt, jogging through the forest, dreaming of things you can buy from catalogues" (3). Part of not being a yuppie lies in simply belonging where you are. Warshawski calls Chicago "my briar patch," Milo's family name dominates Meriwether, Thomas Black, Easy Barnes, and Easy Rawlins cultivate gardens, Dave Robicheaux runs a fishing business on the bayou, Amos Walker and Ben Perkins draw their characters from Detroit, and Hiaasen uses attitudes toward Florida as a test for all of his characters. Part of not being a yuppie, too, lies in doing things. Spenser builds a cabin in the woods, as does Dan Roman in Edward Mathias's *From a High Place* (1985). Ben Perkins has a regular job fixing things at an up-scale apartment complex. V. I. Warshawski straps on a jury-rigged tool belt and at least in one of the books Kinsey Millhone talks about using tools. And Hiaasen demonstrates this in reverse in his books where carelessness or ineptness is a sure-fire sign of characters' lack of worth. These serve as signs of a larger, more important, and fundamental part of contemporary hard-boiled detectives. They do something—or at least try to do something—about the suffering that exists around them.

Like their predecessors, people with wealth and power cause most of the suffering for recent hard-boiled heroes. And it is one of the hall-marks of the hard-boiled story that these people have the resources to cause individual suffering, to inflict it on others (especially the hero), and to both obscure and protect themselves from discovery and punishment. Occasionally this kind of wealth and power enter as the suffering caused to innocents by organized crime. Joe Broz and other Mafia types appear in Parker fairly often from *Promised Land* onward. The wiseguys also show up in Crais's *Lullaby Town*, Paretsky's *Indemnity Only*, Hiaasen's *Lucky You*, and several of Burke's books, for example. Politicians and corrupt cops in their employ play the same role in contemporary books that they did in the first half of the century. James Lee Burke and Mosley both like to focus on corrupt and corrupting politicians, and Paretsky, too, features politicians and their evil schemes in *Tunnel Vision* and *Burn Marks*. Paretsky, Hiaasen, and Emerson all target entrepreneurs, individuals who in their quest for inordinate and obscene wealth inflict individual and collective grief and pain on their communities.

The most powerful archetype of suffering and the most perverse use of power, however, has always been the suffering of children. And with this recent hard-boiled writers introduce something which first generation hard-boiled writers did not, could not treat. While children play no role in original hard-boiled fiction, powerless and exploited, they play a significant, even a dominant role in contemporary works. Child pornography, for example, provides the focus for the action in Frey's *The Long*

Way to Die and Andrew Vachss's *Strega*. Incest and child sexual abuse have become regular themes, seen, for instance, in Paretsky's *Tunnel Vision*, Mosley's *Devil in a Blue Dress*, Emerson's *The Rainy City*, Healy's *Blunt Darts*, Crais's *Stalking the Angel*, and all of Vachss's books. The majority of Parker's books, in one way or another, deal with sordid things that parents or other adults have done to children.

And because they often graphically depict the suffering innocents undergo, some recent hard-boiled writers wrestle with why some people do evil things. This, to be sure, sometimes means engaging in relatively simple solutions. Parker, for instance, tends to go Freudian without a whole lot of provocation. Problems usually trace back to something parents did or didn't do, something that really good and extensive therapy can probably fix. Vachss classifies child molesters and pedophiles as "freaks" for whom the only solution isn't therapy but their extinction. James Lee Burke, on the other hand, tries out a number of answers and solutions to the evil Robicheaux confronts in every book. These range from the concept of evil caused by defective genes, to theological explanations (evil is "something tribal and dark, far beyond the moral ken of a youthful law officer, a glimpse into a time before the creation of light in the world" [*Dixie City Jam* 231]). And his answer usually boils down to following Clete Purcel's dictum of "You see the handiwork and you hunt the bastards down. You bust 'em or grease 'em" (*Heaven's Prisoners* 141). Because of the very nature of the genre, most of the writers, in one way or another, arrive at the same answer: the only solution to evil is violence. And while a number of them ask the question of why evil exists, few of them have any kind of answer. Indeed, uncertainty becomes one of the fundamental ways in which writers like Crais and Crumley and Mosley and Paretsky and even Burke define the basic hardness of the hard-boiled world. Knowing the cause for evil requires moral certainty, and moral certainty doesn't exist unless absolutes, authority, and power accompany it. Reacting against absolutes, authority, and power, though, has defined the hard-boiled hero from the very beginning. Additionally, knowing the cause for evil means that it can be fixed—with therapy, with drugs, with love, with community, with whatever. The very core of hard-boiled understanding, though, rests on the certainty that neither evil in individuals nor evil in the world can be fixed. What writers often do, then, is to acknowledge that in their fallen world evil exists—and that it will always exist. "I have learned some things," Milo says at the end of *Dancing Bear*. "Modern life is warfare without end: take no prisoners, leave no wounded, eat the dead—that's environmentally sound" (228).

But that doesn't mean he or she has to like it. Also, for the hard-boiled hero, it emphatically doesn't mean that he or she should do nothing, or, even worse, adopt the strategies and tactics of the wicked. That's why the term quixotic gets applied so often to hard-boiled heroes: they continue to believe in and to uphold ideals that have been lost, or which never really existed. And most of these ideals and the acts based on them don't need anything as complicated as a code to explain them. Indeed, most of them fall well within the meaning of responsibility. Part of responsibility rests on self-reliance. Thus all of Spenser's talk about "autonomy," and the emphasis placed on heroes' competence, have something to do with responsibility. But in hard-boiled books, responsibility always extends beyond the individual, or else there would be no stories. In recent works responsibility to others manifests itself in a couple of ways. First it comes in symbolic acts, acts like incinerating the Amazing Kingdom of Thrills in *Native Tongue,* or exposing the toxic practices of Xerxes Solvents in *Blood Shot.* Neither action will remove avarice from the catalog of individual and corporate human failings, but as symbols they mean as much as Easy Rawlins's equally quixotic act of quitting his job at Champion Aircraft because he demands to be treated as a man.

Not liking the way the world is also connects with the drive, maybe even the need, one can find in many of the recent hard-boiled heroes to maintain their own childlike, or, more accurately, their adolescent selves. It's pretty overt in Crais with all of Elvis's talk about Pinocchio and his discovery of how to survive combat in Vietnam. It's there in Thomas Black's crab apple fights with Kathy Birchfield's nephews in Emerson's books. For Dave Robicheaux it's fishing in the bayou. For Spenser it's staring unabashedly at women's breasts and bottoms. Spenser offers to do one-arm push-ups for pretty girls, and so does Mike Haller in *California Thriller. The Mexican Tree Duck* begins with Sughrue hauling a jukebox out onto the train tracks because the vendor replaced country western records with a new commercial format. In W. Glenn Duncan it's "Down deep, I'm nineteen. Maybe twenty on a bad day" (*Rafferty's Rules* 28). And the same age comes up in Max Byrd: "I wanted to be nineteen and be the grandson of Philip Marlowe" (*California Thriller* 97). Many of the defining features of adolescence, especially male adolescence, fit the characteristics of the hard-boiled hero: the war with authority in all of its guises; the need to say any thing, any time one wants to; the desire (maybe even the need) to show off; the absorption in the bitter-sweet melancholy of loneliness; the attraction to the power of cars and guns; the perception of the world in clear-cut moral terms; the conviction that sex is infallibly exciting, fun, and fulfilling; the universal impatience and the need to act immediately and decisively; the illusion that people will recognize justice and virtue, and that they will prevail;

the abhorrence of regular, boring nine-to-five jobs; the intense and poignant identification with the loss of innocence in children; and the conviction that anyone and everyone will listen and understand. Okay, let loose a society of adolescents and what you've got is the middle ages. Back then the world was really run by fourteen- and fifteen-year-old males. Nobody in his or her right mind wants to contemplate that. What hard-boiled heroes have figured out, however, is a way to maintain the best parts of adolescence in their heads and make them coexist with responsibility—the quintessential adult virtue—in most of their actions. That's one way the new hard-boiled heroes manage to survive.

But there is another way, too. By the standards of the original hard-boiled writers, one of the most curious facts of the contemporary story resides in the number of adopted children one finds in it. Heroes do not just rescue children, they often take them in, often make them their own. They try to make families. Here a partial list: Spenser rescues and then adopts Paul Giacomin in *Early Autumn*; Dave Robicheaux saves and adopts Alafair in *Heaven's Prisoners*; Easy Rawlins saves Jesus in *Devil in a Blue Dress* and Feather in *White Butterfly* and raises both children as his own; Saxon takes in Marvel in Les Roberts's *Not Enough Horses;* Burke, the Mole, and Michelle collectively adopt Terry in Vachss's *Strega*, Leo Haggerty gains custody of Randi Benson at the close of *All the Old Bargains*; and even Milo adopts Muffin some time before *The Wrong Case*. Except in James Lee Burke, none of the men who takes in children as his own is married. Taking the children to be with them, however, gives them a better chance for life than the perverse circumstances from which they came. Mind you, none of the authors includes accounts of interminable waiting at the pediatrician's, or the badgering about homework and chores, or the whining about CDs or video games or MTV. And there's boarding school for a lot of these kids. Nonetheless, the fact of commitment to the welfare of these children is there, and so is the impulse to build a family where none before existed. The emphasis placed on children and childhood performs an even larger thematic role. At the end of the action of a lot of the books, the heroes don't just saddle up and head off for the territories ahead. James Lee Burke inserts the idyl of Dave and his family back on the bayou. Mosley brings his hero back to first the home and then the family he has fought so hard to achieve and maintain. V. I. Warshawski winds up at a birthday party thrown by Mr. Contreras and her friends. Kathy Birchfield gets into her clown get-up for a birthday party for Angel Nadisky at Thomas Black's house at the end of *The Rainy City*. All of this reflects the conclusion that cultivating one's own garden—that making the smallest, most intimate, and most important parts of life work—remains the only truly meaningful act in a world where the vice and corruption have infected all collective enterprises. That doesn't mean that one should abandon all efforts to change the world at large—it just means that one should abandon all hope of succeeding. Making the other parts of life—family and friendships—work isn't always easy or effortless or even successful, but that doesn't mean that the person who is virtuous, responsible, and brave cannot do it. And in this the hard-boiled books of the last quarter of the century hold out more hope than the writers who invented the form in the first quarter.

WORKS CITED

Allegretto, Michael. *Blood Stone*. New York: Avon, 1990.

Bergman, Andrew. *The Big Kiss Off of 1944*. New York: Holt, 1974.

——. *Hollywood and LeVine*. New York: Holt, 1975.

Blaine, Richard. *The Silver Setup*. New York: Pageant, 1988.

Bruccoli, Matthew. *Kenneth Millar/Ross McDonald: A Checklist*. Detroit: Gale, 1971.

——. *Raymond Chandler: A Checklist*. Kent, OH: Kent State UP, 1968.

——. *Raymond Chandler: A Descriptive Bibliography*. Pittsburgh: U of Pittsburgh P, 1979.

Burke, James Lee. *Black Cherry Blues*. New York: Avon, 1990.

——. *Burning Angel*. New York: Hyperion, 1995.

——. *Cadillac Jukebox*. New York: Hyperion, 1996.

——. *Dixie City Jam*. New York: Hyperion, 1994.

——. *Heaven's Prisoners*. New York: Pocket, 1989.

——. *In the Electric Mist with Confederate Dead*. New York: Hyperion, 1993.

——. *A Morning for Flamingos*. New York: Avon, 1991.

——. *Neon Rain*. New York: Pocket, 1988.

——. *A Stained White Radiance*. New York: Hyperion, 1992.

Butler, Gerald. *Kiss the Blood off My Hands*. New York: Carroll and Graf, 1987.

Byrd, Max. *California Thriller*. New York: Bantam, 1981.

Cain, Paul. *Fast One*. Berkeley, CA: Black Lizard, 1987.

Chandler, Raymond. *Killer in the Rain*. New York: Ballantine, 1972.

——. *Pickup on Noon Street*. New York: Ballantine, 1972.

——. *The Simple Art of Murder*. New York: Ballantine, 1972.

——. *Trouble Is My Business*. New York: Ballantine, 1972.

Coggins, Paul. *The Lady Is the Tiger*. New York: Avon, 1987.

Crais, Robert. *Free Fall*. New York: Bantam, 1994.

——. *Indigo Slam*. New York: Hyperion, 1997.

——. *Lullaby Town*. New York: Bantam, 1993.

——. *The Monkey's Raincoat*. New York: Bantam, 1987.

——. *Stalking the Angel*. New York: Bantam, 1992.

——. *Sunset Express*. New York: Hyperion, 1997.

——. *Voodoo River*. New York: Bantam, 1995.

Crumley, James. *Bordersnakes*. New York: Mysterious P, 1996.

——. *Dancing Bear*. New York: Vintage, 1984.

——. *The Last Good Kiss*. New York: Pocket, 1981.

——. *The Mexican Tree Duck*. New York: Mysterious P, 1993.

——. *The Wrong Case*. New York: Vintage, 1986.

Daly, Carroll John. *Murder from the East*. New York: International Polygonics, 1978.

Dold, Gaylord. *Snake Eyes*. New York: Ballantine, 1987.

Duncan, W. Glenn. *Rafferty's Rules*. New York: Ballantine, 1987.

Durham, Philip. *Down These Mean Streets a Man Must Go: Raymond Chandler's Knight*. Chapel Hill: U of North Carolina P, 1963.

Emerson, Earl. *Catfish Cafe*. New York: Ballantine, 1998.

——. *Deception Pass*. New York: Ballantine, 1997.

——. *Deviant Behavior*. New York: Ballantine, 1990.

——. *Fat Tuesday*. New York: Ballantine, 1988.

——. *The Million-Dollar Tattoo*. New York: Ballantine, 1997.

——. *Nervous Laughter*. New York: Ballantine, 1997.

——. *The Portland Laugher*. New York: Ballantine, 1995.

——. *Poverty Bay*. New York: Ballantine, 1997.

——. *The Rainy City*. New York: Ballantine, 1997.

——. *The Vanishing Smile*. New York: Ballantine, 1996.

——. *Yellow Dog Party*. New York: Ballantine, 1992.

Estleman, Loren. *Angel Eyes*. New York: Pinnacle, 1984.

——. *Downriver*. New York: Ballantine, 1989.

——. *Every Brilliant Eye*. New York: Ballantine, 1987.

——. *The Glass Highway*. Boston: Houghton, 1983.

——. *Lady Yesterday*. Boston: Houghton, 1987.

——. *The Midnight Man*. Boston: Houghton, 1982.

——. *Motor City Blue*. New York: Pinnacle, 1983.

——. *Never Street*. New York: Mysterious P, 1997.

——. *Silent Thunder*. Boston: Houghton, 1989.

——. *Sugartown*. Boston, Houghton, 1984.

——. *Sweet Women Lie*. Boston: Houghton, 1990.

Frey, James N. *The Long Way to Die*. New York: Bantam, 1987.

Gores, Joe. *Hammett*. New York: Putnam, 1975.

Goulart, Ron. *The Hardboiled Dicks: An Anthology and Study of Pulp Detective Fiction*. London: T. V. Broadman, 1967.

Grafton, Sue. *"A" Is for Alibi*. New York: Holt, 1982.

——. *"B" Is for Burglar*. New York: Holt, 1985.

——. *"C" Is for Corpse*. New York: Holt, 1986.

——. *"D" Is for Deadbeat*. New York: Holt, 1987.

——. *"E" Is for Evidence*. New York: Holt, 1988.

——. *"F" Is for Fugitive*. New York: Holt, 1989.

——. *"G" Is for Gumshoe*. New York: Holt, 1990.

——. *"H" Is for Homicide*. New York: Holt, 1991.

——. *"I" Is for Innocent*. New York: Holt, 1992.

——. *"J" Is for Judgment*. New York: Holt, 1993.

——. *"K" Is for Killer*. New York: Holt, 1994.

——. *"L" Is for Lawless*. New York: Holt, 1995.

——. *"M" Is for Malice*. New York: Holt, 1996.

——. *"N" Is for Noose*. New York: Holt, 1998.

Hammett, Dashiell. *The Big Knockover.* New York: Vintage, 1972.

——. *The Continental Op*. New York: Random House, 1974.

——. *The Novels of Dashiell Hammett.* New York: Knopf, 1965.

Harris, Timothy. *Good Night and Goodbye*. New York: Delacorte, 1979.

Healy, Jeremiah. *Blunt Darts*. New York: Pocket, 1987.

——. *The Staked Goat*. New York: Pocket Books, 1987.

Hiaasen, Carl. *Double Whammy*. New York: Warner, 1987.

——. *Lucky You*. New York: Knopf, 1997.

——. *Native Tongue*. New York: Knopf, 1991.

——. *Skin Tight*. New York: Fawcett, 1990.

——. *Stormy Weather*. New York: Knopf, 1995.

——. *Strip Tease*. New York: Knopf, 1993.

——. *Tourist Season*. New York: Warner, 1986.

Hilary, Richard. *Snake in the Grasses*. New York: Bantam, 1987.

Kantner, Rob. *The Back-Door Man.* New York: Bantam, 1986.

Kittredge, William, and Krauzer, Steven, eds. *Great American Detective*. New York: New American Library, 1978.

Latimer, Jonathan. *The Lady in the Morgue*. New York: International Polygonics, 1988.

——. *Solomon's Vineyard*. New York: International Polygonics, 1988.

Madden, David, ed. *Tough Guy Writers of the Thirties*. Carbondale: Southern Illinois UP, 1968.

Mathias, Edward. *From a High Place*. New York: Ballantine, 1987.

Mosley, Walter. *Black Betty*. New York: Norton, 1994.

——. *Devil in a Blue Dress*. New York: Pocket, 1991.

——. *Gone Fishin'*. Baltimore: Black Classics, 1997.

——. *Little Yellow Dog*. New York: Norton, 1996.

——. *A Red Death*. New York: Norton, 1991.

——. *White Butterfly*. New York: Norton, 1992.

Mundell, E. H. *A List of Original Appearances of Dashiell Hammett's Magazine Work*. Kent, OH: Kent State UP, 1968.

Nolan, William, ed. *The Black Mask Boys*. New York: Morrow, 1985.

Norman, Geoffrey. *Blue Chipper*. New York: Avon, 1994.

Paretsky, Sara. *Bitter Medicine*. New York: Morrow, 1987.

——. *Blood Shot*. New York: Delacorte, 1988.

——. *Burn Marks*. New York: Delacorte, 1990.

——. *Deadlock.* New York: Dell, 1992.

——. *Guardian Angel.* New York: Delacorte, 1992.

——. *Indemnity Only.* New York: Ballantine, 1982.

——. *Killing Orders.* New York: Dell, 1993.

——. *Tunnel Vision.* New York: Delacorte, 1994.

Paretsky, Sara, ed. *A Woman's Eye.* New York: Dell, 1992.

Parker, Robert B. *A Catskill Eagle.* New York: Delacorte, 1985.

——. *Ceremony.* New York: Dell, 1983.

——. *Crimson Joy.* New York: Delacorte, 1988.

——. *Early Autumn.* New York: Dell, 1987.

——. *God Save the Child.* New York: Berkley, 1976.

——. *The Godwulf Manuscript.* New York: Berkley, 1975.

——. *The Judas Goat.* New York: Dell, 1983.

——. *Looking for Rachel Wallace.* New York: Dell, 1981.

——. *Mortal Stakes.* New York: Dell, 1983.

——. *Pale Kings and Princes.* New York: Delacorte, 1987.

——. *Pastime.* New York: Putnam, 1991.

——. *Perchance to Dream.* New York: Berkley, 1993.

——. *Playmates.* New York: Putnam, 1989.

——. *Poodle Springs.* New York: Berkley, 1993.

——. *Promised Land.* New York: Berkley, 1978.

——. *A Savage Place.* New York: Dell, 1982.

——. *Sudden Mischief.* New York: Berkley, 1999.

——. *Taming a Sea Horse.* New York: Delacorte, 1986.

——. *Valediction.* New York: Delacorte, 1984.

——. *The Widening Gyre.* New York: Delacorte, 1983.

Pronzini, Bill, ed. *The Arbor House Treasury of Detective and Mystery Stories from the Great Pulps.* New York: Arbor House, 1983.

Ray, Robert. *Bloody Murdock.* New York: Penguin, 1987.

Reilly, John M., ed. *Twentieth-Century Crime and Mystery Writers.* 2d ed. New York: St. Martin's, 1985.

Roberts, Les. *An Infinite Number of Monkeys.* New York: St. Martin's, 1987.

Ruhm, Herbert, ed. *The Hard-Boiled Detective: Stories from the Black Mask Magazine 1920-1951.* New York: Vintage, 1977.

Schutz, Benjamin. *All the Old Bargains.* New York: Bluejay, 1985.

——. *A Tax in Blood.* New York: St. Martin's, 1987.

Vachss, Andrew. *Blue Belle.* New York: Signet, 1988.

——. *Flood.* New York: Donald Fine, 1985.

——. *Hard Candy.* New York: Signet, 1990.

——. *Strega.* New York: Knopf, 1987.

INDEX

alcoholism, 168-70
Allegretto, Michael, 210

Bellem, Robert Leslie, 2
Bergman, Andrew, 4
Black, Thomas. *See* Emerson, Earl
Blaine, Richard, 4
Brown, Fredric, 1, 2
Bruccoli, Matthew, 2
Burke, James Lee, 130, 159-284, 208,
  209, 216, 218, 220; *Black Cherry
  Blues*, 161, 162, 164, 165, 168,
  170, 176, 178, 180, 182, 183; *Burning Angel*, 166, 171, 172, 176, 177,
  178, 181; *Cadillac Jukebox*, 174,
  177; *Dixie City Jam*, 160, 162, 166,
  168, 177, 178, 179, 180, 182, 183,
  219; *Heaven's Prisoners*, 160, 163,
  165, 166, 167, 171, 172, 175, 177,
  178, 179, 180, 181, 182, 183, 219;
  *In the Electric Mist with Confeder-
  ate Dead*, 161, 166, 167, 168, 174,
  176, 177, 178, 179, 181, 182; *A
  Morning for Flamingos*, 160, 164,
  165, 166, 168, 171, 174, 178, 179,
  181, 211, 214; *Neon Rain*, 161,
  166, 168, 174, 176, 182; *A Stained
  White Radiance*, 165, 167, 168,
  170, 171, 172, 174, 175, 176, 177,
  178, 179, 181
Butler, Gerald, 1
Byrd, Max, 206, 207, 208, 210, 216,
  220

Cain, Paul, 1, 2, 15
Chandler, Raymond, 1, 2, 3, 10, 12,
  29, 49, 67, 119, 121-22, 135, 141,
  147, 159, 205, 206, 217
childhood, 208-9, 218-19

Coggins, Paul, 216
Cole, Elvis. *See* Crais, Robert
Crais, Robert, 141-58, 207, 208, 220;
  Free Fall, 142, 144, 146, 150, 152;
  Indigo Slam, 149, 151; *Lullaby
  Town*, 144, 146, 147, 148, 152, 218;
  The Monkey's Raincoat, 142, 144,
  145, 147, 151, 152, 154; *Stalking
  the Angel*, 143, 144, 147, 150, 151,
  152, 219; *Sunset Express*, 145, 149,
  152; *Voodoo River*, 150, 151, 152,
  154
Crumley, James, 29-47, 77, 130, 207,
  209, 216, 217, 218; *Bordersnakes*,
  29, 33, 36, 42, 45, 48; *Dancing
  Bear*, 29, 31, 32, 33, 34, 37, 39, 40,
  41, 42, 45, 210, 213, 215, 219; *The
  Last Good Kiss*, 29, 30, 31, 32, 34,
  36, 38, 40, 41, 43, 46, 212; *The
  Mexican Tree Duck*, 29, 34, 36, 42,
  45, 46, 215, 220; *The Wrong Case*,
  29, 30, 31, 32, 33, 36, 37, 38, 39,
  40, 41, 42, 43, 46

Daly, Carroll John, 2
depression. *See* manic depression
Dold, Gaylord, 4
Dooley, Dennis, 3
dreams, 19, 206, 215, 216, 220
Duncan, W. Glenn, 19, 206, 215, 216,
  220
Durham, Philip, 3

Emerson, Earl, 77, 121-40, 208, 209,
  216, 218, 220; *Catfish Café*, 125,
  129; *Deception Pass*, 133, 134;
  Deviant Behavior, 121, 123, 128,
  129, 130; *Fat Tuesday*, 122, 125,
  126, 127, 128, 129, 130, 131; *The*

227